John Hotta
The Art of Director Excellence

The Alexandra Lajoux Corporate Governance Series

Edited by
Alexandra Reed Lajoux

John Hotta

The Art of Director Excellence

Volume 1: Governance – Stories from Experienced
Corporate Directors

Foreword by Douglas K. Chia, President, Soundboard
Governance LLC and Senior Fellow, Rutgers Center for
Corporate Law and Governance

DE GRUYTER

ISBN 978-3-11-068910-5
e-ISBN (PDF) 978-3-11-068912-9
e-ISBN (EPUB) 978-3-11-068916-7
ISSN 2629-8155

Library of Congress Control Number: 2023941013

Bibliographic information published by the Deutsche Nationalbibliothek
The Deutsche Nationalbibliothek lists this publication in the Deutsche Nationalbibliografie;
detailed bibliographic data are available on the internet at http://dnb.dnb.de.

Advance Praise for *The Art of Director Excellence, Volume 1: Governance – Stories from Experienced Corporate Directors*

"This book brings board effectiveness to life! Corporate governance begins with regulations, structures, and processes, but really understanding what makes for an effective board takes years, if not decades, in boardrooms. The book brings the dynamics of the boardroom to the written page, through stories and insights from experienced and highly respected board members."

> – **Susan Angele**, Board Director, Board Chair of the 30% Coalition;
> former executive of The Hershey Company

"John Hotta has strung the finest pearls of wisdom on Board Governance in this book."

> – **Subash Anbu**, NACD.DC.; Board Director,
> Private Directors Association

"*The Art of Director Excellence: Volume 1 – Stories from Experienced Corporate Directors* provides an extraordinary opportunity for executives at all levels to develop and strengthen their leadership skills. It's a must-read for emerging business leaders."

> – **Christopher Clark**, Senior Consultant,
> Stuart Levine & Associates

"John Hotta has written the definitive book on board governance for all levels and different business models. It is the post-SOX book I wish I had when I started covering corporate governance as a reporter and a book I will no doubt refer to often as I embark on my own board-service journey."

> – **Judy Warner**, an editorial consultant specializing
> in coverage of corporate governance issues and
> the former editor in chief of
> NACD *Directorship Magazine*

https://doi.org/10.1515/9783110689129-202

Foreword

More of an Art Than a Science

Board directors are tasked with performing a job that has existed for centuries without definition, other than the abstract concept of fulfilling "fiduciary duties," and for which there are no proven methods that, even when applied with precision, will always lead to the intended outcomes. Instead, directors must rely on applying what common law refers to as "business judgment," based on their own expertise and experience, to fact patterns where the same decisions made in analogous situations may lead to strikingly different outcomes. Directors have a duty to monitor management's compliance with an ever-expanding set of requirements and responsibilities, but they must do so relying primarily—sometimes exclusively—on information provided by the very management they are monitoring. This means that even a well-qualified board with strong leadership that follows best practices can make decisions that end in failure or fail to take actions to forestall crises.

If corporate governance were a science, then those failures and crises should never happen. But when placed in the hands of individuals in boardrooms, where the pursuit of excellence is inevitably impacted by pressure and influenced by bias, governance becomes more art than science. Art is abstract, subjective, and the product of human emotion and imagination. It cannot be defined. It is there to be judged. Science is objective and data driven. It can be defined—even proven—and is meant to exist in an objective, judgment-free zone. Board governance would be much more efficient and predictable if it could be boiled down to and conducted like a science. Experts have proposed an array of processes and procedures to make it more so. And scholars have produced studies based on empirical data to support these proposals, but their studies are only able to demonstrate correlation between practices and results, never causation.

There are gray areas in corporate governance where a director's business judgment must be supplanted by their moral and ethical judgment. Doing the right thing is not a science. Healthy corporate culture cannot be reverse engineered. At the end of the day, the foundation of good governance is trust. Trust among the board members. Trust between the board and management. Trust in the board by the shareholders. There are many ways to establish this, none of them proven. Governance is more of an art than a science. Thus, John Hotta has chosen an apt title for this book, *The Art of Director Excellence*: a work that brings to life what boards of directors do, both collectively and as individuals, and gives readers an inside look at how they strive for excellence in an area that has no tested formulas or algorithms, as told by the directors themselves.

https://doi.org/10.1515/9783110689129-203

What Can Be Observed

Legendary shareholder activist and advocate, Nell Minow, applies the "observer effect" from quantum mechanics to boards when she says, "Boards of directors are like subatomic particles; they behave differently when they are being observed." But this scientific concept can only apply to the extent that boards can be observed. While directors exist to serve and protect the interests of the company and its shareholders, shareholders have no right to observe directors in action even though the shareholders elect the directors. Unlike the occupants of elected offices that we are more familiar with, corporate directors have no obligation to interface with their electorate. Their meetings are private affairs where the only non-directors invited in are top level management, independent auditors, and sometimes outside counsel or other advisors. Public company boards typically end their meetings in "executive session" where everyone, including the CEO (even if they are also the board chair), is asked to leave the room to give the independent directors their private time to discuss matters in confidence. Not even the corporate secretary, whose main job under most corporate bylaws is to take the official minutes of these meetings, is allowed to stay for the executive session. Instead, the secretary can only record that an executive session took place and rely on the independent director who presided over it to report to the secretary whether something was said or done that merits memorializing.

Like the game of baseball where the action only starts when the pitcher releases the ball from their hand, corporate governance is a game where the action necessarily starts in the hands of the board of directors. The board has the sole authority to hire, pay, and fire the CEO. The shareholders can meet to act collectively, but only after the board calls and gives notice of a shareholder meeting. If a shareholder wishes to sue the board, derivatively on behalf of the corporation, the decision for that derivative suit to proceed must go through the board itself. But going back to Minow's application of the observer effect to boards, corporate governance is a game where no one else gets to observe the players in action on the field. There are no fans, critics, or scouts observing from the stands, listening on the radio, or watching on television. Owning shares does not mean that you also get tickets to the games. *The Art of Director Excellence* gives readers what everyone outside the boardroom craves—a look at board directors in action.

Noses and Fingers

There is much conventional wisdom about what boards of directors do, who should be on boards, and what the most effective ways are for boards to govern a corporation. Shareholders in particular have strong opinions that shape the conventional wisdom around corporate governance. Sometimes the conventional wisdom is summed up with pithy phrases like "one size does not fit all," "sunlight is the best disinfectant," and "culture eats strategy for breakfast." One such phrase uses four words to describe how directors should do their job: "noses in, fingers out." So commonly is this phrase repeated among the corporate governance set that it appears at least 35 times in the director interviews excerpted in this book. What does this strange analogy to anatomy mean? "Noses in, fingers out" means that directors should closely observe how management is doing its job without interfering or actually doing the job for them. Directors should get their faces close enough to the action to the point where they can see how the factory is being run and catch a whiff of any off-putting odors. Their noses must be trained to pick up on the scent of molding bread before it turns green and detect smoke before actually seeing it. But being so close and giving in to the temptation to reach in with hands and fingers would cross the line from monitoring to managing. Directors must look (and smell), but they may not touch.

That directors should do their jobs with "noses in and fingers out" is a universally held principle and makes for convenient shorthand when one is speaking on a panel at a corporate governance conference. But how does it work in practice? How deep into the business should a director's nose poke? What if their nostrils get so close that management can feel breaths on the backs of their necks? Should that nose always be present but never seen, or would being seen have potential benefits (like the observer effect)? Should an extremely zealous director be given free rein to sniff around like a canine cop? And aren't there going to be times when their fingers will be required to lift the tarp from under which a noxious smell is coming, especially if the director actually sees smoke? Using direct quotes from his interviews with board directors, Hotta fleshes out how the phrase "noses in, fingers out" is interpreted and applied. Readers may be surprised to see how directors have a range of approaches to operationalizing the noses-fingers mantra and will be challenged to think about the nuances and complexities that directors must grapple with.

Disagreements and Differences

Disagreement among directors is one of the most valuable things that *The Art of Director Excellence* brings to light. Through seeing the differences in how directors respond to Hotta's questions, readers will understand how boards and directors can be extremely effective without applying every agreed-upon, common sense principle of good corporate governance. Directors will have contrasting philosophies and make different judgments on which ones to apply based on the circumstances, including the type of company and its stage of maturity. *The Art of Director Excellence* shows us this through interviews with directors of a vast assortment of public, private, and not-for-profit companies, some that are rarely examined this closely. Within these broad categories, each of which comprise thousands of corporate entities, Hotta gives readers excerpts from interviews with directors representing activist investors, directors of companies going from public to private (and vice versa), directors backed by private equity firms, directors of startup companies, family-owned company directors, directors of SPACs, and directors of state-owned organizations, to name just a few subcategories.

The bulk of corporate governance literature and media coverage focuses on board failures at the largest companies like Penn Central, Enron, Lehman Brothers, Wells Fargo, and Viacom, or the made-for-streaming con jobs like Theranos and We-Work. By parsing through how directors at a wide range of companies approach the job, *The Art of Director Excellence* draws out the differences in how these types of companies are governed.

Governance Is . . .

There is a saying to explain what governance is: "Governance is governance." While at first glance this definition is circular and unhelpful, it happens to be the title of a widely read monograph (originally a speech) by Kenneth M. Dayton, the former chairman and CEO of the Dayton Hudson Corporation (known today as Target Corporation), published by the Independent Sector in 1987. Dayton unpacks this saying when he writes,

> Governance is governance. That's more than a title—it's a deeply held conviction. It's a conviction first of all that governance is not management and, second, that governance in the not-for-profit sector is absolutely identical to governance in the for-profit sector.

Dayton expounds on this by saying,

> [G]overnance is governance no matter what the institution—be it government, corporation, or nonprofit (be it health agency, organized religious group, arts institution, foundation, or advocacy group).

The Art of Director Excellence reaffirms Dayton's view of governance but goes deeper to illustrate that while "governance is governance" no matter the type of organization, there are idiosyncrasies that only those who have been responsible for the governance of multiple types of organizations can fully appreciate and explain with authority. Hotta has done a valuable service by presenting us with explanations from this exclusive cadre of professionals who know first-hand what "governance is governance" really means.

Flaws and Gaps

The Art of Director Excellence also lays bare the flaws in the board governance system and the gaps that continue to exist, even after the many rounds of corporate governance reforms and enhancements made in recent decades, as well as the shortcomings of directors themselves. These are imperfect actors with their own conscious and unconscious biases.

After every corporate failure, the question quickly arises "Where was the board?" As we see in *The Art of Director Excellence*, even when a board is up to the task and doing the very best it can, sometimes that will not be enough. "Best practices" work in theory but come with major caveats when applied in real life, and newly conceived practices often have unintended consequences. Readers will see that while governance is governance, governance only works to a point, even when carried out by the most capable directors. But when governance fails is when we can find clues for how to improve it. *The Art of Director Excellence* may be another trove of hidden clues for all of us to find.

An Update of Myth and Reality

In 1971, Harvard Business School Professor Myles L. Mace published the book *Directors: Myth and Reality*, which was the product of two years of field research consisting of more than 75 in-depth interviews and several hundred shorter discussions with corporate directors and executives. Professor Mace summarized the key findings from his book in a 1972 *Harvard Business Review* article where he wrote,

> Over the years, businessmen, business associations, lawyers, and scholars have turned out literature attempting to describe more detailed functions for directors . . . Much of it describes the roles that boards should play, not those that they really do . . . [T]he generally accepted roles of boards . . . have taken on more and more the characteristics of a well-established myth, and there is a considerable gap between the myth and reality.

Professor Mace revisited and updated his research for a 1979 *Rutgers Law Review* article (observing that "board practices have changed little" since his original findings) and a second time in 1986 (again concluding that there had been "no significant modifications in what boards do and do not do.") To what extent do Professor Mace's words from then ring true today?

The Art of Director Excellence essentially updates Professor Mace's inside look at corporate boards with words directly from today's directors who are faced with many more challenges than were their predecessors in the 1970s and 1980s and from a wider array of stakeholders. Board composition has changed considerably over the past four decades in terms of independence and diversity, as has the legal and regulatory landscape for corporate governance as a result of landmark court decisions, such as In Re Caremark International Inc. Derivative Litigation, and major federal corporate governance legislation, most notably the Sarbanes-Oxley Act of 2002 and Dodd-

Frank Act of 2010. *The Art of Director Excellence* is an important contribution to the canon of corporate governance literature and will serve as a valuable resource for both the actors and observers of the corporate governance system.

Douglas K. Chia
President, Soundboard Governance LLC
and Senior Fellow, Rutgers Center for Corporate Law and Governance
March 8, 2023

Contents

Appendices

1 Introduction and What Board Directors Do

1.1 Introduction

I started serving as a board director while I was a leader at Microsoft. Since the 2010s, I have served on boards of multi-billion-dollar private and nonprofit organizations.

When I became a board director, I turned to books to understand my role and responsibilities. The books I read did not make sense to me. Firstly, I did not recognize my board in them because most corporate governance books describe public company boards. Secondly, corporate governance books are academic, not practical. Finally, other books are written by professional service providers whose goal is to sell a product or service. So these books are narrow rather than comprehensive. When I read textbooks today, they still feel removed from my experience as a board director.

This book addresses the wide range of boards at public companies, private companies, and nonprofit organizations. I authored this book after interviewing over 50 board directors, including board chairs and CEOs. It compiles all their wisdom and practical knowledge.

My interviewees are based in North America, Asia, and Europe. Many are shining stars in public company boardrooms; I am honored to call these directors my friends. Others serve on private company and nonprofit organization boards. They are equally smart, talented, and experienced.

Interviews were conducted during the pandemic as well as during global recovery. I asked my friends and colleagues: (1) "What do you want to say to students of corporate governance?" and (2) "How would you compare what you expected of board service versus the reality?" I hope the reader will benefit from the great content and insight I received.

The board directors shared my belief in the importance and value of good corporate governance. They contributed their time and thoughts because they also wanted to pass on their hard-earned wisdom to students of corporate governance. Students (and their professors) in executive education, graduate, and undergraduate corporate governance classes will find this collection of interviews immensely insightful.

The Art of Director Excellence is designed to be used with standard textbooks. I have included an Appendix, which cross references commonly used textbooks to show how this book matches their contents. Professors can assign their favorite corporate governance textbook and add this as a complementary book of interviews with real-world wisdom and experience. Students of corporate governance will benefit from the over 300 years of cumulative board director experience in this easy-to-read book.

> **"Channing"**: I'm just glad that you have a book that is based on current real-world experience, because with a push to diversify – which used to mean women and now it means people of

https://doi.org/10.1515/9783110689129-001

color – I think that there's going to be a tide . . . The generations are shifting so we're going to see some non-traditional choices being made for people in director seats.

Maybe not at the public-company level, because there's still a huge level of audit governance compliance and risk that those companies need.

But I think we're going to see a shift in the types of directors that are being tapped . . . . It's going to be an interesting time in corporate governance. So having you write a book like this is super helpful, because the more we can help this generation of directors understand there's some differences.

Before new board directors go into the boardroom, you know how to play a little bit about what the rules are. That's going to help the companies that need them. Because when directors make a mistake, it can cost the company depending on what the company is doing. I'm glad you're doing this.[1]

Effective board director and CEO partnerships can lead businesses to greater impact and higher results. I have seen the value of businesses and organizations increase significantly because of good corporate governance. Owners, shareholders, and stakeholders receive the financial value and service benefits from good governance.

1.2 Book's Purpose

Michael Marquardt (addressing a CEO): My long-term goal is for you as CEO to say . . . in five years . . . we have achieved the unachievable . . .It was the partnership and the effectiveness of this board of directors that allowed us to arrive at the right strategy in a way that everybody bought in and we were true partners.[2]

I find Marquardt's quote inspiring as it features many of the key messages of this book. The board and CEO can work together in partnership to "achieve the unachievable," and board directors can work constructively together when they focus on strategy.

It is the board and CEO's responsibility to develop the right strategy, ask constructive questions, and monitor developments so they can achieve remarkable results and significant impact. Boards should work with management to develop their strategy annually and monitor the results, at least quarterly. And, of course, boards should work to continually improve governance.

Ryan Patel: It's not about you, the board director. You're in service . . . I think that you got to keep that in mind. Because sometimes when you look at corporate governance the board director says "I made it. I'm at the top of this company."

You're not top of any company truthfully. You are reporting to stakeholders. Your job is to be in service.[3]

---

1 Board director/CEO interview conducted in September 2020.
2 Board director/CEO interview conducted on 4 February 2021.
3 Board director interview conducted on 30 October 2020.

What Ryan says rings true. The misconception is that the CEO reports to the board, and when I joined the board of a company that's what I thought. (I thought I was more important than the CEO but I am embarrassed to admit this now.)

Instead, the board represents the owner's and stakeholders' interests. These owners and stakeholders[4] are not in the boardroom. The board and CEO must work in partnership to achieve the best results.

> **Anna Catalano:** The most important thing . . . is the importance of being accountable to shareholders and responsible to stakeholders.[5]

For public and private companies, boards represent owners, investors, and shareholders. For nonprofit organizations, boards represent the community and other stakeholders.

I point to Professor Christine Mallin's chapter, "Owners and Stakeholders" in her textbook, *Corporate Governance* from Oxford University Press.[6]

> **Michael Marquardt:** Let's say the company has 2,000 shareholders. It is not practical for those 2,000 shareholders to monitor what's going on at the company, to be involved in decision-making. So, they have to pick five, six, seven, eight, nine, ten, eleven people that will represent them as owners.
>
> Those people will be in the boardroom. Those people will be meeting with management. Those people will oversee what's going on. Management is accountable to P&L and everything else.
>
> It is their job, the board representing those shareowners that own the business. And obviously select the CEO; that's the most important obligation.[7]

For public companies (owned by investors), there was a time when boards believed they should focus only on shareholders,[8] but there has been a shift since the 2020s from shareholders to consider employees, supply-chain vendors, environmental concerns, and social justice issues.[9]

> **Anna Catalano:** I tell people when they ask, "what is it exactly that boards of directors do?" I say we represent people who cannot be there in the room.
>
> We are accountable in a company that has investors. We are accountable to the investors or public company shareholders. It used to be back in the Milton Friedman days it was shareholders only. And the only thing we needed to do is maximize the bottom line.
>
> And the world has changed and that's no longer true.
>
> People and investors care not only about what happens to their money. Investors care how companies behave in the communities. How they operate with employees. How they treat customers.

---

4 Stakeholders include shareholders, employees, customers, community members, suppliers, etc.
5 Public company board director interview conducted on 3 June 2021.
6 Christine Mallin, *Corporate Governance, sixth edition.* Oxford, UK: Oxford University Press. 2019.
7 Board director/CEO interview conducted on 4 February 2021.
8 An extreme form of shareholder primacy.
9 Sometimes called stakeholder capitalism.

So, the role of directors has broadened quite a bit. I've been doing this for over two decades. It has broadened an awful lot.[10]

Michael Marquardt: What's really from an owner's perspective? From a shareowner shareholders perspective?

Ask yourself the basic question, why? Why does the board exist? Why do the committees exist?

Some people lose track of that because they get caught up in the whole theater of it all. I don't forget who you're working for as a director. You're there to represent.

I prefer shareowners and business owners who have given you their proxy literally to make decisions on their behalf as shareholders. The shareholder makes it almost sound like you're holding something.

This is this your business. And this is serious business.[11]

As experienced corporate directors, Catalano and Marquardt say board directors represent owners. Owners are typically shareholders. The primary responsibility is to protect the owners' and shareholders' investment and ensure the company's success.

1.3 What Board Directors Do

When an experienced board director is asked, "what do you do?" they might reply with "ask questions," "oversee management," "noses in, fingers out."[12] From the board directors I interviewed, I define what that means.

1.3.1 Understand the Difference Between Governance and Management

There is a line between governance and management. Boards are focused on governance, while the CEO is the leader of the organization and manages the team and the company.

Anne Hamilton: Let me tell a compelling story. My role as a trustee[13] has been easier than I anticipated.

---

10 Public company board director interview conducted on 3 June 2021.
11 Board director/CEO interview conducted on 4 February 2021.
12 "Noses In, Fingers Out" means that a board director asks questions and investigates but does not touch operations See LinkedIn article, 'Noses in and Fingers out: The importance of boundaries between a board and CEO', by Joanna Andrew, 6 April 2017, https://www.linkedin.com/pulse/noses-fingers-out-importance-boundaries-between-board-joanna-andrew.
13 "Trustee" is a board director for a Nonprofit, in this situation a college.

In my early days, I found a lot of frustration with the "line."[14] As a trustee I grew more distant from the college . . . . than when I served on the foundation board.[15]

On the foundation board, my role was clear. I was there to raise money for students, programs, etc. So, it was easy for me to drop into the welding people say, hey, would you mind making some garden art for us to sell the plant sale. Or drop in on a class and check in with people to have casual conversations with instructors and students and the like.

As a trustee . . . that's not strictly verboten. But it comes with a different sense of obligation when I have a conversation with faculty, who may be part of a union. Or if I say something to a student; I have to think from a different lens and a different position.

So, in some ways being a board director has given me more distance from institutions that I love. I thought I was doubling down and getting into the trenches in my volunteer[16] work as a trustee. As it turns out that I'm actually a little more removed.[17]

Barbara Adachi: For board directors who have had prior management roles, a key learning is to let go of what we are used to doing, which was managing and executing. The role of governance is simply oversight and strategy. We are no longer involved in execution and implementation.[18]

Phil Haas: Governance is focused on the bigger picture and the whole organization. Management is operating and watching the quality, services, and price of the business; it's just a different view.

Outside stakeholders (e.g., board directors) bring experience in life and leadership. Inside employed management stakeholders know about the inside of the organization and sometimes need to look at the broader picture outside of the organization. That's the magic that board members bring to governance.[19]

"Halsey": I think the organization was pretty good about respecting that Venn diagram, for lack of a better term, between governance and management. The board asked enough questions and got pretty involved and I'm sure we sometimes drove the CEO nuts. For the most part we didn't meddle other than to ask questions, seek data, or cogitate[20] over what our decision should be.[21]

The board's role is to ask questions, as described below. In almost every situation, the board should not direct the CEO and senior management to do something. The following story is a good example.

Evelyn Dilsaver: This story is when board members happen to be more directive.

The board was telling a CEO we want you to hire a COO. And after many times telling him to hire a COO, the CEO finally said:

---

14 "Line" in this situation means the line is between management and the board.
15 When trustees and foundation boards are separate, the foundation does not have fiduciary responsibility. This governance structure is covered in Chapter 7, "Board Leadership and Culture."
16 Most Nonprofit board members are unpaid per my discussion in Chapter 6 "Compensation Committee."
17 Trustee interview conducted on 6 June 2021.
18 Public company board director interview conducted on 5 May 2021.
19 CEO/Board director interview conducted on 9 January 2023.
20 "Cogitate" means to think deeply.
21 Anonymous board director/CEO interview conducted on 6 May 2021.

"Tell me what you're worried about? Are you worried that I don't have a succession plan? Or are you worried that I can't get the big projects done when I'm on the road with investors and so forth . . ."

"Because there's two different answers. 1 If you're worried about a COO, I can hire a COO. But I'm not ready to do that yet. 2 But if you're worried about how I can get the projects done at a company, I don't need to hire a COO. I can create an operating structure and operated committee, have one of my executives lead, and they can make sure the projects get done while I'm gone."

And it was an eye-opener for us because we were being very directive coming up with a solution for the CEO when the reality was there are multiple solutions depending on what you're trying to solve.

From a governance point of view, we've learned to ask the questions: "Here's what I'm worried about. How do you get projects done when you're gone? How do you know that they're really working?"[22]

By asking questions which are insightful and strategic, board directors fulfill their oversight responsibilities to guide the company toward success. Board directors should be prepared, focus on strategic issues, and be respectful and professional.

> **Further reading on the difference between governance and management**
> See chapter "The Proper Role of the Board" in Michael E. Batts's *Board Member Orientation: The Concise and Complete Guide to Non-Profit Board Service*.[23]
> Chapter "Governance and Management" in Bob Tricker's *Corporate Governance: Principles, Policies, and Practices*, Fourth Edition.[24]
> Chapter "The Board's Role in Management" in John L. Colley, Wallace Stettinius, Jacqueline L. Doyle and George Logan's, *What is Corporate Governance?*[25]
> Chapter "The Role of the Board" in Betsy Atkins's book, *Be Board Ready: The Secrets to Landing a Board Set and Being a Great Director*.[26]
> Chapter "Functions of the Board" in Bob Tricker's *Corporate Governance: Principles, Policies, and Practices*, Fourth Edition.[27]
> Chapter "Clarifying the Rights and Roles of the Board and the Shareholders" in Deborah Hick Midanek's *The Governance Revolution: What Every Board Member Needs to Know, NOW!*[28]

---

22 Public company board director interview conducted on 6 November 2020.
23 Chapter "The Proper Role of the Board" in Michael E. Batts, *Board Member Orientation: The Concise and Complete Guide to Nonprofit Board Service*. Orlando, FL: Accountability Press. 2011.
24 Chapter "Governance and Management" in Bob Tricker, *Corporate Governance: Principles, Policies, and Practices*, Fourth Edition, Oxford, UK: Oxford University Press, 2019.
25 Chapter "The Board's Role in Management" in John L. Colley, Wallace Stettinius, Jacqueline L. Doyle, George Logan, *What is Corporate Governance?* New York, NY: McGraw-Hill, 2005.
26 Chapter "The Role of the Board" in Betsy Atkins, *Be Board Ready: The Secrets to Landing a Board Set and Being a Great Director*. Chicago: NEWTYPE Publishing, 2019.
27 Chapter "Functions of the Board" in Bob Tricker, *Corporate Governance: Principles, Policies, and Practices*, Fourth Edition, Oxford, UK: Oxford University Press, 2019.
28 Chapter "Clarifying the Rights and Roles of the Board and the Shareholders" in Deborah Hick Midanek, *The Governance Revolution: What Every Board Member Needs to Know, NOW!* Berlin, GE: De Gruyter Press, 2018.

1.3.2 Ask Questions

Experienced corporate directors know that asking questions is essential, and perhaps one of the greatest tools for board directors to understand a situation and the depth of skills and knowledge of a leader.

Joyce Cacho: Your job is not making statements. Your job is to ask questions. So, if you have come up in through the executive ranks, your career experience may have been to be the expert in the room by making declarative statements.

Then you might have to pick up "question asking skills" as you think about a board director journey.[29]

R. Omar Riojas: It's important for board members to exercise their fiduciary duty. In doing so they have an opinion.

My role as a board member is to have an opinion and to ask questions of management because I think the solutions often are in the answers.

The questions themselves can oftentimes refine strategy or lead the organization in a different direction.[30]

Rich Horan: This may sound strange to some people, but I think the question is more important than the actual answer.

What's important is how management comes up with an answer. What is their rationale, what inputs and variables did they use to come up with an answer?

If the answer is thought out, you can maybe throw out a couple other questions as well. What about this? What about that? If they have thought out answers to all questions, that's good.[31]

Evelyn Dilsaver: This story is a recent one. We were talking about our 10-Q.[32] Included in our disclosures was how big a particular customer's revenue was for our company. That customer represented 20% of the revenue.

One of the board members said our company had to disclose publicly the precise percentage. I asked the board member, "what are you worried about when we disclose it?" And he said, "oh, I'm not really worried."

Then two minutes into his answer he said, "what I'm really worried about is that our competitors will know that number and can start to sell against us giving those percentages."

So, if you started out by asking "What are you worried about" you can get a better answer. So, that's been a lesson for me.

Asking questions respects the different roles of board directors and management (CEOs, senior management). Asking questions will help the CEO and senior management to focus on what is important to owners and stakeholders.[33]

---

29 Board director interview conducted on 16 February 2021.
30 Board director interview conducted on 25 November 2020.
31 Board director Interview conducted on 15 February 2021.
32 10-Q is a US financial report, which is filed quarterly to the federal Securities and Exchange Commission (SEC).
33 Public company board director interview conducted on 6 November 2020.

By asking questions and understanding different experiences and perspectives, the board can have healthy discussions.

> **Barbara Adachi**: As a board director your role is to probe and ask questions, without making "statements" or taking a specific position around decisions that are management's responsibility. You must learn how to reframe your questions in the boardroom, so it sounds constructive versus accusatory or attacking of management. This was an important learning for me as there is truly an art of asking the right questions.[34]

> **Minaz Abji**: I think you have to have a relationship and cordial relationship with all the board members. You have to respect them when they say something. Not argue with them. Listen to what they're saying. I think you learn by listening to what others say and contribute. But I think you have to get along with people.
> You cannot be a person to join a board and criticize. You can suggest. You can ask questions. But not to criticize anybody and to have a relationship. Otherwise, you won't have a collegial relationship.[35]

Each board has a strong culture, which is described in Chapter 6, "Board Leadership and Culture." Oversight of a company often means having challenging, healthy discussions. Board directors can challenge and debate without arguing, bickering, and clashing – this is disagreeing without being disagreeable.

Oversight of a company means having challenging, healthy discussions.

> **R. Omar Riojas**: I've always believed that the management and the board . . . exist because it's a healthy check. I think that's good governance.
> I think it's good for capitalism. A health check between management and the board . . . . to maximize shareholder value. That's a healthy check and that's why I think boards and management exist to have that healthy dynamic.
> We've decided as a society to have this healthy balance. The result is an organization that can then be successful. We've seen over the past few decades that this has been a good thing, right?
> Obviously not perfect. And there needs to be, you know, tinkering.
> That's the interesting part of management and board governance is that it's a checks and balances approach.[36]

> **Erin Essenmacher**: When you want to have a difficult conversation – introduce something that may not be popular or something people have not thought about – think about the audience.
> I'm here in the boardroom because I want to provide effective oversight which sometimes means challenging assumptions. But I want to consider how is my message is going to be best received by (1) my fellow board members, (2) the independent board chair, but also (3) the CEO . . . . Hopefully, you're working in a very collaborative way. At the end of the day challenging the status quo is an important role of most boards.[37]

---

34 Public company board director interview conducted on 5 May 2021.
35 Public company board director interview conducted on 20 January 2021.
36 Board director interview conducted on 25 November 2020.
37 Board director interview conducted on 27 October 2020.

See J. Lyn McDonell's chapter on asking questions, "The Art of Asking Questions as a Director" in *The Handbook of Board Governance: A Comprehensive Guide for Public, Private, and Not-for-Profit Board Members* by Richard Leblanc.[38]

1.3.3 Limitation of Noses In, Fingers Out

The phrase "noses in, fingers out"[39] is commonly used by CEOs to describe the board's role. I think the "noses in" part means asking questions. But the "fingers out" part is wrong in many situations, depending on the life stage of the company, and if the organization is a private company or nonprofit.

In many situations, the CEO asks a board director to be "hands-on" and perform a task. This is appropriate for CEOs because the board's role is to help the CEO and organization.

> **Lisa Chin**: The noses in, fingers out stuff is difficult in small privately held organizations . . . . you could roll up your sleeves and hire the VP of sales, which I helped to do.
>
> I think one of the biggest lessons for me is learning that there's always a line when you're invited in as a board director. You're singing for your supper for your equity slice . . . .
>
> But you're still a director of the organization. You still have to be mindful . . . . as much as we want to run and manage things . . . you are still a consultant. That's one of the biggest lessons I've learned being a consultant in every director position I've had.[40]

PE (i.e., Private Equity) who may own a company does not necessarily believe in "fingers out."

> **Larry Taylor**: I have a short story about a PE (private equity) board that I serve. Private equity has a different view of the world.
>
> Private equity still thinks that shareholder primacy rules us. The mantra of nose in fingers out, doesn't apply so much.
>
> Private equity-owned companies have smaller boards. They have a shorter-term view versus long-term view. They want to get their money out and that small board is digging deep into management.[41]

---

38 J. Lyn McDonell "The Art of Asking Questions as a Director" in Richard Leblanc, *The Handbook of Board Governance: A Comprehensive Guide for Public, Private, and Not-for-Profit Board Members*, Second Edition, Hoboken, NJ: Wiley, 2020.

39 "Noses in, fingers out means that board members should have their noses in the business. They should know what's going on, understand risks, trends, issues, and wins. They should understand the market and the capabilities. They should understand what's working and what is not. They should be sniffing around. Fingers out means that board members should not disempower management from running the business by running it for them. It means don't interfere, don't second guess every decision or try to control every move. Keep your fingers out." (Jamie Flinchbaugh, "Noses In, Fingers Out" www.jflinch.com. Blog 27 April 2010.)

40 Board director/CEO interview conducted on 30 September 2020.

41 Board director interview conducted on 27 October 2020.

"Flynn": I've heard so many people talk about noses in, fingers out. A number of people say "bullshit" to the whole noses in and fingers out thing.

Noses in, fingers out does not apply when you start up a company.

The board's role is oversight. But in the beginning start-up stage it's "fingers in" with management's agreement. In the start-up stage it's an oversight role with fingers in.

The noses-in part is true. How does the board sniff around?[42]

"Blake": I'm going to talk a little bit of the cliche noses in fingers out mantra, okay? A board member has to be noses-in for smelling crap . . . . smelling for things that don't make sense.

But fingers out? Not touching anything? Is it really adding value to be noses in fingers out?[43]

Erin Essenmacher: I think what it means to be engaged does differ based on the company type and where they are in their life cycle.[44]

Again, experienced corporate directors agree on "noses in." But "fingers out" does not describe what board directors are asked to do by owners and investors. CEOs and senior management may resist "noses in" information gathering by asserting "fingers out."

Lisa Chin: I was also . . . very close to the family that owned a family-owned business. So even though it was "noses in fingers out" . . . . the family owners were asking, can you please fix this? So, the owners of the company were asking me to do this.

The CEO of the family-owned business will outwait the board director. The CEO will know how to keep you from being a pesky board member.[45]

Julian Ha: The phrase I've heard many times; it's supposed to be "noses in fingers out" for board members, right? You're supposed to make sure you know what's going on, sniff around.

It's not really your job to push things, – that's management. And we were obviously respectful of that as outside board members.

But I think we felt we had to push a little bit more to get that assurance – get that additional information – whether it's from our lawyers or from management. It was a learning process.

Management was trying to say, "why do you need to know all this?" We said we need to know this because that's the role of independent board directors. And we will create more shareholder value including the value to you. Because your management are significant shareholders in this business.[46]

---

42 Board director interview conducted in February 2022.
43 Board director interview conducted in September 2020.
44 Board director interview conducted on 20 October 2020.
45 Board director/CEO interview conducted on 30 September 2020.
46 Board director interview conducted on 20 January 2021.

1.3.4 Manage Your Altitude

As the section above describes, there is a limitation to "noses in, fingers out." "Noses in" is consistent with what the board directors said. But "fingers out" depends on the wishes of the organization's CEO, shareholders and owners, and other stakeholders.

I think "manage your altitude" is better than "noses in, fingers out." I credit public board director Anna Catalano with using this expression "manage your altitude".

> **Anna Catalano**: But in times of crisis, such as having a special committee investigating the CEO for sexual harassment situations, you're not going to be hands-off. You're going to get in there and say: "what the hell is going on," right?
>
> I have no aversion to getting in the weeds when needed, but then quickly understanding the situation you raise your altitude and go back up. It's kind of like an eagle that's flying. Every once in a while, you got to go down but then you go back up.
>
> I think it generally describes what boards do. I think that it's important for people to understand that when things are falling off the rail, fingers get in real quickly. Board directors are very capable of putting fingers in when needed. It's just not one of those things that's in our normal job description.
>
> What's the right altitude to maintain? I think being high, but capable of getting down to the surface of the water to grab the fish but then they go right back up. If you're down too low, your CEO and senior management aren't going to learn anything. They're not going to have the space. If you're up too high, there could be all kinds of crap going on down there that you don't realize. You've just got to manage that altitude.[47]

Other experienced board members concur with this opinion. There is a difference between management and governance, as described above. But board directors need to take a "deep dive."

> **Evelyn Dilsaver**: We already talked about whether you're more directive versus inquisitive. It really depends on the company and the industry whether a board member needs to dive in to be more directive and depends on the experience of the management team.
>
> A mature board leader can judge the capability of the management team. And be able to say, "I need to dive deeper."[48]

If the reader does not like "manage your altitude," another board director Bonime-Blanc suggests "leaning in."

> **Andrea Bonime-Blanc**: Everybody talks about "noses in, fingers out". I prefer to use a slightly different phrase. I like people who are leaning in.[49] Board members who are leaning in are not sitting back. Sitting back board should be a thing of the past.

---

47 Public company board director interview conducted on 6 June 2021.
48 Public company board director interview conducted on 6 November 2020.
49 "Lean in" means asserting oneself https://www.merriam-webster.com/words-at-play/words-were-watching-lean-in.

"Noses in, fingers out" continues to be very prevalent. But I think we need to be so much more proactive today than we even were two years ago. It includes all of these other issues including ESG & T,[50] which includes cyber, AI, etc.[51]

Bonime-Blanc continues: But getting to the point about "noses in fingers out", there were noses out and fingers out in Germany at Wirecard.[52] It's a huge scandal. We call it the Enron of Europe because it's a multibillion-dollar company that collapsed. The supervisory board was leaning back . . . . That can't be done in a world as complex, risky, and challenging as the world that we live in today.

It goes back to the velocity of change – technological breakthroughs happening everyday changing everything. Are we able to keep up as human beings with everything that's going on.

With the velocity of everything, boards have to be more proactive. They can't be sitting back even with a noses in. They need to be talking to people in management. They need to have practices where they can glean more out of what's going on.

They can't just expect to "smell the coffee".[53] What if there's poison in the coffee? The coffee might still smell well, but there's poison in there. That's a good analogy.[54]

1.3.5 Learn and Look for Opportunities

"Asking questions" and "Noses in" are clearly within the scope of the board director's role. Board directors should take advantage of as many learning opportunities available. In addition, many events are public, such as investor calls if you are a shareholder, and information that is publicly available via search engines. Setting up a Google Alert on your company and competitors is an excellent way to keep informed.

Here are some examples of seeing what's happening and learning what's going on:

Hon. Carlos C. Campbell: Warren Bennis says, "Managers do things right. Leaders do the right thing." So, for board directors, it is a question of knowing what has to be done.

I can give an example. We were in a canola plant business at one company and I went out, I never knew what canola was. I went up to North Dakota to see the operation.

We built a huge facility, invested hundreds of millions of dollars. I had to get a feel for what it was like. I had to see the trains where they load up the products, the seeds, and the oil, and the different things that we do and how they take it to market. I had to see the cradle-to-grave operation. I learned.

---

50 ESG&T is Environment, Social, Governance, and Technology https://www.youtube.com/watch?v=2D18gD4Kb48 .
51 Board director interview conducted on 8 January 2021.
52 Wirecard scandal: https://en.wikipedia.org/wiki/Wirecard_scandal#:~:text=The%20Wirecard%20scandal%20was%20a%20series%20of%20corrupt,The%20company%20was%20part%20of%20the%20DAX%20index.
53 "Wake up and smell the coffee" means pay attention to what is happening https://idioms.thefreedictionary.com/Wake+up+and+smell+the+coffee!
54 Board director interview conducted on 8 January 2021.

I went out to our oil and gas facilities in Colorado. I could see the equipment, which they could read the settings remotely. They had a tank for gas, one for the oil, and one for the water. You have to see how it's separated . . . .

We acquired a lending facility, like a federal savings bank or something in New Jersey, and went out to see the operation. What are they doing? . . . I believe in hands on. You don't meddle, you stay hands off . . . .

The CEO . . . . left us board directors alone. He does not micromanage . . . I think the hands-on experiences of seeing how people interact their behavior, their character. I think that's important.[55]

Board directors can take advantage of board site visits and employee events that they are invited to attend.

"Flynn": One of the boards invited me to employee events all the time . . . . At least once. I generally didn't say anything to anybody . . . . Just the equivalent to talk about the weather.

I always got so much out of those meetings because people will just talk if you just listen. I was listening what they were saying in the room, at the reception . . . Again, I had zero people talking to me but they're talking around me.

You just learn so much by sitting in those things. I would be informed about whether the culture was good or culture is bad. If the employees were happy or not happy. You don't want to interact with people, you just listen and hear what people are saying.[56]

1.3.6 Oversee the Organization

The CEOs role is the most important in the organization. The board director's role is to support the CEO, provide oversight, and work on behalf of people not in the boardroom.

Joyce Cacho: The fiduciary responsibility is usually expressed in: Duty of Care; Duty of Loyalty.[57] I am increasingly raising the duty of oversight. Because we still need to talk about strategy and the future . . . to see around the corner.

Board directors are hired by the company. But by law board directors discuss the company strategy and risk taking, including seeing around the corner.[58]

The board's job is to provide oversight. To oversee the organization board directors should ask questions and "manage their altitude." Board directors are responsible for supervising the organization on behalf of owners and stakeholders.

---

55 Public company board director interview conducted on 29 October 2020.
56 Anonymous board director interview conducted in February 2022.
57 The duty of care and the duty of loyalty are described in Chapter 2.
58 Board director interview conducted on 16 February 2021.

> **Christine Martin**: My experience as a consulting CEO is sometimes I show up and ask questions. I ask "what's going on" and the board says "I don't know." Two weeks later, I say the organization can't make payroll next month. So that's a real-life example where a fairly astute set of board leaders were not paying attention.
>
> The nonprofit board was not getting the right information. They were not getting updated financials. The fundraising or the revenue person in the organization was making a lot of promises about what was coming in. But there was no detail.
>
> Those board members didn't ask questions and they didn't question what they received. I think there's lots of examples of that because they cared about the mission of the organization. It took an outside resource coming in to say this is not a sustainable business mode first of all. And you don't have the cash in the bank you thought you did. You're not going to be able to make payroll in two weeks and all of those commitments you heard about around philanthropy revenue coming in are also unlikely to happen.[59]

The board also provides oversight to faltering companies.

> **Rich Horan**: Sometimes the board is the responsible adult in the room. We see all sorts of examples. I think there's a mindset to develop a company. As a board director I'm not going to tell them how to do it. I'm going to listen to what the company is doing. I'm going to listen, is it a reasonable approach? . . . I don't have all the inputs. I learn as much as I can and ask questions.[60]

Board directors in public companies represent shareholders and owners (see Chapter 2, "Public Companies"). Board directors in private companies represent investors and owners (see Chapter 3, "Private Companies"). Nonprofit board directors represent many stakeholders, including their communities, donors, employees, and more (see Chapter 4, "Nonprofit Companies").

1.3.7 Directors Represent Owners and Stakeholders

This chapter covers how board directors represent owners and stakeholders; the duty of care and the duty of loyalty; and corporate governance in different countries.

It later focuses on public companies. Chapter 3 discusses private and family-owned businesses. And Chapter 4 discusses nonprofit organizations, state-owned enterprises, and hybrid B Corporations.

Public, private, family-owned businesses, nonprofits, state-owned enterprises, and B Corporations need boards. Board directors represent different owners and/or stakeholders depending on the type of organization. Table 1.1 summarizes public, private, and nonprofit organizations with owners, investors, and stakeholders.

---

59 Board director/CEO interview conducted on 28 November 2020.
60 Board director interview conducted on 16 February 2021.

Table 1.1: Owners, stakeholders and their representatives in public, private, and nonprofit organizations.

	Boards Represent Owners and Investors	Boards Represent Stakeholders	Notes
PUBLIC			
Large public companies	X		e.g., Fortune 500
Institutional investors	X		e.g., California State Teachers' Retirement System
Funds, including indexed funds	X		e.g., BlackRock, State Street, Vanguard
Micro-caps and small-to-medium public companies	X		e.g., Russell 3000 at the lower end
Public to private companies	X		e.g., Levi's, Dell
PRIVATE			
Start-ups (including founder-led)	X		There can also be founder-led nonprofits
Family-owned	X		There can be family-controlled public companies
ESOPs	X		Companies partially owned by employees. ESOPs can be private or public
Private equity (PE- backed companies)	X		
Private to public (including IPOs and SPACs)	X		
HYBRIDS			
B Corps	X	X	
NONPROFITS			
Mission-driven organizations		X	Communities served by the organization
University boards		X	Students, faculty, staff, alumni, community
Professional and trade associations		X	
State-owned enterprises		X	

The organizations in Table 1.1 are described in Chapters 2, 3 and 4. Board directors in these organizations represent different owners and stakeholders, the characteristics of which are described in each section.

> **Further reading on board oversight**
> There are chapters regarding fiduciary duties in Robert Nii Arday Clegg's *Corporate Governance: The Boardroom, The Bottom Line, and Beyond*[61] about the alignment of board directors to shareholders and stakeholders.
> One of my favorite books about corporate governance is Brown and Casey's *Corporate Governance: Case and Materials*, Second Edition.[62]

Laws, regulations, and stock exchange policies differ for public, private, and nonprofit organizations. For example in the United States, exchange policies require listed companies to have audit, compensation, and nominating and governance committees. In addition, laws differ in the states where the company is incorporated. Laws and regulations change regularly in the many locations of incorporation around the world.

1.4 Duty of Care and Duty of Loyalty

The experienced corporate directors I interviewed do not focus on laws and stock exchange policies. Corporate secretaries, company staff, and hired professional services ensure the company or organization complies with frequently changing global laws and regulations.

Directors follow the duty of care and the duty of loyalty, which are defined below. The general concepts of duty of care and duty of loyalty arise from equity law and jurisprudence and are captured in state corporation statutes. In the United States, legal requirements vary between states. This is why many companies are incorporated in Delaware, where there is a focus on business law and perhaps more consistency and predictability.

The duty of care is:

> The principle that directors and officers of a corporation in making all decisions in their capacities as corporate fiduciaries, must act in the same manner as a reasonably prudent person in their position would.
>
> Courts will generally adjudge lawsuits against director and officer actions to meet the duty of care under the business judgment rule.
>
> The business judgment rule stands for the principle that courts will not second guess the business judgment of corporate managers and will find the duty of care has been met so long as the fiduciary executed a reasonably informed, good faith, rational judgment without the presence of a conflict of interest.[63]

---

61 Robert Nii Arday Clegg, *Corporate Governance: The Boardroom, The Bottom Line, and Beyond*. Philadelphia, PA: Self Published, 2020.
62 Robert J. Brown, Lisa L. Casey, *Corporate Governance: Cases and Materials*, Second Edition. Durham, NC: Carolina Academic Press, 2016.
63 Duty of Care, Legal Information Institute, Cornell Law School, https://www.law.cornell.edu/wex/duty_of_care.

Duty of care outlines that board directors should know the state of their organization, ask reasonable questions, know company risks, and make reasonable decisions. The duty of care requires no conflict of interest, which is important for boards to self-monitor at least annually. The duty of loyalty further describes conflicts of interest.

The duty of loyalty is:

> The principle that directors and officers of a corporation, in making all decisions in their capacities as corporate fiduciaries, must act without personal economic conflict.
>
> The duty of loyalty can be breached either by making a self-interested transaction or taking a corporate opportunity.
>
> To prevent a violation of the duty of loyalty, if a fiduciary wishes to make a self-interested transaction or take a corporate opportunity, the fiduciary must first fully disclose both the facts of the conflict, and the details of the transaction. The transaction must then be approved by either a majority of disinterested directors or a majority of disinterested shareholders.
>
> If the duty of loyalty is found to be violated, courts may order the offending fiduciary to pay restitution, and may impose punitive damages to deter future violations.[64]

In plain language board directors should not act or make decisions for their personal or family's benefit (unless it is a family-owned business). Again, board directors should act as the representative of owners or stakeholders and not their personal interest. At a minimum, potential conflicts should be communicated to the company secretary. Board directors should abstain from voting on matters that benefit themselves or their families.

There may not be a law against self-dealing (violating the duty of loyalty) in the country where a company is incorporated or operates. But this book is written assuming that good board directors will follow the duty of loyalty.

> **Hon. Carlos C. Campbell:** What I liked about the company we put together was probably the best board I've ever served on. Not to disrespect any other board. But he had a bunch of really bright people. And they were all hand-picked. And they would seriously question anything that looked like a related party transaction a violation of the duty of loyalty. And they came down hard.
>
> So, the independence factor was alive and well. We followed SEC guidance and that was replaced and superseded with Dodd Frank. The company embraced it. What they truly embraced was corporate governance.
>
> As far as my experience in corporate governance is concerned. I think the number one rule: understand the duty of loyalty, the duty of care, and the business judgment rule.[65,66]

Board director Hon. Carlo C. Campbell says what many board directors say, following the duties of care and loyalty is following laws and regulations. Of course, many lawyers and company secretaries would say there is more. But board directors follow the

---

64 Duty of Loyalty, Legal Information Institute, Cornell Law School. https://www.law.cornell.edu/wex/duty_of_loyalty.

65 See Oversight described throughout this book, including Financial Oversight, section 5.2.

66 Public company board director interview conducted on 29 October 2020.

duties of care and loyalty principles and, therefore, comply with the majority of corporate governance laws and regulations around the world.

1.5 Business Judgment Rule

In the United States, I follow the guidance of my friend and colleague Carlos Campbell. In addition to the duties of care and loyalty, a board director follows the business judgment rule.

> **Hon. Carlos C. Campbell**: I think the number one responsibility for board directors is to understand the duty of loyalty, the duty of care and the business judgment rule.[67]

The business judgment rule:

> In lawsuits alleging a corporation's director violated their duty of care to the company, courts will evaluate the case based on the business judgment rule. Under this standard, a court will uphold the decisions of a director as long as they are made (1) in good faith, (2) with the care that a reasonably prudent person would use, and (3) with the reasonable belief that the director is acting in the best interests of the corporation.[68]

In other words, board directors should not be engaged in fraud, not have conflicts of interest, attend entire board and committee meetings, and investigate unethical behavior and wrongdoing.

> **Hon. Carlos C. Campbell**: We were building single-family homes in the Central Valley . . . . I could see what we were doing was no longer abstract. For a director to really represent the duty of care and to exercise the business judgment rule . . . . you have to be engaged, you cannot be abstract, you have to be able to put names to faces and understand the culture and the behavior, you know, how to people do things.[69]

Board and committee meeting minutes are crucial, because minutes are proof of board discussions.

1.6 Corporate Governance in Different Countries

In addition to corporate governance laws and regulations, companies must follow taxation and operational laws and regulations around the world. Companies hire professional services firms to ensure they comply with these operational laws in different countries.

---

67 Public company board director interview conducted on 29 October 2020.
68 Business Judgment Rule, Cornell Law School https://www.law.cornell.edu/wex/business_judgment_rule.
69 Public company board director interview conducted on 29 October 2020.

There is a difference between legal responsibilities and corporate-governance practices. When looking around the world, there are significant differences in specific corporate-governance laws between states, regions, and countries. The board directors I interviewed have experiences with companies and organizations based inside and outside the United States.

Andrea Bonime-Blanc: We've just written a piece for Directorship[70] about Wirecard. Are you familiar with that story? Read the article because it's basically a poster child for all things going wrong. And the board has a big role to play in it. It's a German company.

They have a supervisory board structure. And then they have the executive board which is the management. To me at the end of the day, the executive board is really the executive team, and the supervisory board is really the board.

From a corporate-governance standpoint in Germany, their supervisory board is even more removed than the boards that we have typically here in the US. In our piece, we kind of talked a little bit about the lack of duty of care.[71]

The legal requirements vary significantly between countries. Multinational companies take advantage of consumer markets, capital markets, manufacturing, and operational efficiencies.

Further reading on corporate governance in lower-middle and low-income countries can be found on academia.edu.[72]

Further reading on governance in different countries

See the section on international corporate governance in Christine Mallin's *Corporate Governance.*[73]

See chapters on international corporate governance in David Larker's and Brian Tayan's *Corporate Governance Matters: A Closer Look at Organization Choices and Their Consequences*, third edition.[74]

See Robert Monks's and Nell Minow's *Corporate Governance*, fifth edition.[75]

See the chapter on corporate governance around the world in Bob Tricker's *Corporate Governance, fourth edition.*[76]

See my colleague Hari Panday's chapter, "Cross-Border Corporate Governance" in Richard LeBlanc's *The Handbook of Board Governance: A Comprehensive Guide for Public, Private, and Not-for-Profit Board Members, Second Edition.*[77]

---

70 Andrea Bonime-Blanc and Michael Marquardt, Directorship. May/June 2021.

71 Board director interview conducted on 8 January 2021.

72 Corporate Governance. https://www.academic.edu/Document/in/Corporate_Governance.

73 Christine Mallin, *Corporate Governance, sixth edition.* Oxford, UK: Oxford University Press. 2019.

74 David Larker and Brian Tayan, *Corporate Governance Matters: A Closer Look at Organization Choices and Their Consequences*, Third Edition, Pearson Education FT Press, 2020.

75 Robert Monks and Nell Minow, *Corporate Governance, Fifth Edition*, Wiley, 2011.

76 Bob Tricker, *Corporate Governance, Fourth Edition*, Oxford University Press, 2019.

77 Richard LeBlanc, *The Handbook of Board Governance: A Comprehensive Guide for Public, Private, and Not-for-Profit Board Members*, Second Edition, 2020.

2 Public Company Board Directors

2.1 Overview

This chapter provides an in-depth examination of public companies. The United States is very lucky to have a robust public market and there are many types of public companies representing different categories of investors.

As described in Chapter 1, board directors oversee a business or organization on behalf of its owners and stakeholders. A public company is one in which ownership is organized via shares of stock that are traded on a stock exchange or over-the-counter markets.[1]

2.2 Board Directors in Public Companies Representing Activist Investors

In this chapter, I describe public companies relative to their owners, investors, and shareholders.[2]

Based on interviews with public company board directors, this section and the next describe board directors who (1) represent activist investors and (2) think like an activist to optimize company performance. Even if a board director does not represent an activist, a board director should think like an activist.

Most activist investors are interested in short time frames. These investors look at quarterly and annual returns on their money. Some activist investors may seek quick financial gains by cost-cutting, asset sales, share buybacks, or dividend increases. These short-term activist investors may focus on immediate returns and may exit their positions quickly after objectives are achieved.

Some activist investors may take a longer-term approach. For some activist investors, long-term may mean five-to-seven years, which is considered short- or medium-term for many companies. Long-term activist investors may work with management and the board to implement changes that drive long-term growth and shareholder value.

Board directors who represent activist investors in large public companies must balance the objectives of the activist investors and the best interests of all shareholders. Board directors who represent activist investors will have extra focus on management performance and suggest strategic and operational changes. Board directors

---

1 https://www.investopedia.com/terms/p/publiccompany.asp.
2 In this book, I use the word "owners" to match Professor Christine Milan's use of owners. Investors and shareholders are owners.

https://doi.org/10.1515/9783110689129-002

representing activists will focus on strategy, including changes in cost-cutting, divestitures, and operational improvements.

> **Bala Iyer**: Activist attacks are becoming more frequent. When a high-performing, local company was under attack, the board met more than 50 times. Today's activist attacks are not uncommon. For instance . . . . when a very high performing local was under activist attack, that board met 100 times in that year.[3]

> **Sheila Hooda:** I have been on a public, a large private board. I've been on boards for private equity and activist investors. And when you think long-term you are thinking like 10–20 years. For investors you're thinking of 7-, 10-, 20- years. I haven't been on a board with long-term focus.
>
> Every US public company has the BlackRocks and State Streets being 20–30 percent of the investors. You call them the long-term, passive, and patient. Everyone has those and they are very engaged with on the shareholder engagement side.[4]
>
> I am talking about private equity and activists. And they are seldom long-term. They can't because they are a managed fund. And they've got to return to their investors between perhaps three to seven years. Five may be the average before they want to exit.
>
> When representing activists the concept and the themes of the discussions change.[5]

The impact of activist investors on corporate governance is described in a few books. See Further Reading below.

Further reading on activist investors
See *The Activist Directors: Lessons from the Boardroom and the Future of the Corporation*[6] by Ira Millstein; and my colleague Thomas Bakewell's and James Darazsdi's chapter, "Activist Shareholders and Their Role in Governance," in their book *Claiming Your Place at the Boardroom Table: The Essential Handbook for Excellence in Governance and Effective Directorship.*[7]

2.3 Board Directors in Public Companies Thinking Like an Activist

Though most public company board directors do not represent activist investors, board directors continue to represent owners and shareholders who want to optimize their investment. Board directors on large public company boards represent owners and therefore, can "think like an activist" so that their company does not become a target for activist investors.

---

3 Public company board director interview conducted on 8 January 2021.
4 See section 2.4: Board Directors and Institutional Investors.
5 Public company board director interview conducted on 28 November 2020.
6 Millstein, Ira. *The Activist Director: Lessons from the boardroom and the Future of the Corporation.* New York, NY: Columbia Business School Publishing, 2016.
7 Thomas Bakewell, James Darazsdi. *Claiming Your Place at the boardroom Table: The Essential Handbook for Excellence in Governance and Effective Directorship.* New York, NY: McGraw Hill, 2014.

David Rosenblum: If you go back to what is the role of directors in a public setting, it is to provide a force alignment of the behavior of management with the long-term interest of shareholders.[8]

Anna Catalano: It is no longer only important what companies do in terms of providing services and goods. The primary function of a company is to make these things and sell them to customers that need these things.

 We are also responsible for how we do things in addition to what we do and as institutions in our society continue to fail at what they're supposed to do. Let's say education. Let's say government. Let's say infrastructure. Let's say you name it, okay? This is what tax money is supposed to do, as those institutions don't deliver what a lot of what people need in their lives.

 People look at enterprise to fill in the void. They look for us to help in creating community activities for kids after school. They look for us to create opportunities for single mothers that don't have a way to make ends meet. They look for business and enterprise to fill the void that many of our existing institutions can't seem to do well. And that is a newer role for business than we've had in the past.

 It was a 'nice to do' if you could do it. It's almost a need to do now because we have too many parts of our society that aren't working well, whether it's access to education, access to jobs, all kinds of things.

 What happened to mail delivery? The post office can't do everything. So you have the growth of DHL and Federal Express and UPS. They fill that need that government institutions can't meet the needs of today's society.

 I also think that there is a growing importance of how we conduct ourselves when it comes to how we treat employees. I mean, this began back in the Industrial Age when labor unions emerged. But it goes beyond that because it's no longer just the living wage.

As a society are we creating opportunities equally accessible to all pockets of our society, and all types of people in our society? Are we giving those opportunities in an equitable way, so that everyone has the same opportunity to succeed or fail?[9] The challenge is to increase the value of shares fast enough to satisfy owners, including activists. Public company directors must focus on shareholder value which includes decreasing organizational costs, focusing on strategy, divesting assets, and preparing for activism. This means engaging constructively with activists and preparing for possible shareholder campaigns.

If activist investors believe that the CEO and board are not optimizing for shareholders, they can take action via shareholder proposals and proxy fights.

When shareholders proposals are anticipated or filed, the company's investor relations team become more active. Hopefully the investor relations team has ongoing discussions with investors such as institutional investors and private equity firms. But if there are anticipated shareholder proposals or proxy fights, the need for investor relations to communicate investors becomes more important.

---

8 Public company board director interview conducted on 11 November 2020.
9 Public company board director interview conducted on 3 June 2021.

Activist investors are raising issues that they believe are not being adequately addressed by the public company. Shareholder proposals are used to raise concern about a specific company policy or practices. The goal is to get a majority of shareholders to vote for the proposal and put pressure on the company to make changes. Proxy contests are a more aggressive tactic if they believe the company is not responding to activist concerns.

If activist investors wants to gain control of the board of directors they will start a proxy contest and nominate director candidates to the board.[10] An activist investor may recommend a slate of investors to the board. Or activists can attempt to replace the entire board. This is a way for activist investors to change the company's senior management and strategy.

If a proxy contest does occur, the board should work closely with its legal and financial advisors. But frankly such proxy contests are disruptive to the company and board directors. The best way to avoid this disruption is to think like an activist and communicate with shareholders.

> **"Valen"**: When there was a whiff of a proxy fight the investment management team and CEO went into overdrive. These things take a lot of time and a lot of meetings.
>
> Frankly it's just better to spend time with shareholders and investors before such a thing occurs. A lot of the things which activists want about are things are good things for the company. So [the company] should definitely be talking to investors to do the right thing for shareholders.[11]

Public company directors must understand shareholder perspectives. Working with investor relationships, experienced board directors should listen to shareholder concerns, and gather feedback to better represent shareholder interests. Of course the board and senior management should always act in the best interest of the shareholders.

> **Further reading on public company director leadership**
> Regarding public company directors, see Ram Charan, Dennis Carey, and Michael Useem's book *Boards That Lead: When to Take Charge, When to Partner, and When to Stay Out of the Way.*[12]
> See also the chapter, "The Governance of Listed Companies" in Bob Tricker's book *Corporate Governance, fourth edition*[13] and the chapter "Proxy Scorecards Will Empower Investor" by James McRitchie in Richard LeBlanc's book *The Handbook of Board Governance.*[14]

---

10 At the time this book is being published, the impact of universal proxy has not yet been measured. With universal proxy, it may be easier for activists to elect board directors.

11 Public company board director interview conducted in December 2020.

12 Ram Charan, Dennis Carey, Michael Useem, *Boards That Lead: When to Take Charge, When to Partner, and When to Stay Out of the Way*. Boston, MA: Harvard Business Review Press. 2013.

13 Bob Tricker, *Corporate Governance, Fourth Edition*. Oxford, UK: Oxford University Press, 2019.

14 Richard LeBlanc, *The Handbook of Board Governance: A Comprehensive Guide for Public, Private, and Not-for-Profit Board Members, Second Edition*. Hoboken, NJ: Wiley, 2020.

2.4 Board Directors and Institutional Investors

Board directors do not usually interact with institutional investors. Investor relations teams, CFOs, and CEOs usually interact with institutional investors. Sometimes, at the request of CEOs and investor relations teams, an Independent Chair[15] or Lead Director[16] may interact with institutional investors' staff.

Though board directors do not interact with institutional investors, they should understand the impact of institutional investors on shareholder value. Institutional investors may monitor board compensation and company strategy.

The board directors I interviewed did not say anything about institutional investors. But there are many books on the impact of institutional investors on corporate governance such as:

Carol Nolan Drake wrote a chapter for directors "The Long-Term Relationship Between Directors, Companies, and Institutional Investors" in Richard LeBlanc's book *The Handbook of Board Governance*.[17]

Both Christine Mallin's book *Corporate Governance*, Sixth Edition[18] and Jill Solomon's *Corporate Governance and Accountability*, Fifth Edition[19] have chapters called 'The Role of Institutional Investors in Corporate Governance'. Deborah Hicks Midanek's book, *The Governance Revolution*,[20] has a chapter called 'The Rise of Institutional Investors'. Midanek also has a book *Speaking Out on Governance: What Stakeholders Say About the Revolution*,[21] with an article from Anne Sheehan, former CEO of institutional investor CalPERS, called "How is it That We Earned the Return"?

2.5 Board Directors and Indexed Funds

Indexed funds managed by BlackRock, State Street, and Vanguard now own many public US companies. As public board director Sheila Hooda said these indexed funds are passive and patient. This means that these indexed funds let public companies

---

15 A board chair who is not the company CEO.

16 When the company CEO and the board chair are the same person, one of the directors is identified as Lead Director.

17 Richard LeBlanc, *The Handbook of Board Governance: A Comprehensive Guide for Public, Private, and Non-for-Profit board Members, Second Edition*. Hoboken, NJ: Wiley. 2020.

18 Christine Mallin, *Corporate Governance, Sixth Edition*. Oxford, UK, Oxford University Press. 2019.

19 Jill Solomon, *Corporate Governance and Accountability, Fifth Edition*. Hoboken, NJ, Wiley. 2020.

20 Deborah Hicks Midanek, *The Governance Revolution: What Every board Members Needs to Know, NOW!*, Boston, MA, De Gruyter Press. 2018.

21 Deborah Hicks Midanek, *Speaking Out on Governance: What Stakeholders Say About the Revolution*. Boston, De Gruyter Press. 2020.

operate as the company chooses.[22] But because indexed funds own a substantial percentage (20 to 30 percent) of US public companies, it makes sense for investor relations teams to listen to indexed-fund managers.

Not much is written about the impact of indexed funds on corporate governance. But my colleague Chris Lee spoke discussed what board directors should know about indexed funds.

Chris Lee: I would just highlight a couple of topics that I feel quite passionate about. Officially, it's also the LinkedIn post that I did recently back in October 2020.[23] This is about corporate governance in the age of index funds.

So, index funds were a financial product that not too many people cared too much about ten years ago. And now it has become very big.

So, they are basically investors who take the view that picking stocks in the market is a waste of time. You should just invest into an ETF Exchange Traded Fund and that would give you probably the best returns over time, especially people who are not interested in finance and do investment as their day job.

And even a lot of the very successful investors like the CIO Chief Investment Officer for Yale University, David Swensen has also famously said that for an average investor or for non-professional is better off for them to put their money with an index fund. And even Warren Buffett has also said that too.

Everyone is going to own some kind of index-related product just like every one of us now uses ATM machines. So, the capital-markets dynamics is going to be completely different when your largest shareholder is an index fund . . . . not a human.

So, this is a very big paradigm shift in terms of how boards should get to know their biggest investors.

So evolutionary change is something that board members have underestimated. It's not a revolution that we're talking about. It is an evolutionary change. So, it's changing very slowly. And then boards have to really catch up and learn about what's the change in dynamics.

And you know, this is a very technical subject. I wanted to first raise the awareness that this is complex and technical. Ask questions like how is the NASDAQ different from the Dow? What is the indexation methodology of the Dow? And who gets to be included in the S&P? And if you are included into the S&P, what is your composition? And how to calculate the weight because that is going to determine the buy/sell decisions of the index funds.

If the index fund manager is selling Microsoft shares, it's not because Microsoft is not doing well. It's just that the index weight in the S&P has gone down. So, in order to keep up with the index, they have to sell shares.

These are the things that I want to share with boards. I've been doing this for more than two decades and I feel that it is important especially in global markets for ETFs.

I also feel that some foreign firms have done a better job than American firms in understanding the index funds development. From investor relations to index fund managers, there's a

---

22 Indexed funds, in the past few years, have made directional ESG (Environmental, Social, and Governance) and DEI (Diversity, Equity, and Inclusion) statements, which I will describe in the chapter on strategy.

23 LinkedIn, 'Is the Rise of Index Funds at Odds with Good Corporate Governance?' Christopher Lee, (22 October 2020), LinkedIn. https://www.linkedin.com/pulse/rise-index-funds-odds-good-corporate-governance-christopher-lee/.

short article that I published on LinkedIn[24] that you could definitely refer to and I will be happy to add a little bit more to that.[25]

Chris Lee continues: I'll begin with the traditional, activists fund managers piece first, and then I will expand it to the index funds piece.

Before, the advent of an index fund there were already many activist funds: Pershing Square, Joe Ackerman, and Nelson Peltz and they were very active engaging with boards and the management team on how to change the business, what strategies they need to review and they have very active discussions with management teams on basically the business of the company. So that's one type of very influential investor that is interacting with the boards.

In terms of reacting to those investors, boards have to react and also respond to activist shareholders in terms of board composition, diversity, etc.

Index funds also play a similar role. And in fact, if you look at the global assets under management by activist funds, it is actually very small compared to the size of index funds. So we're talking about like $150B in active versus almost 10 trillion dollars with a trillion in passive.

To my point about this being evolutionary, it's not just a revolution that all of a sudden the boards have to now react to investors and know our investors and do more with IR investor relations work.

We're just saying that you have to expand beyond just dealing with the activist shareholders by including the calculation agents, and all the indexes like FTSE, S&P 500 . . . and all the rating agencies.

It's a little like back in 2008, before the financial crisis. People just look at the ratings of the bond. This is a BB- or this is an AAA-rated bond and are happy with it. But they don't actually go into the methodologies on why this is rated AAA.

So that was the failure because the rating agencies were not really doing their jobs in terms of rating these bonds. So now we're just going in a little bit more into the index company and ask them: "So, how do you actually do your index methodology?"

Microsoft is a good company. Why is the weight only 2%? Why shouldn't we increase the weight to 5% of the index. So that's the kind of discussion that I think boards can definitely have. And people on boards that I know have the capacity to do that. It's just that they may not have the appreciation or maybe the time to get there yet.[26]

Because index funds own such a large percentage of US public companies, I believe Director Lee has a thoughtful approach and is on the leading edge of discussing the impact of index fund on corporate governance. Because index funds own so much of US public companies. See academia.edu for further research published about the impact of institutional funds on corporate governance.[27]

---

24 Christopher Lee, LinkedIn, (October 2020). *Is the Rise of Index Funds at Odds with Good Corporate Governance?* https://www.linkedin.com/pulse/rise-index-funds-odds-good-corporate-governance-christopher-lee/.

25 Public company board director interview conducted on 7 December 2020.

26 Public company board director interview conducted on 7 December 2020.

27 Academia.edu, https://www.academia.edu.

2.6 Board Directors, Micro-Caps and Small-Cap Companies

Board directors of Micro-Cap and Small-Cap companies have unique challenges. Of course, there are limited financial and human resources. The company may provide a new product or service in a competitive market. With increased competition and fewer resources there may be increased risk and it might be more difficult to access to capital.

> **Michael Marquardt:** Here's a hypothesis of mine and why I'm framing it. Probably me and Adam Epstein[28] are very much on the same page on this. It seems like a majority of advice for corporate directors and corporate governance advice that's out there from NACD or by Spencer Stewart or by Pearl Meyer or whatever is aimed at large public company boards. But it is presented as if it applies to everybody.[29]

I recommend reading my colleague Adam Epstein's book about small-cap companies, *The Perfect Corporate Board: A Handbook for Mastering the Unique Challenges of Small-Cap Companies*.[30] And you can read Jo Iwasaki's chapter, "Governance of Small- and Medium- Sized Entities" in Richard LeBlanc's book, *The Handbook of Book Governance*.[31]

I agree with Michael Marquardt and Adam Epstein that most advice and books are written for public company boards, which is why I started this book. There are many kinds of organizations with boards that represent different owners and stakeholders.

The numbers of micro-caps and small-cap companies are much greater than the number of public companies. And as board director Michael Marquardt says, there is less literature on micro-caps. But micro-caps and small-cap companies are essential to the public company ecosystem. The US SEC (Securities Exchange Commission) aims to increase the number of public companies, which means more small- and medium- enterprises in the future.

> **"Earnest":** Being a board member of a micro-cap is harder than you think. I am a jack of all trades to make this company work.
>
> I am frequently helping the CEO find new talent. I am surprised that we find good people even during tough times in 2019–2020. But they don't always stay, so we are always looking for new talent.
>
> I have been advising the CEO and CFO to look at going private. There is so much private capital available now.[32]

28 Adam J. Esptein, globally recognized small-cap expert and boardroom advisor, https://adamjepstein.com/.

29 Board Director/CEO interview conducted on 4 February 2021.

30 Adam Epstein, *The Perfect Corporate board: A Handbook for Mastering the Unique Challenges of Small-Cap Companies*. New York, NY, McGraw-Hill Education, 2012.

31 Richard LeBlanc, Richard. *The Handbook of board Governance: A Comprehensive Guide for Public, Private, and Not-for-Profit Board Members*. Hoboken, NJ, Wiley, 2020.

32 Board director interview conducted in June 2021.

Micro- and small-cap companies may not have the financial resources to offer the same compensation, benefits, and growth opportunities as larger companies. So, board directors may have extra challenges when helping the CEO find talent.

> **"Adler":** I am friends with the CEO, and we do what we can to get the right board members. Right now we are looking for people who have a little deeper finance skills to help our CFO and our Audit Committee.
>
> We have a pretty good board that covers most of the bases. But it's a challenge to prepare both for sale and as well be viable 10 to 15 years from now.[33]

Micro-cap and small-cap companies have smaller boards, which means there may be less skills, knowledge, experience, and diversity on boards. This means that boards may be less able to provide guidance on strategy and not able to help the CEO with needed projects.

> **"Francis":** The other thing that we did was we distributed a big dividend every month. And basically we were distributing. If you bought the stock at $10 we were distributing 10% of the value, which is a very high dividend yield of 9–10%.
>
> And when I saw the amount of cash we were generating from the business and the capital improvements we had to do, we were distributing 100% of what we're making. So we're actually taking on more debt every year.
>
> Our goal said on paper was we want to make sure that we have 70% to 80% of our cash flow that we're distributing so we can reinvest. But we never got there.
>
> We bought these hotels because we wanted to grow in the market very fast. They underestimated how much capital they had to put into the hotels in the putting more capital into the hotels than they thought. Then they distributed it.[34]

I include Francis's story because this is a real public company. The company generates solid, consistent returns. And when a company generates solid returns, investors may not look into the details of how the company generates returns. We will return to Director "Francis's" story later in this book.

> **"Brook":** What made us different was that we were not the normal public company. First, we were a micro-cap. This company should never have been public. It became public as a reverse acquisition into a public company shell.
>
> Our first litigation was with a company that took us public. It was a sham, right? They were buying public company shells and then taking unsuspecting unwitting country bumpkins and saying we can make you multimillionaires if you give us your millions.
>
> And that's how this company started. It started with this guy who had about $xx million worth of assets. And somebody came to him and said we'll put you in this public company, pump up the stock, dump it, and you'll make multiples of what your property is worth.
>
> That's how this company started as a sham and it is ending as one. So that's a story in and of itself.

---

33 Board director interview conducted in May 2021.
34 Board director interview conducted in January 2021.

Micro-caps have their own Gestalt, which made us different. We had no employees. We had one full-time corporate secretary who's really like an administrator and we had one contractor, who was our CFO.

We were at completely thinly traded stock. There were groups of beneficial shareholders, so in essence there were like four or five shareholders and then a whole bunch of little, tiny shareholders. In the 80s where you buy penny stocks the company was mostly trading in pennies.

At one point when the two new directors joined, we solved our auditor problem. When we solved our SEC problem, we started filing with the SEC again. Then the company was basically back on track. We actually rose to about three dollars a share. So, we were actually creating value and that's what we used to say "Oh, look, we're doing a good job. We're doing the right thing. We're right."

And then, you know people's personalities got in the way again. So, we were thinly traded. As I said we started off as a scam and we ended up in bankruptcy.

What made us the same as all public companies is that we had an accountability to shareholders. And most of us never took our eyes off that ball. We had an accountability to the SEC. And we worked very hard to clear our problems with the SEC. We communicated with them a lot.

We had an outside auditor. And we had all the same rigor of independence and professionalism with our auditor that at Fortune 50 company would have. So, we followed that. We have the same time legal exposure that any public company would have and in our case probably a little more.

And what made us the same as large public companies is that we actually conducted a formal audit committee investigation. And we engaged one of the best professional firms with the guy that probably had the number one reputation for audit committee investigation. You can only imagine how interested he was in the fact structure of this $XX-million-dollar market cap company for the number one audit committee investigation lawyer in the country to take us on as a client. And it didn't disappoint.[35]

Of course, most micro-caps do not have these kinds of problems. The stories of both Francis and Brook show the need for board directors. They both serve as board directors to get their companies back on track to become more sustainable.

From a corporate-governance perspective, duty of care is needed because their companies must follow government regulation and listing agency guidance to access public capital markets. And sometimes micro-cap and small-cap companies must pay for top-notch professional services to comply. I will return to Francis's and Chris's stories throughout this book.

2.7 Cross-Border Corporate Governance

Corporate governance in the United States differs from that in other countries. In the US there is emphasis on shareholder primacy, but there is increasing prominence in stakeholder capitalism. (See Purpose in Section 9.1.) There is also significant differ-

---

35 Board director interview conducted in December 2020.

ence in regulation between countries; in the US there may be increased disclosure and transparency. Also, board structure differs especially between the number of independent directors and inside directors.[36]

> **Chris Lee**: I think especially some of the UK basic regulation is very useful.
>
> I would also bring in the two-tier board structure in Germany,[37] right? And I think people are acutely aware of the fact that there is a supervisory board at BMW and Deutsche Bank. All these companies include employee representatives and also regionally representatives. It is a very different structure compared to the boards that were familiar with in the US
>
> So it's worth mentioning that . . . . the UK are focusing a bit more on the stakeholder model as opposed to just the Delaware shareholder model, right?
>
> The Delaware Court says shareholder primacy model is the dominant model and the UK and the German model are very different.[38]

The UK model requires that public-listed companies disclose how they have complied with regulations and codes or explain why they have not met the code.[39] In 2018, the UK Corporate Governance Code was designed for sustainable growth between companies, shareholders, and stakeholders.[40]

In Germany and other countries, there is a two-tier structure.[41] There is an executive board composed of management for day-to-day business operations and a supervisory board elected by the shareholders and employees to supervise the executive board. The CEO and board chairs are always separate roles. Comparing the German and US models, the US board of directors is often equivalent to the German supervisory board.

Some of the board directors I interviewed sat on US boards of public companies based in other countries; for example, a Chinese company with a US board to take advantage of the US capital markets. This occurs because the companies operate in the US due to increasing globalization. This kind of cross-border corporate governance is likely to increase.

---

36 Inside directors are employees, including officers, of a company https://www.investopedia.com/terms/i/insidedirector.asp.

37 The Structure of the Board of Directors: Boards and Governance Strategies in the US, the UK and Germany, Harvard Law School Forum on Corporate Governance, https://corpgov.law.harvard.edu/2021/04/12/the-structure-of-the-board-of-directors-boards-and-governance-strategies-in-the-us-the-uk-and-germany/.

38 Public company board director Interview conducted on 11 January 2023.

39 SSRO corporate governance framework, Gov UK, https://www.gov.uk/government/publications/ssro-corporate-governance-framework/corporate-governance-framework.

40 UK Corporate Governance Code (July 2018), Institute of Directors, https://www.iod.com/news/governance/uk-corporate-governance-code-july-2018/.

41 The German Supervisory Board, University of Oxford, https://blogs.law.ox.ac.uk/blog-post/2022/12/german-supervisory-board#:~:text=Germany%20has%20a%20two-tier%20board%20system.%20This%20system,the%20supervision%20and%20control%20of%20the%20management%20board.

Board directors in the US who sit on the boards of companies based in China represent the shareholders of the US capital market. As described in the interview below, the CEO is likely Chinese and other board directors are likely from the US and China.

> **"Hayden":** There were three US independent board directors. It was me and another gentleman, who is a US-based American from Connecticut. He was the operator guy and the financial expert was somebody who was Swiss. Eventually he changed out for various reasons, so we did have a shift to an Audit partner who was American.
>
> But he and I both spoke Chinese (the second Audit chair). We were the three independents – the majority independent.
>
> The CEO who was on the board. He was Chinese. And there was another gentleman who was essentially the COO, head of Biz Dev, he was Chinese. It was a six-member board.
>
> It was helping companies – dirty industries – recycle their outputs, reduce pollution, and generate energy from equipment that the company would install.
>
> [Private equity firm] was obviously interested in the sector and there was a six-member board because [private equity firm] had a seat as well.
>
> We had good outside counsel. It was an American law firm; a respected top 50 American law firm. We all had the diligence. There is a level of opaqueness that is normally reduced when it's a pure American company.
>
> So given that it was not a US company, given that things were in a different language, we wanted to make sure that there was a respected reputable American law firm behind all this. Securities law firm that would make sure that all the Ks and the Qs . . . . 8-Ks were filed properly when they needed to be US government regulations. An important piece for us even agreeing to step on.
>
> It is more than due diligence before joining the US board. More diligence coming in and more effort on going to continually justify these legal bills. It was just that additional thing that you wouldn't have to necessarily deal with if it's a standard US company.
>
> That will create more shareholder value. including for yourselves. It was just the process of educating everybody in terms of what drives value, what is our role especially as a first-time board for a previously private company, now publicly listed, but still with a significant closely held share from management and founders.
>
> And as US laws and regulations change, the board directors continue to partner with the CEO and the China-based company to make changes as long as the company participates in US capital markets.[42]

> **"Xio"** in a similar situation said: Chinese management would say, "why do you need to know all this?" While we said we need to know this because that's the role of independent board directors.[43]

This idea is the most important; creating more value for the company and shareholders. As public board directors Hayden and Xio say, the US board directors are responsible for ensuring the China-based company complies with US fiduciary laws and listing regulations. The board directors ensured that the company had the right professional services guidance and partnered with the China-based CEO to explain why

---

42 Public company board director interview conducted in 2021.
43 Public company board director interview conducted in 2021.

certain changes were made. And as US laws and regulations change, the board directors continue to partner with the CEO and the China-based company to make changes as long as the company participates in US capital markets.

> **Further reading on international corporate governance**
> I recommend my colleague Hari Panday's chapter, "Cross-Border Corporate Governance" in Richard LeBlanc's *The Handbook of Board Governance.*[44] There are multiple chapters about global corporate governance in Jill Solomon's *Corporate Governance and Accountability.*[45]

2.8 Board Directors for Companies Going Public to Private

There are significantly fewer public companies today than twenty years ago. Some public companies, such as Dell and Levi's, move from private companies to public companies and back to private again.[46] By becoming private, some companies believe they have enough private capital and can create a more valuable company by changing strategy and operations with less regulation and less focus on quarterly and annual earnings.

> **Chris Lee:** One thing that is clear is that the number of listed companies now is a fraction of what it used to be. I can look up the data for you, which is like maybe ten to twenty years ago 7,000 listed companies on NASDAQ and NYSE combined. But nowadays it's probably less than 50 percent.[47]

> **"Robin":** Levi's went public because they needed the public company status. But operating a public company is also a lot of work for the CEO and could be a distraction, sometimes even to the detriment of the core business of producing blue jeans and nice garments. So they went private if you remember.
>
> This is the struggle for many family-owned companies[48] and businesses. If they don't need the capital from Wall Street and they don't need the financing, they already have the name and the brand and the credibility with their lenders and their financial partners.
>
> What is the incentive for them to be a publicly listed company? Given that there are more regulations and also perhaps more cost.[49]

---

44 Richard LeBlanc, *The Handbook of board Governance: A Comprehensive Guide for Public, Private, and Not-for-Profit board Members, Second Edition.* Hoboken, NJ: Wiley. 2020.

45 Jill Solomon, *Corporate Governance and Accountability, Fifth Edition.* Hoboken, NJ, Wiley. 2020.

46 Private companies do not have shareholders in US capital markets. Private companies are described in Chapter 3.

47 Public company board director Interview conducted on 7 December 2020.

48 Family-owned companies are described in Chapter 3. Family-owned companies can be public or private companies, but are more often private companies.

49 Public board director interview conducted in December 2020.

Board directors of the public company continue to represent their shareholder owners until they become private. To represent public-capital-market shareholders, the board directors should optimize the payment to shareholder owners to take a company private. The duties of care and loyalty apply to optimizing payment to shareholder owners. If it is a US company, the law requires board directors only approve decisions that optimize the payment to public company shareholder owners. The exception to optimizing shareowner value is B Corporation status, which is described in Chapter 9.

3 Private Company Board Directors

3.1 Overview

There is a long-term trend for private companies to remain private, as stated in Chapter 2. Some private companies become public via IPOs and SPACs (described later in this chapter) and some private companies become public and then return to being private.

Board director Lee, who also teaches, describes the increasing number of private companies. There are many more private company directors than public company directors. There are approximately six million private companies in the US with less than 50 employees.

> **"Robin"**: It's a fraction of what it used to be (number of public companies) because of the regulatory compliance costs and partly because the cost of going public in terms of financial costs . . .
>
> Some companies choose to stay private because they just don't have the right mix of skill set. For example, the right people who could function as an acceptable board . . . In addition, there are legal and perhaps financial reasons against being a public company . . . .
>
> I talked with my board member on M. If you're like me anyway, you grew up on that kind of thing.
>
> M is now in the fifth generation. They run M almost like a public board . . . . Even though M is a private company, they have independent directors, and they also invite members of the board to give them advice and guidance, very much similar to a public company board.
>
> I think there are good examples in the marketplace of private companies who choose to stay private because they don't need the distraction from the capital markets.
>
> I'm a capital markets guy. I get a lot of criticism from corporate CEOs saying that we are too short-term; we focus too much on quarterly earnings.
>
> They private companies wanted to avoid that distraction . . . the inefficiencies in the stock market by staying private.
>
> At the same time, they would still embrace a corporate governance model that is very similar to a large public company.[1]

> **"Valen"**: A lot of companies don't need to have that public money, right? There's enough money in the private equity world where they can tap into . . . .
>
> This is my opinion. But . . . I think a lot of it's around control. They just want to maintain more control over their company. And that's a real driver right beyond the cost.[2]

Is it about control rather than representing investor interests? Some board directors and CEOs will confidentially say it is about control and others will say that investors will benefit more by keeping CEOs and private boards in control.

---

1 Public company board director Interview conducted in December 2020.
2 Board director interview conducted in December 2020.

https://doi.org/10.1515/9783110689129-003

3.2 Similarities and Differences Between Public and Private Company Board Directors

Many corporate director books focus on public company directors. Public companies may be larger. But there are more private than public companies in the US. And the number and percentage of public companies is decreasing.

Like public company directors, private company directors represent investors. Investors are chiefly concerned with financial return.

Private companies do not have the regulation and compliance requirements of public companies. Moreover, private company directors and investors have less focus on stakeholder interests.

Most private company directors do not discuss regulation and compliance and in many cases, private companies will hire staff and professional services to ensure that private companies comply with laws.

An investor understands the company's business model, revenue and profit projections, and management capability. An investor may understand a business more than someone recruited to join a public company board.

Private company directors are also asked to identify new investors. Board directors learn more about a company when they bring in new investors. Potential new investors often ask questions that push the company to expand in new operational areas or customer markets.

Private-company directors may be asked to augment the additional skills and experience (e.g., finance, recruiting) of the company's CEO and senior management team, or they may find alternative resources. This includes both short-term needs (i.e., advisors, consultants) and long-term roles (human-resources executive, information-technology executives, etc.). Sometimes board directors are asked to recruit and interview senior leaders. CEO and private-board director Chin is an active recruiter upon request from her CEO and board chair.

> **Lisa Chin**: The "noses in fingers out"[3] stuff is difficult in small privately held organizations because you roll up your sleeves. For example hire the VP of sales, which I helped do. That's one of the biggest lessons for me; learning that there's always that line and only to help the CEO when you're invited in . . . .
>
> You're singing for your supper or working for your equity slice . . . . But you're still a director of the organization. You still have to be mindful that it's not your decision. It's the CEOs decision. As much as the board directors want to run and manage things.
>
> You are still just a consultant. So that's one of the biggest lessons I've learned.
>
> I observe that line only because . . . I've been a director on privately held companies . . . Even when I've been asked by the lead investors or the leaders in the family to go in and "do X" and I did it right. I functioned as a consultant who rolled my sleeves up. I helped write a sales plan. I help with marketing. I did all this other stuff. Even though I was doing the work of man-

---

3 See Section 1.3 for "noses in, fingers out".

agement. I was still a director. And I still had an equity stake . . . You cannot stop being a director even when you're invited in.

Management treats you differently. You can be invited in to perform a role, but that's a point in time. It never changes.

So that is the balance of being a consultant and you are a director.[4]

Private company board directors may be asked to find short-term and senior-level advisors and consultants to augment the CEO and senior management. Board directors are expected to have a large network from which to draw talented advisors. For example, board directors likely know experienced advisors for taking private companies to public companies. Our board directors know advisors on how to shape CEO performance management and compensation to align with company strategy and execution.

Public company directors are more esteemed but not necessarily more talented. Investors may investigate the background of public company directors to ensure that the directors have the necessary skills, experience, and integrity to oversee the company and make decisions in the best interests of shareholders. Private companies do not have the need for such esteemed backgrounds.

The compensation of private company directors can be significantly greater than public company directors. Public company directors are compensated similarly to well-paid employees, i.e., 50 percent or more of the public company's director's compensation may be in stock.

A private company director may own a substantial portion of the private company. So, in addition to being paid (similar to modestly paid employees), the private company director may receive a substantial payout when a private company is sold.

As explained in Chapter 2 on public companies, there seems to be a long-term trend for private companies to remain private. But some private companies became public via IPOs and SPACs (defined in the following pages) while others became public and returned to being private. These public companies become private again to decrease shareholder and activist demands, reduce regulatory burden, and improve operational flexibility.

Further reading on private company governance

See Dennis Cagan's *Boards of Directors for a Private Enterprise*,[5] Adam Epstein's *The Perfect Corporate Board: A Handbook for Mastering the Unique Challenges of Small-Cap Companies*,[6] Elizabeth Hammack's *The Private Company Board of Directors*,[7] Roger Ford's *Boards of Directors and the Privately Owned Firm*[8]

---

4 Board director/CEO interview conducted on 30 September 2020.
5 Dennis J. Cagan, *The Board of Directors for a Private Enterprise*. Bloomington, IN: Author House. 2017.
6 Adam Epstein, *The Perfect Corporate Board: A Handbook for Mastering the Unique Challenges of Small-Cap Companies*. New York, NY: McGraw-Hill Education. 2012.
7 Elizabeth Hammack, *The Private Company Board of Directors*. Granite Bay, CA: Self Published. 2019.
8 Roger H. Ford, *Boards of Directors and the Privately Owned Firm: A Guide for Owners, Officers, and Directors*. New York, NY: Quorum Books. 1992.

and Richard LeBlanc's *The Handbook of Board Governance: A Comprehensive Guide for Public, Private, and Not-for-Profit Board Members, Second Edition.*[9]

3.3 Private Equity (PE) Backed Company Directors

Board director Rosenblum describes the close alignment of investors, directorates, and CEOs.

David Rosenblum: What you've seen is the rise of private equity and arguably the principal advantage of private equity is a reduction of this agency problem . . . .[10]

The agency problem is when agents (e.g., company management) don't fully represent the best interests of principals (e.g., shareholders). Principals (e.g., private equity firms and private company directors) hire agents (e.g., CEOs) to represent their interests and act on their behalf . . . .[11]

And when you talk with people on boards of private equity-owned companies, who also have public company experience, they tell me, "We spend a lot more time on strategy than we do on compliance compared to public companies."

And most of the research I've seen would say, as an asset class, private equity has done extremely well with companies because you've reduced the gap. The private equity-backed executives are, in fact, significant owners.

They have significant economic incentives to do things lined up with the interests of the shareholders, which ultimately, in private equity are endowments, pension funds, and private offices.[12] Third parties that have turned cash over to private equity firms to act as their agents.[13]

Private equity owners expect more from their boards of directors than most investors.

Larry Taylor: I serve on a PE (private equity) board, and they have a different view of the world. They tell you shareholder primacy rules. The mantra of "noses in fingers out," doesn't apply so much.

They are smaller boards. They have a shorter-term view versus long-term view. They want to get their money out and that small board is digging deep into management.

---

9 Richard LeBlanc, *The Handbook of Board Governance: A Comprehensive Guide for Public, Private, and Not-for-Profit Board Members, second edition.* Hoboken, NJ: Wiley. 2020.
10 The agency problem is a conflict of interest that occurs when agents (e.g., company management) don't fully represent the best interests of principals (e.g., shareholders). Principals hire agents to represent their interests and act on their behalf. The Agency Problem: Two Infamous Examples. Investopedia. 15 April 2021. Blog https://www.investopedia.com/ask/answers/041315/what-are-some-famous-scandals-demonstrate-agency-problem.asp#what-is-the-agency-problem.
11 *The Agency Problem: Two Infamous Examples.* Investopedia. 15 April 2021. Blog https://www.investopedia.com/ask/answers/041315/what-are-some-famous-scandals-demonstrate-agency-problem.asp#what-is-the-agency-problem.
12 A private office or a family office is a private wealth management firm that serves ultra-high-networth individuals (HNWI).
13 Public company board director interview conducted on 11 November 2020.

> The board I serve on is an aerospace board. I'm often asked to go down into the shop floor and talk to managers and bypass the CEO on all kinds of things. Because private equity firms want to really know what's going on. Many times, that's beneficial to profitability. The shareholders get higher returns often.[14]

Private equity firms select companies to buy. So, selecting and managing board directors is one way to protect the private equity firm's investment.

Private equity firms invest in companies because they see substantial growth and financial returns. They provide industry and competitor information to CEOs and board directors to augment company information.

When a private equity firm invests, it has its sights on an exit.[15] The exit is when the firm will earn most of its financial return. Most private equity firms want a return on their investment in three-to-five years, which drives company strategy, execution, and CEO performance.

There is close alignment between board directors and private equity owners. Private equity firms select and compensate the board directors.

Private equity firms focus on the strength of the CEO. The CEO leads the business to execute the strategy and achieve results. A private equity firm will thus consider how board directors will best augment the CEO's skills and experience.

The compensation of CEOs and board directors is dependent on achieving the financial goals the PE firms expect.

Further reading on private equity-backed company governance
See Simon Witney's *Corporate Governance and Responsible Investment in Private Equity*.[16]

3.4 Start-up Board Directors

> **Minaz Abji**: The start-up mentality is survival. Start-up mentality is "I need cash to pay the bills." And they're not able to afford all the other things that they may want to do . . . .
>
> I would say to the people who are going to read your book, they're most likely going to end up with small start-ups. And the small start-ups don't do everything that students of corporate governance are taught.
>
> Start-ups don't have the budgets or the resources to do all the stuff that the large companies do. The large boards have a lot more resources. And start-up boards do a lot more work.

---

14 Board director interview conducted on 27 October 2020.
15 An exit strategy is an executed by an investor, trader, venture capitalist, or business owner to liquidate a position in a financial asset or dispose of tangible business assets once predetermined criteria for either has been met or exceeded. https://www.investopedia.com/terms/e/exitstrategy.asp.
16 Simon Witney, *Corporate Governance and Responsible Investment in Private Equity*. Cambridge, UK: Cambridge University Press. 2021.

What they'll have to figure out is what's so important. What should be part of the board's charter? How can the charter be better than it is? Is there missing stuff? What's something you cannot live without?[17]

Directors serving on the boards of start-ups are investors, coaches, and connectors. Perhaps the most important connections that start-up board directors make are for more investment. Connections to private equity firms are highly valued. In addition, start-up board directors may be asked to augment operational roles, such as IT and recruiting.

The number of private companies and start-ups have been increasing. CEO and private company director Chin describes the wide range of private companies.

> **Lisa Chin**: I do think that Silicon Valley is different . . . And I agree with you that a lot of the tech guys roll their sleeves up and they say "do this, this, and this . . . . and this is how we're going to make money."
>
> Whereas the other ones in other industries are different because the pace is slower. The time to market is different. In Silicon Valley what's productized is different.
>
> In financial services, relationships are based on trust . . . So financial services are very traditional. We had a Trust Department. It's multi-generational wealth; that is not going to work with a Silicon Valley model.
>
> I would argue that start-ups and business models vary by industry because whatever you're selling, whatever the product or service, the director's involvement has to reflect the values or the objectives of what the company is trying to serve.[18]

The experience of start-up board directors varies as much as companies differ. The start-up-board director differs by industry, geography, competition, financial environment, and other aspects.

> **Barbara Adachi**: In joining a start-up, it was the first time they set up a board with independent directors. In this type of environment, the CEO uses us as a sounding board, but there is very little formal structure and communication between meetings.
>
> An example would be the first financial package which contained a lot of numbers, but no benchmarks, comparison to plan or budget, etc. The package has evolved over time but required a significant amount of direction from the board.
>
> As most of the board members had significant operating roles in the past, we still must be careful not to overstep. Our role is to oversee, not manage. At times, it is hard to let go of "managing" but we remain committed to our governance oversight responsibilities.[19]

Another significant aspect of start-up board directors is founders. My interviews contained many stories about working with founders. The relationship between board directors and founders will be captured in the second book in this series, The Art of Director Excellence, Volume 2.

---

17 Public company board director interview conducted on 20 January 2021.
18 Board director/CEO interview conducted on 30 September 2020.
19 Public company board director interview conducted on 5 May 2021.

The investors of many start-ups are family members because they are willing to risk the loss of their investment to support the family member starting a business. The next section focuses on private companies that are family-owned businesses.

> **Further reading on startup board governance**
> There is a good book, specifically on the startup board. Brad Feld, Matt Blumberg, and Mahendra Ramsinghani wrote *Startup Boards: A Field Guide to Building and Leading an Effective Board of Directors, Second Edition.*[20]

3.5 Family-Owned Business Directors

The board directors of many family-owned businesses are family members and frequently, independent board directors of family-owned businesses are family friends.

Over time, the board directors of family-owned or family-controlled firms will not be family members or friends. This change in board composition is because board directors represent all investors.

An independent director describes working in a family-owned business as a "non-family board member":

> "**Channing**": No matter what, the family is always right.
> I learned that the hard way. No matter what. Families are families. It is an entity like no other.
> Because if you were to stand back and be a fly on the wall, you could tell "who took whose blocks" when they were younger.
> Family members never get over those issues. And this weeds into governance. Especially if they're fortunate enough to have a family company and its multi-gen[21] . . . .
> Even though you could be right and say, "if we don't do this, we're going to have to sell the company." You could be right, but that doesn't matter. What matters most is an understanding of the family dynamics.
> How do you balance your responsibilities for the organization as Director versus serving at the pleasure of the family is a very tricky thing. Ultimately the family wins even if they're at each other's throats. The family wins . . . .
> That's the challenge. There was a lot of disagreement in the family, and it had nothing to do with the balance sheet. It had nothing to do with the problems that were actually brought to the Directors. It actually had to do with stuff outside of the boardroom.
> We didn't realize this for the first couple of years that we were dealing with some of the dynamics. We couldn't understand why, all of a sudden, four siblings and some in-laws were on

---

20 Brad Feld, Matt Blumberg, and Mahendra Ramsinghani, *Startup Boards: A Field Guide to Building and Leading an Effective Board of Directors, Second Edition.* Hoboken, NJ: Wiley. 2022.
21 multigenerational

the board. And there were five outside directors. We couldn't understand why one family member would just come in guns a-blazing and always not seek to bring the problem up early.

When I went in, I made the choice that I'm with one of the family members who is chairing the board and their spouse.

I just stuck with them because morally, I was thinking, they know what they're doing. They may not be doing the best job of running the company and keeping the legacy open, but they're not attacking anyone.

They're not going to cause the company to tank. We're not going to make the news because of what they're doing. We might not make a lot of money but that seems rational.

There was another director who chose to be with the firebrand who actually had experience as a CEO and lost his company because the board fired him.

It was very challenging because you have an equity stake. You care about the company and might have relationships with multiple generations, which I did.

Some would rather break the company apart so they have more money. Others, want to preserve the legacy. Others don't care and they're being forced to care. So, it really depends on why you're on the board in the first place.

I was on the board because I have a deep love for some of those people and I was happy to do whatever I could to help them, keep their company and family name out there and honor the founder's legacy. So, the choice was easy for me because the board member – the family member – who was ripping everything up was, did not bring me in.

My loyalty was to the family members that did bring me in . . . .and because they weren't doing any harm. They really were choosing to do what they believed the company values were. The other person believed in what they were doing too but was quite destructive.

How family members talk to each other was kind of disrespectful . . . . and in front of outside Directors.[22]

This second story for classroom discussion describes a global family-owned business:

"Hayden": When I joined . . . it was a company in this relatively small town.

I met with the family a few times because I only wanted to join if we all thought I could add value. I didn't want to just be occupying a board seat without being able to contribute.

Some of them were from the [US] community. Some were long-standing family friends and always had their broader interests at heart.

I was the last one to join the board before the exit.

This private Family-Owned Business was really fascinating. I'm no longer on it because we helped them exit. They were acquired by a large European conglomerate. I think I was on that board for maybe about three or four years.

What I found interesting about them is they were relatively small – about $100 Million or so in annual revenues. For a relatively small company it was pretty global and complex in the sense that they had operations in Germany and China. And they had manufacturing there. They made this special type of machinery.

The patriarch, the guy who started this company was a board member, as were two of his sons. And what's also interesting is a son-in-law was running the company. His daughter was not on the board. But the daughter's husband (the son-in-law) was the CEO. So again for a relatively small company it was pretty complex because of operations on three different continents and this kind of family dynamic.

---

22 Board director interview conducted in September 2020.

I found it a fascinating challenge, which I was happy to take on. I learned it's a very different shareholder model. It's your duty to the family and the business.

Trying to figure out the dynamics within the family is also very interesting. Without going into too much detail, there were different family members with different strengths and skills . . . . And there were actually five other outside board members.

I was always trying to make sure that we spent more time on the strategy rather than on the tactical stuff . . . . I felt some of the meetings were a little bit more tactical, more just reporting, rather than let's talk about where we want to be. Let's take a step back. And you know this time next year, what kind of results do we want or things like that?

In the end, we did a good job. How we helped them exit, which I know was one of the goals. There was a little bit of a catch-up that I had to do in the first year.

The family members cashed out and went different entrepreneurial ways. I think it's a happy ending. I still keep in touch with some of them, just to check in.

It was, I think, a very interesting journey and maybe the point for your audience is, don't forget about family-owned business opportunities.[23]

When a family owns the majority of shares in a company, it is considered family-owned. At some point, a family may not own the majority of shares but the family may continue to control the company. A company may have articles of incorporation or bylaws specifying that the majority of board directors may be elected by the family. Or there may be dual-class stock structure with one class having more voting power than the other. Company bylaws[24] become crucially important at this point. In the US, companies are required to have Bylaws, which must be reviewed and approved by board directors.

Most bylaws include standard and good governance provisions such as "one share, one vote."[25] But some bylaws keep company control with the founder and the founder's family. Bylaws may include initial shares that have more votes than subsequent shares. For example, dual-class[26] stock allows initial shareholders the ability to veto future shareholder initiatives.

Board director Lee works and lives in California in Silicon Valley, and explains further:

> **Chris Lee**: There is a "Silicon Valley" attitude to retaining control of a company while accepting capital from public markets. Even though a Founder (or the family of a founder) may own only ten percent of the shares but retains voting control of the company.[27]

---

23 Board director interview conducted in 2021.
24 Rules established by an organization to regulate itself. https://en.wikipedia.org/wiki/By-law.
25 https://en.wikipedia.org/wiki/One_share,_one_vote.
26 Dual-class stock: When multiple share classes of stock are issued, typically one class is offered to the general public, while the other is offered to company founders, executives, and family. The class offered to the general public often has limited or no voting rights, while the class available to founders and executives has more voting power and often provides for majority control of the company.
27 Public company board director interview conducted on 7 December 2020.

"Earnest": Companies like Facebook, Google and a lot of the tech firms have dual share class structure. Whereby the founders' class has maybe ten times more voting rights compared to the average common shares. So from a corporate governance point of view I think it is an inferior model.

We believe in one-share one-vote and every shareholder should be treated equally. So Founders who have only five percent or maybe ten percent of the whole should not have the majority voting power.[28]

Family-controlled companies can be either private or public.

Family members on a board of directors in a family business have the same responsibilities as other board directors. However, there are additional interpersonal complexities between board directors who are family members. Navigating these interpersonal complexities is covered in my second book, The Art of Director Excellence, Volume 2: Roles.

> **Further reading on family-owned business governance**
> There are a number of books on being on the board of a family-owned business. See Leon Danco's and Donald Jonovic's book, *Outside Director in the Family-Owned Business*.[29] Or see the chapter on *Family-Owned Firms* in Christine Mallin's book *Corporate Governance*.[30]

3.6 ESOP Board Directors

An ESOPs (Employee Stock Ownership Plans) is:

> An employee benefit plan that gives workers ownership interest in the company. ESOPs give the sponsoring company the selling shareholder and participants receive various tax benefits, making them qualified plans. Companies often use ESOPs as a corporate finance strategy to align the interests of their employees with those of their shareholders.[31]

Board directors of ESOPs are representatives of the owners of the company, including employees who own a significant part of the company. Most ESOPs are closely held private companies. But ESOPs can be offered by public companies. Board director Essenmacher describes her ESOP board experience.

"Darian": The company is 40% ESOP. Part of the reason that the board was formed was because the CEO understood that the company was at an inflection point. The industry is changing and

---

28 Board director interview conducted in June 2021.
29 Leon A. Danco, Donald J Jonovic, *Outside Directors in the Family-Owned Business*, Cleveland, OH: The University Press, Inc. 1989.
30 Christine Mallin, *Corporate Governance*, Sixth Edition. Oxford, UK: Oxford University Press. 2019.
31 Akhilesh Ganti, *Employee Stock Ownership Plan (ESOP)*. Investopedia. (April 29, 2021) https://www.investopedia.com/terms/e/esop.asp.

customer base are changing . . . . The CEO was thinking about the future – things like strategy and succession planning.

The trustee for the ESOP basically said "you need a board" because employees are an important group of stakeholders. This company has been structured based on stakeholders – thanks to the work and vision of the CEO . . .[32]

The National Center for Employee Ownership is the best information source about ESOPs in the United States.[33] There are nuances in serving with board directors who represent workers.

These are captured in The Art of Director Excellence, Volume 2: Roles.

3.7 Private Companies Moving to Public Markets Including IPOs and SPACs

Some private companies become public via IPOs and SPACs. Though the number of public companies will likely continue to decrease, there were still IPOs and a significant amount of private capital funding SPACs at the time of interviews.

IPOS are:

Initial public offerings (IPOs) are a company's first sale of stock to the public. Securities offered in an IPO are often, but not always, those of young, small companies seeking outside equity capital and a public market for their stock.[34]

SPACs are:

Special Purpose Acquisition Companies (SPACs) are companies formed to raise capital in an initial public offering ("IPO") to use the proceeds to acquire one or more unspecified businesses or assets to be identified after the IPO.[35]

Board directors help companies change from private to public companies.

Chris Lee: I think the public versus private discussion is definitely something that is going to be ongoing. . . .

Given the IPO cycle that you are seeing now in the market, there will be many young companies like the Airbnbs and DoorDashs of the world. They will need to upgrade their corporate governance.

---

32 Board director interview conducted in November 2020.
33 https://www.esop.org/.
34 Initial public offering (IPO). NASDAQ. https://www.nasdaq.com/glossary/i/initial-public-offering.
35 Ramey Layne, Brenda Lenahan (July 2018), *Special Purpose Acquisition Companies: An Introduction* Post Harvard Law School Forum on Corporate Governance. https://corpgov.law.harvard.edu/2018/07/06/special-purpose-acquisition-companies-an-introduction/.

This is going back to the point we made earlier. A lot of engineer Founders were very good at doing products and building businesses. But corporate governance is not just about building a better mouse mousetrap and increasing sales. Corporate governance is about a lot of other things.

So that's the transition and the evolutionary step into corporate governance that I think they have to take.[36]

Private company directors should work with CEOs to determine short- and longer-term strategies. The decision to seek public-equity market funding is a key strategic decision for CEOs and board directors. There is a close relationship between CEOs and board directors during this time, as CEO and board director Chrostowski describes.

Andrew Chrostowski: I don't think it's ever premature to plan for the future, right? We're a hyper-growth company. We're scaling as we speak. . . . And we're probably not atypical with a venture-backed early start-up.

This is where governance is somewhat complicated. Depending on your tranches of investment . . . what rights you have. It's fairly complicated when you go into an IPO.

Or now a lot of discussions about SPACS as one method of getting to public markets.

But in either case, you create a collapse of the governance structure. When going public that change would absolutely cause needs for new board members. And the SEC would require all kinds of things that would also be to the benefit of the companies.

So we certainly plan for those kinds of transactions.

If there was another raise . . . we'd certainly add another board member. So for us, it's going to be about how we add capital to drive our growth. And it's a question of which way that capital comes into the company that will determine how we move forward.

Clearly, you pick up all the public governance structure when you move down the IPO or SPAC path versus what you might do if you continue to grow as a private company. But in any case, the board will expand with increased investment.

And when we do that, I always embrace the concept of making sure we have good diversity on the board.[37]

Private company directors stay tuned to investors as their companies move from private to public.

"Earnest": I have brought other companies public before. I have done this many times. Each time I learn something new.

I learned the importance of good corporate governance. This is something that investors want.

I have now learned that investors want to know about ESG. It seems like every conversation is about ESG, though sometimes they are really asking about the company's purpose. . . . and have a diverse board. That seems like a no-brainer these days.[38]

---

36 Public company board director interview conducted on 7 December 2020.
37 CEO/ board director interview conducted on 20 January 2021.
38 Board director interview conducted in June 2021.

"Sam": Interesting research that I'm doing that is a work in progress is that I see how some companies go from private to public. All the tech firms, they're on a road to IPO which is definitely something that the founders and also the engineers want to embark on. And over time after the public company for maybe ten years, they would actually entertain the idea of going private again.

An interesting case because Levi's went public because they needed the public company status and also the governance now operating a public company is also a lot of work for the CEO and could be a distraction. Sometimes even to the detriment of the core business of producing blue jeans and nice garments. They went private if you remember, right?

This is kind of the struggle for many family-owned companies and businesses as well. If they don't need the capital from Wall Street, and they don't need the financing. And they already have the name and the brand and the credibility with their lenders and also their financial partners.

What is the incentive for them to be a publicly listed company? Given that there are more regulations and also more perhaps cost right?[39]

Board directors can help a private company prepare for an IPO by guiding management and professional advisors with the timing and structure of the offering. They can help assess SPAC offers by ensuring the SPAC's offer is fair and reasonable and communicate the benefits of the SPAC merger to investors.

3.8 SPAC Board Directors

In 2020 and 2021 when initial interviews were conducted, board directors were recruited to take private companies to join public companies. SPACs are created specifically to take private companies to public markets.[40]

Board members for SPACs are investors, investing $200K USD or more. SPAC board directors have an expectation for compensation, which can include zero or low compensation while the company (or companies) are a SPAC, and an expectation of compensation when a company goes through the de-SPAC process.

Though SPACs have existed for decades, many SPACs came into existence in the early 2020s with many more directors involved.

"Adler": I thought an interesting way to get my toe wet on a public company board was to join a SPAC board. As you know, SPACs are everywhere; there may be too many SPACs.

I put in $xxx thousand to join the SPAC board. I know there is a risk that I will lose some or all of my money. But I like the other people on the SPAC board, and I think we will find good companies to bring public. We all have a passion about healthcare.[41]

---

39 Board director interview conducted in November 2020.
40 Special Purpose Acquisition Companies ("SPACs") are companies formed to raise capital in an initial public offering ("IPO") with the purpose of using the proceeds to acquire one or more unspecified businesses or assets to be identified after the IPO.
41 Board director interview conducted in May 2021.

In 2020, many private companies were ready for public capital markets. This means they had to report revenue costs to Wall Street analysts, be ready to comply with US Securities and Exchange Commission (SEC) government regulations.

For these companies to be ready for US capital markets and US government regulation, it was easier to de-SPAC.

During this de-SPAC process, there is frequently a change in board directors. For regular public companies, there is an expectation of esteemed public board directors. Public company board directors represent investors and work with the CEO to increase company value.

Later in 2020, 2021, and 2022 there were fewer companies ready for US Wall Street analysts and US government regulation compliance. It was harder for these companies to become public and go through the de-SPAC process. At the end of 2022, many SPACs liquidated before even acquiring their targets.[42] When a SPAC finds a company to acquire, the de-SPAC process includes post-merger integration, establishing corporate governance, engaging with investors, and complying with regulatory requirements.

Many SPAC board directors do not get compensated until after the transaction. Moreover, the terms of compensation of SPAC board directors may change when companies transition from private to public companies. After the de-SPAC process, these companies have a different board composition and board directors have public company board director responsibilities.

---

42 "SPAC Boom Ends in Frenzy of Liquidation," Wall Street Journal, 25 December 2022. https://www.wsj.com/articles/spac-boom-ends-in-frenzy-of-liquidation-11671917668.

4 Nonprofit Board Directors

4.1 Overview

In the United States, nonprofit organizations are non-governmental organizations (NGOs) that are mission-driven with a social service. See the chapter "Focusing on Results: The Power of Purpose" in John Carver's book Boards *That Make a Difference: A New Design for Leadership in Non-Profit and Public Organizations.*[1]

For-profit and nonprofit boards are similar yet different. Both non- and for-profit boards provide fiscal oversight. Board director Martin who has served as CEO for many nonprofits, explains:

> **Christine Martin:** In the for-profit space, they're focused on making money for an organization. The for-profit board has an obligation to shareholders, be they public shareholders or be they private shareholders and investors . . . . In the nonprofit space the board is also responsible for the fiscal stability of an organization.
>
> In both cases, boards care a lot about the mission. I would argue that in the for-profit space, mission is sort of synonymous with making money; it's very clear that's how you make decisions.
>
> In the nonprofit space as a board member, it is not always so clear. There is somewhat less flexibility in terms of how nonprofits make money. And it is more uncertain.
>
> In the nonprofit space, board members also get very anxious about organizations that are operating at a loss. (For-profits can operate at a loss for a limited amount of time.) Being a board member at a nonprofit is getting comfortable with being in a more risky situation. This is something that board members need to adapt and learn from.

For nonprofits, board directors are responsible to investors. In nonprofits, investors are often donors. Just as for-profit board directors represent the interest of investors, nonprofit board members work to fulfill donors' intent and serve the mission. In addition, nonprofit board directors ensure the organization complies with government regulations to maintain nonprofit status.

> **Christine Martin** continues: I guess the last thing I want to point out is that in addition to the duty of fiscal oversight responsibilities and governance, the main difference is nonprofit board members are responsible to the state and to the feds for upholding the charitable deductions and charitable responsibilities for the organizations that they're serving.
>
> And essentially if you think about it, nonprofits are funded either by donations . . . or funding from state and federal governments . . . or other grant makers.
>
> As a nonprofit board member your job is to make sure that those contributions are stewarded in the individual's or entity's intent.
>
> It's a pretty significant difference between a for-profit and nonprofit because of that duty for ensuring that the charitable purpose of a nonprofit – whether it's the Red Cross or the YMCA

1 John Carver, *Boards That Make a Difference: A New Design for Leadership in Nonprofit and Public Organizations, Third Edition.* San Francisco, CA: Jossey-Bass. 2006.

https://doi.org/10.1515/9783110689129-004

or your school's PTA – that the charitable donation is made appropriately, recorded appropriately, and that the money that is being used in the way that it is intended.[2]

As board director Martin says, nonprofit board directors represent investors who are philanthropists who donate money to support the organization's mission. Board directors ensure that philanthropist donations are spent efficiently and effectively and in small part, nonprofit board directors ensure the investor/philanthropist experience with the organization is positive.

Another difference between a for-profit and a nonprofit board is the number of board directors.

For-profit boards usually pay board directors. Increasing the number of board directors increases for-profit company costs. So for-profit companies have a smaller number of board directors.

Nonprofit board directors are usually unpaid. They are asked to invest or donate to the nonprofit and, therefore, add revenue to the organization. So nonprofit organizations usually have a large number of board directors. Board director Adachi questions if a nonprofit board can govern with a large number of directors.

> **Barbara Adachi:** With larger nonprofit boards, every constituency is represented in the room. Prior to joining a corporate board, my only experience was with large national nonprofit boards like the American Cancer Society ranging from 30 to 45 members. The decision-making process is longer, focusing on gaining consensus of a large board. Nonprofit board experience is helpful in building your network and learning basic governance principles, but the strategic issues and board culture will be very different when compared to a smaller public or private company corporate board with eight to ten members.[3]

Because nonprofit board directors are a revenue source, there is an incentive to have a larger board and a different performance expectation. For example, there may not be performance expectations, or performance objectives may be unclear. There may not be annual performance discussions and there may not be an effort to remove board directors.

> **"Rene"**: Nonprofit boards tend to be larger. And people, unless they just act out egregiously, don't get removed.[4]

> **"Ridley"**: Nonprofit organizations have a separation of governance and fundraising boards. I think nonprofit organization we've gotten in trouble in the past is when some of the big fundraisers we're also on the fiduciary board . . . .
>
> I've also served on boards that are smaller and we don't have big fundraisers. We have some fundraisers on our board, and we have some operators, and we have other stakeholders, and it just works.[5]

---

2 Board director/CEO interview conducted on 28 November 2020.
3 Public company board director interview conducted on 5 May 2021.
4 Board director interview conducted in 2020.
5 Board director interview conducted in January 2023.

R. Omar Riojas: I think it's good to have a board with different skill sets . . . everyone's contribution should be valued, you know, equally and differently, right? . . . It's a good process to add board directors who bring fundraising capabilities . . . . board directors who have a network . . . and they have good intentions. In other words, these are folks who really care passionately about the nonprofit's mission and have been long-time supporters. That's key – long-time supporters.[6]

See the "Non-Profit vs. For-Profit Boards – The Fundamental Difference" in Dennis Cagan's book *The Board of Directors for a Private Enterprise*[7] for another perspective on nonprofit and for-profit differences.

4.2 Nonprofit Board Director Responsibilities

Nonprofits today are beginning to have performance objectives for board directors. See the article "The New Work of the Nonprofit Board" by Barbara E. Taylor, Richard P. Chait, and Thomas P. Holland from Harvard Business Review.[8]

Board directors of nonprofits have a significant responsibility to be "investors" in the organization as private company board directors are expected to be investors and donors. Unlike private company board directors, nonprofit board directors do not own the nonprofit, nor do nonprofit board directors receive financial benefit from the organization.

Like public company board directors, nonprofit board directors have a significant duty of care. This requires disclosure of any conflicts of interest or benefits the board directors or their families may receive from the nonprofit. In the United States, the tax benefit given for nonprofits is contingent on the board director's and employee's focus on the mission.

Like public board directors, nonprofit board directors are esteemed members of the community. Like public companies, the directors serving on the nonprofit board are part of the organization's brand. The character and actions of nonprofit board directors reflect on the organization.

Like private company directors, nonprofit board directors are expected to bring in more donors to the organization, which is commonly called fundraising. Nonprofit board directors bring in donors rather than investors.

---

6 Board chair interview conducted on 11 January 2023.

7 Dennis J. Cagan, *The Board of Directors for a Private Enterprise*. Bloomington, IN: AuthorHouse. 2017.

8 Barbara E. Taylor, Richard P Chait, and Thomas P. Holland. *The New Work of the Nonprofit Board*, Harvard Business Review, September – October 1996. Cambridge, MA: Harvard Business Review Press. 1996.

David Rosenblum: If you're talking about nonprofit boards, the principal objective role of the board – beyond oversight of strategy and oversight of the CEO and risk – is really fundraising.[9]

Board director oversight responsibilities of the CEO, strategy, and risk (as described in this book) remain the same for nonprofits. See William Bowen's book, *The Board Book: An Insider's Guide for Directors and Trustees*.[10] In particular, see the section: "Are For-Profit and Non-Profit Board Practices Converging?"

Like public and private company boards, nonprofit boards should work with management to develop strategy and manage risks. The aspirational opening quote in the Introduction by Michael Marquardt[11] is relevant for nonprofits. The board and nonprofit management should work together to put strategy that works annually as well as long term.

Nonprofit board directors are responsible for representing stakeholders. Stakeholders include the people served by the nonprofit's mission; the employees and volunteers who work in the nonprofit and philanthropists/donors as noted earlier.

At many nonprofits, board directors are asked to augment management responsibilities. Like a private company start-up, a nonprofit CEO may ask board directors to augment the organization.[12] For example, if the nonprofit organization needs legal advice and a board director is a lawyer, the nonprofit CEO may ask the board director lawyer for advice.[13,14]

---

9 Board director interview conducted on 11 November 2020.

10 William G. Bowen, *The Board Book: An Insider's Guide for Directors and Trustees*. New York, NY: W.W. Norton. 2012.

11 Board director/CEO interview conducted in 2021.

12 See the section: *"Trustees Are Acting More Like Managers"* which is in "Chapter 1: First Principles" in "Governance as Leadership" *HBR's 10 Must Reads*. Cambridge, MA: Harvard Business Review Press. 1996.

13 In general, when a nonprofit board director performs service for the organization, they are usually not compensated. But if the board director performs a service and is compensated, such an agreement should be public knowledge and be disclosed. Moreover, if there is compensation, to ensure there is no conflict of interest (duty of care) a board director may take a leave of absence or resign from the nonprofit board.

14 I am frequently asked by people who are new to board service if they should join a nonprofit board. My answer and first question are "Do you believe in the organization's mission?" For example, "would you be (or are you) a donor or a volunteer, if not serving on the board?" My second question is "Does the board develop strategy, manage risk, manage CEO performance, and represent stakeholders?" Unfortunately, the answer to this second question is "no" for many nonprofits, which may mean the board director is a funding source rather than a board director. And if the answer is "no", the future board director will not learn many skills and experiences relevant to future board service. If the answer is "yes" to both questions, then I recommend volunteering for nonprofit board service. In addition, I think other talented people will serve on these kinds of boards. With such talent, this is a good entrance to other boards. For additional insight from my board director interviews about joining boards, see my second book, The Art of Director Excellence, Volume 2: Roles.

There are a surprising number of books on nonprofit governance. Please see Further Reading below.

Further reading on nonprofit board governance
See Michael E. Batts's book *Board Member Orientation: The Concise and Complete Guide to Non-Profit Board Service.*[15]
See John Carver's book *Boards That Make a Difference: A New Design for Leadership in Non-Profit and Public Organizations*, Third Edition.[16]
See Richard P. Chait et al.'s *Governance as Leadership: Reframing the Work of Non-Profit Boards.*[17]
See Richard LeBlanc's, *The Handbook of Board Governance: A Comprehensive Guide for Public, Private, and Not-for-Profit Board Members, Second Edition.*[18]

4.3 College and University Board Directors

There are many types of nonprofit boards. Directors on college and university boards represent many stakeholders.[19] College and university board directors, usually called trustees, represent donors, alumni, students, employees, and the community. College and university boards are interesting because of the institution's multiple sources of power and authority. College and university boards represent many stakeholders, which adds to their complexity. University trustee Taylor describes this complexity.

> **Larry Taylor:** On my university board, there is shared governance, which I had to learn. You've got three governance systems and the faculty is too often an adversary to the board. And administration has their own kind of governance. So the three of us have to get along and I wasn't used to that; I did learn to adjust to that. I had sidebars with other board members who said, "Larry you can't do that."[20]

In general, colleges and universities can attract esteemed and talented board directors. Talented board directors are well-suited to manage the performance of college and university presidents. Many trustees[21] have been in the top leadership of their organizations and can do an excellent job in evaluating President[22] performance. Col-

---

15 Michael E. Batts, *Board Member Orientation: The Concise and Complete Guide to Nonprofit Board Service*. Self-published. 2011.
16 John Carver, *Boards That Make a Difference: A New Design for Leadership in Nonprofit and Public Organizations, Third Edition*. San Francisco, CA: Jossey-Bass. 2006.
17 Richard P. Chait et al., *Governance as Leadership: Reframing the Work of Nonprofit Boards*. Hoboken, NJ: Wiley. 2004.
18 Richard LeBlanc, *The Handbook of Board Governance: A Comprehensive Guide for Public, Private, and Not-for-Profit Board Members, second edition*. Hoboken, NJ: Wiley. 2020.
19 Most colleges and universities are Nonprofits. There are some for-profit colleges and university, which should be treated as private-company boards.
20 Board director interview conducted on 27 October 2020.
21 Board directors are called Trustees at many colleges and universities.
22 CEOs are called Presidents at most colleges and universities.

lege presidents and senior leadership should welcome input and guidance of board directors in developing strategy and managing risk.

As described earlier, nonprofit board directors are usually asked to contribute to the organization. When trustees at colleges and universities donate, there may be confusion between the trustee's governance responsibilities and the donor's role.

> **"August"**: My half-sister and I have the same father but different mothers. And her mother remarried somebody else who is a very wealthy man call him "Juan". He is a trustee at XX University and being a trustee is really more about how much money you have.
>
> It is interesting to compare notes with him because I'm a trustee of a state-owned university.
>
> It felt really different. It was interesting to talk to him. There's the "Juan" Art Center, which is the building that he and his wife built at the University. It was amazing – the different flavors of the kind of work that we do as trustees, which is really about helping more people get access to college versus his perspective . . . looking to build out a legacy with buildings with his name on it . . . Does he have any empathy or understanding about students?
>
> Juan feels like he's making an investment. They have a different stake in the university. Does he and his wife think that they could dictate the art?[23]

The college, university board, chair and president provide guidance to trustees about governance responsibilities and donor interests. Given the high caliber of college and university trustees, this should be an easy discussion.

It could, however, be a difficult discussion If there is confusion between governance and fundraising responsibilities. In my second book, *The Art of Director Excellence*, Volume 2: Roles, there is an additional discussion about this potential conflict between governance and fundraising responsibilities.

4.4 Professional and Trade Associations Board Directors

When I interviewed my 50 friends and colleagues for these books, I told interviewees that the audience for my books would include undergraduate and graduate students studying corporate governance. With this audience in mind, a few interviewees mentioned board directors of professional and trade associations.

Board directors in professional and trade associations are representatives of their careers, organizations, and communities. They work for the benefit of workers in their professions and trades.

For people who want to join bboard service, joining a relevant professional and trade association with the intention of being a governance leader (chair, vice chair, committee chair, etc.) may be a worthwhile learning experience as described by board directors below:

---

23 Board director interview conducted in June 2021.

Julian Ha: Trade associations are a creature of D.C.[24] as you can appreciate. And most of the time you serve because your employer is a member . . . .

You're there because you really believe in your profession or industry. Right now I'm on three association-type boards; one is the US-ASEAN Business Council . . . My fellow board members, they're all either senior business leaders within Fortune 500 companies or heads of government affairs. And so it's a different type of experience, which I think is also positive.

It's all about . . . . How can you represent this industry?

When the head of Chubb or Coke flies to Vietnam or Indonesia or Thailand, this Council has on-the-ground resources to help them meet with foreign ministers and ambassadors and transact and conduct more business.[25]

Melinda Yee Franklin: I'll talk about the San Francisco Chamber of Commerce because I started off as a board member – regular board member – with 70+ fellow board members who are all senior executives in their firms from small-medium-large businesses.

It was great to spend time with people to learn about their businesses. How can board directors work together to collaborate on projects that were helping the greater good? For example focus on helping small businesses or mentoring. For instance there was a women's leadership program that I've been very involved with to help bring other women into corporate America. I was able to handpick the areas that I thought I could contribute to.

I have a real interest in the public policy committee. It was important to me because we were addressing the issues of the day (tax issues and different business issues). This is the fabric of doing business in San Francisco, including some controversial things like minimum wage and labor issues. We're making sure that the business community has a voice and a seat at the table.

So yes, I found being a member of a board was very beneficial.[26]

Board directors of professional and trade associations learn more about governance and board service. And it provides an opportunity to do social good.

4.5 State-Owned Organization Board Directors

There are many state-owned organizations around the world. Some of the largest energy companies in the world are state-owned.
- A state-owned enterprise (SOE) is an entity formed by the government to engage in commercial activities.
- The government usually takes either full or partial ownership of any SOEs, which are typically approved to engage in specific activities.
- SOEs represent the government in commercial endeavors and sell physical resources to trading entities and corporations.

---

24 The District of Columbia in the United States.
25 Board director interview conducted on 20 January 2021.
26 Board director interview conducted on 7 March 2021.

- SOEs operate in all countries but are especially prolific in China, the United States, New Zealand, South Africa, India, and Russia.[27]

The responsibilities of state-owned organization board directors are similar to those described so far for public, private, and nonprofit directors. Many state-owned companies and institutions have boards, with board directors representing the community, the public, and the state. In some situations, the board directors represent the politician or political party that appointed the board director. But better corporate governance is if the board director represents all members of the community.

I have heard from many board directors of state-owned enterprises that "your values must match" with the government that appoints directors. I agree that if your values don't match those of the government, then don't join. Resigning after joining a state-owned enterprise board of a state-owned enterprise is not ideal. Giving up a board role could be misinterpreted, and it's not good governance.

Let's return to **"August,"** who is an appointed state-owned university board director who discusses "Juan," her extended family member and private university board director and explains the perception versus reality of board directors who are state appointed:

> Juan said to August "Oh, you're an appointed official" and August's response was "hmmm." Juan was skeptical about whether or not that was the right thing. I said I was appointed by the state and he said he was "elected" – elected by the other university trustees/board Directors. . . .
>
> Juan said "you people who are appointed. That means you are political beings, right? That means you have these loyalties to the person that appointed you." August said "That's just not true in our system . . . We have none of those politics. There's no money to go around. We see it as more of our volunteer work than a resume builder . . . . Or get your name on a building . . . . We're not that kind of trustee."[28]

The most important stakeholder for board directors in state-owned organizations is the person or group who appointed the director. And board directors should represent residents of the state as well as investors, employers, consumers, and many other stakeholders.

Board directors of state-owned organizations must ensure the service is provided in a reliable and efficient manner to meet the needs of the public. Board directors may need to ensure organizations meet the state's laws and regulations and operate in a transparent manner.

---

27 State-Owned Enterprises (SOE) (30 September 2020), Investopedia, Will Kenton, https://www.invest opedia.com/terms/s/soe.asp.
28 Board director interview conducted in June 2021.

4.6 Temporary Board Directors

Christine Martin, an interim CEO and board director, mentioned appointing a temporary board. She described an organization that was going through significant financial strain. In this situation, many board directors began to resign. So, she appointed a new temporary board.

Because the organization was a nonprofit, the board of directors represented community interests to get the organization out of a financial hole. A temporary board was necessary to focus the organization on a financially sustainable business model and ultimately merge the organization with another entity. The temporary board experience is described by CEO and board director Martin.

> **Christine Martin**: We brought in a temporary board, which I've never done before including former board members who still cared about the organization.
>
> A couple of former staff members and that team held the organization together with some support from me over four months. Then we merged the entity into a much healthier larger place. The work we were doing educating middle school and high school students about impact of climate change on the environment . . .
>
> Sometimes a board with lack of attention and lack of focus can lead to fairly catastrophic results in an organization. CEOs do a lot of that work. We kind of have to do some truth-telling to the board and identify where they're not engaged.[29]

A board is essential to an entity. This situation and solution are interesting as the board's role becomes more focused on the lifecycle stage and the organization's specific needs.

---

29 Board director/CEO interview conducted on 28 November 2020.

5 Audit Committee

5.1 Board Committees

When joining a board, new board directors should understand that most of the work is conducted in committees. Board directors are selected not only for their experience and insight across an enterprise but for specialized skills and expertise. So when joining a board, a new board member is usually assigned to a committee.

> **"Harper"**: I spend the majority of my time in committees. I attend committees. I attend follow up meetings for committees. I ensure that documents are accurate and then we have those documents sent to the full board for review.
>
> People think that the action happens at full board meetings. But that's not true. Most of the action happens in the committees, then actions are ratified at the full board level.[1]

Many US public companies have Audit, Compensation, and Nominating and Governance Committees. But organizations have many variations to this committee structure, described in Chapter 8 about the Nominating and Governance Committee.

Because committee work is so important, this book includes a section devoted to Audit, Compensation, and Nominating and Governance Committees, with one chapter dedicated to each topic. In addition, this section of the book describes the many possible ad hoc committees focused on CEO selection, CEO onboarding, and other topics.

Because board committees are so important, chapters on this topic are included.[2]

5.2 Financial Oversight

Because board directors represent owners and stakeholders, perhaps at the top-of-mind of board directors is the financial performance of organizations. This includes not only public and private but also nonprofit organizations.

> **Christine Martin**: Board members have a duty . . . . a fiduciary duty as an appointed board member, whether they're working for pay for-profit entity or a nonprofit entity to provide oversight and stewardship of financial resources.[3]

---

1 Board director interview conducted in July 2022.
2 "The Importance of Board Committees," in Mark A. Pfister's, Across the Board: The Modern Architecture Behind an Effective Board of Directors, Port Jefferson, NY: Pfister Strategy Group, 2018. And "Board Committees" in Michael E. Batts, Board Member Orientation: The Concise and Complete Guide to Nonprofit Board Service. Orlando, FL: Accountability Press. 2011.
3 Board director/CEO interview conducted on 28 November 2020.

https://doi.org/10.1515/9783110689129-005

The CEO and CFO are responsible for managing the organization's financial performance. But the board provides financial oversight of the CEO and CFO on behalf of owners and stakeholders.

Financial oversight has always been a primary board responsibility, but there has been a shift in how boards have exercised this duty. When boards were composed mostly of company employees and advisors, CFOs and financial advisors always had a seat at the table. Following the development of independent boards, the duty of financial oversight shifted to independent audit (and sometimes finance) committees that included such expertise but without such strong company ties. Members of such committees can ask difficult questions that employees and advisors may be reluctant to ask.

> **Ryan Patel**: I feel like that person should be challenged by other people. Likewise, a business needs to be challenged If it is a mature business, you need someone with finance expertise . . . . The director chairing the audit committee needs to be strong. We need to have more savvy people like that.[4]

The Audit Committee provides a deep dive on behalf of the board to dig into the organization's financial health. My friend and colleague Tom Bakewell recalls a time when he and his fellow directors spent years working with a company that evolved from being a "sleepy tradition-bound company on life support" to one of "robust health with annual revenues that grew from $8 million to $90 million with enviable margins and earnings."[5]

Special attention should be paid to start-up and entrepreneurial organizations. Founders have laser-like focus on building their business and may too easily accept net losses.

> **Michael Pocalyko**: The trick for entrepreneurial companies is to be able to move from being a managerial process board to becoming an effective oversight board. More often than not this process requires adding or replacing directors. Not making that transition is a big failure of many entrepreneurial companies.[6]

Adding board directors with accounting or finance expertise is a relatively quick fix. An advisory committee focused on finance can also help. Recruiting board directors and setting up an advisory committee is described in Chapter 6 regarding the Nominating and Governance Committee.

In addition to financial expertise, board directors need to understand the overall organization and have financial literacy. Although financial literacy is not required of all directors by any current law listing standard, it has been recommended by the National Association of Corporate Directors and other governance

---

4 Board director interview conducted on 30 October 2020.

5 Chapter "The Importance of Finance to Exemplary Directorship," Thomas Bakewell and James Darazsdi, *Claiming Your Place at the Boardroom Table: The Essential Handbook for Excellence in Governance and Effective Directorship*. New York, NY: McGraw Hill, 2014. The quote is from the introduction to the book, pages xv to xvi.

6 Public company director interview conducted on 13 January 2021.

organizations.[7] Jason Masters has a good chapter, "Financial Literacy and Audit Committees: A Primer for Directors and Audit Committee Members" The Handbook of Board Governance: A Comprehensive Guide for Public, Private, and Not-for-Profit Board Members, second edition by Richard Leblanc.[8]

5.3 Fraud and Wrongdoing

Even though financial oversight of public company is now accomplished through independent audit committees (and in some cases finance and/or risk committees), most boards today are finance-heavy.[9]

A red or yellow flag should be raised in the unusual situation where no (or few) board directors have financial expertise. The worst case is that senior management is engaged in financial wrongdoing and is trying to evade detection.

To be candid and direct, board directors, especially on the audit committee, should be looking for fraud. Amongst the board directors interviewed for this book, more than one has discovered intentional fraud.

> **"Skylar"**: How did we find out fraud? We ended up doing an audit committee investigation because our auditor said there's something fishy in Denmark. He said, "I can't release the audit until you guys confirm or deny what I think is going on." So thank God for our auditor, who actually brought this to our attention. We were a little bit blindsided by it.[10]

> **"Skylar"** continues: We conducted a formal audit committee investigation. And we engaged one of the best professional service firms, with the guy that probably has the number one reputation for audit committee investigations. You can only imagine how interested he was in this situation, because we were a small market cap company. It was unusual for the number-one audit committee investigation lawyer in the country to take us on as a client. And it didn't disappoint. That's when we learn that the fox was in the henhouse.[11] It was only because of that audit committee investigation that we actually learned that the enemy was within.[12]

The audit committee and, in particular, the audit committee chair are asked to clean up problems in organizations. There are systematic ways to detect fraud and wrongdoing, including internal audit and whistleblowing programs. These kinds of pro-

---

7 The recommendation of financial literacy for all directors was first made three decades ago by NACD in the Report of the NACD Blue Ribbon Commission on Director Professionalism (NACD, 1996).
8 Jason Masters, "Financial Literacy and Audit Committees: A Primer for Directors and Audit Committee Members," Richard Leblanc, *The Handbook of Board Governance: A Comprehensive Guide for Public, Private, and Not-for-Profit Board Members*, second edition. Hoboken, NJ: Wiley. 2020.
9 Spencer Stuart: https://www.spencerstuart.com/-/media/2020/december/ssbi2020/2020_us_spencer_stuart_board_index.pdf. See chart on p. 7.
10 Board director interview conducted in December 2020.
11 "Fox in the henhouse" means someone in the company attained personal gain.
12 Board director interview conducted in December 2020.

grams are described below. But audit committee chairs and members can play an important role in detecting fraud by remaining open to people in the organization.

> **Michael Pocalyko**: In my judgment, the audit committee chair has a broad charter. I'll give you a specific example that happened to me: I became audit chair of a troubled company. We brought in new directors and a new chairman, and in two years the company recovered. I'm fond of telling this story. I had interviewed with the previous chair a couple of months prior. He definitely did not want me on the board. I initially wasn't sure why, but then it became apparent about four or five months later when he was fired by the majority shareholders. That company was about 70 percent private equity owned, although it was a distinguished public company. The chair who rejected me was an unprincipled authoritarian who was in way over his head. He wanted no challenge to his authority, no truly independent directors, no one who might cast doubt upon his questionable decisions and his need to control.
>
> The new chair called me on New Year's Eve. The company was reeling. Its previous audit chair had died in office. The founding chair was under indictment and the firm was debarred from doing business with the Department of Defense, working under an administrative order from the courts—this was a major defense contractor. There had been three chairs within the last six months. The new chair asked: Will you join the corporate board as our audit chair? Now, precisely because of the many problems and challenges with which we were faced, my scope of authority became very broad and wide. Among other critical actions, within the next ten days I acted to fire the SEC auditor. We changed SEC audit firms within my first thirty days on that board.
>
> The authorities of an audit chair will always vary depending on the circumstances that are being addressed within the company. But I firmly believe that audit chairs need to speak to everybody in the company—just as firmly as I believe that you have to circumscribe the ability of all directors from snooping around in the company. The audit chair needs to be able to take anybody's call. As the audit chair of a global manufacturing corporation's board of directors, I used to hand out my business card with my mobile number on it to anybody on the shop floor.[13]

Some CEOs and board chairs may believe that board directors handing out business cards with their contact information violates the maxim "nose in, fingers out". Of course, board directors must pass most issues to management to resolve. But directors may hear significant concerns if they pass out business cards. CEOs and board chairs need to agree this behavior is appropriate.

The board director's effort to identify fraud is described in two chapters of Richard Leblanc's *The Handbook of Board Governance: A Comprehensive Guide for Public, Private, and Not-for-Profit Board Members*. See the chapters: (1) Dr. L. S. (Ai) Rosen: "Accountant's Advice to Company Directors: Directors' Obligation to Detect Top-10 Frauds"[14] and (2) James Hunter "Ten Tell-Tale Signs of Possible Fraud: A Director's Primary."[15]

---

13 Public company board director/CEO interview conducted on 13 January 2021.
14 Chapter "Accountant's Advice to Company Directors: Directors' Obligation to Detect Top-10 Frauds," Richard Leblanc, *The Handbook of Board Governance: A Comprehensive Guide for Public, Private, and Not-for-Profit Board Members*, second edition. Hoboken, NJ: Wiley. 2020.
15 Chapter "Ten Tell-Tale Signs of Possible Fraud: A Director's Primary," Richard Leblanc, *The Handbook of Board Governance: A Comprehensive Guide for Public, Private, and Not-for-Profit Board Members*, second edition. Hoboken, NJ: Wiley. 2020.

5.4 Auditors and Other Professionals Supporting the Audit Committee

As the previous stories from experienced board directors suggest, the right professional services help is critical. For the audit committee to do its job, management and the board must select talented professional services firms. Board directors must spend time and effort finding talented firms to conduct audit and investigations. board directors must spend time and effort finding talented firms to do audit and investigations.

> **"Skylar"**: The auditors were bad. The lawyers were bad. The investigators they used were bad. Everything was done on the cheap without consideration for quality. And my father used to say, "I'm too poor to be cheap." So, you have to go for the highest quality that you possibly can and when we get to the audit committee investigation.
>
> I said no more second-tier guys. We are going for the top-shelf liquor.[16] We're going for the top shelf and we are going to get ourselves out of this problem; not by finagling back doors with questionable deals and second-tier, third-tier, fourth-tier professionals. We're going to do it right.[17]

When working with professional services firms, it is best-practice (and currently common-practice) for the audit committee to meet with them without management. This gives them freedom to speak to the board about possible management wrongdoing.

> **Michael Pocalyko**: Another best practice that I've always done . . . and I've been a public and private audit committee member and audit committee chair of both . . . is to insist on meeting with the charge auditor alone outside of the executive meeting.
>
> And I insist on meeting with the associates of the outside accounting firm—the people who have actually been in the company performing the audit field work—outside of the presence of their charge partner. One of the questions I always ask them is "What have you been told not to tell me?" Most of the time I get a smile and the answer is a straightforward and honest "Nothing." But you'd be surprised that maybe about a third of the time they look around at each other before beginning to say something like, "Well, we had some internal discussions . . ." They usually won't say much more until I give them a rhetorical finger in the sternum[18] and make it clear that the audit committee requires full transparency of the auditors' work and discussions in every respect.[19]

To state the obvious, questioning professional services people does not violate "noses in and fingers out." They are not company employees and as mentioned above, there needs to be further assessment of the mix "noses in, fingers out" which is discussed in Chapter 7, 'Entire Board Responsibilities'.

---

16 "Top shelf liquor" means high quality.
17 Board director interview conducted in December 2020.
18 "Rhetorical finger in the sternum," an image of poking someone in the chest, means being forceful.
19 Board director/CEO interview conducted on 13 January 2021.

For more information about working with professional service firms, see the chapter "Organizational Wrongdoing" in the book *Corporate Governance: A Pragmatic Guide for Auditors, Directors, Investors, and Accountants* by Vasant Raval.[20]

5.5 Integrity as an Organizational Value

The experienced directors interviewed for this book consider business ethics to be important. But when I listened to directors talking about this topic, they were referring to culture and the organizational value of personal integrity.

These values cumulatively help shape organizational culture, of which Peter Drucker famously said, "culture eats strategy for breakfast," meaning that culture has more impact than strategy on organizations.

One area in which culture and integrity come into focus is the area known broadly as mergers and acquisitions, or M&A, which also includes divestitures and spinoffs. Some acquisitions are simple but in other cases, many financial transactions may occur in sequence, including last-minute transactions to complete the deal.

> **"Avery"** (speaking of an M&A transaction): I thought things were a bit unusual and then when things got close to the end of the process, the board members decided they needed to reward themselves for their good work. They started putting in place various sorts of incentives for the board.
>
> I was not a board member here. In this situation, I served as a senior executive. But I was in the boardroom for all of these conversations . . . .
>
> The buyers saw some of this in various documentation that was provided to them and . . . moved on.
>
> But to me, it was a real lapse of governance. This is something that I found distasteful to be honest. Had I been on the board rather than in a situation where I was closely advising the board from the in-house position on the senior executive team, I probably would have spoken against this sort of strategy. But in this case, everyone was involved. So it just happened.[21]

Regarding Avery's situation, even though an organization may be acquired and cease to exist soon as an independent entity, the time before acquisition is not a time to violate the Duty of Loyalty. Board directors should not take personal advantage of a temporary situation. Integrity is critical always

Another area in which personal integrity can be useful is when it comes to the reporting of material weaknesses. Public companies must report material weaknesses

---

20 Chapter "Organizational Wrongdoing," Vasant Raval, *Corporate Governance: A Pragmatic Guide for Auditors, Directors, Investors, and Accountants*. Boca Raton, FL: CRC Press, 2020.
21 Public company board director interview conducted in October 2020.

to the US Securities and Exchange Commission (SEC).[22] A material weakness is a deficiency that may result in a financial misstatement.[23]

Material weaknesses represent a significant deficiency in internal controls over financial reporting that could result in a misstatement of financial statements. Owners and stakeholders want to know organizational weaknesses because they have an investment in the company. They may also be interested in significant deficiencies, although the SEC does not require these to be reported.[24]

But the line between material weakness and significant deficiency is debatable. So, this is a situation in which integrity may help guide board directors.

> **Michael Pocalyko**: Board directors consider the issue of materiality. Is it a material weakness? A material weakness must be reported to the public through the company's SEC filing, in the period in which it was identified. But falling somewhere below a material weakness is a "significant deficiency."
>
> So where is the threshold between a significant deficiency and a material weakness? Well before the SEC auditor gets to make that report; that is a decision that should be made by the audit committee of the board, along with executive management, the risk management committee, the executive committee of the board, and the board at large. The company must effectively arrange its detection capabilities and its decision processes. But it is the board of directors' decision whether something is a material weakness or not. Period. You never want to find out about a material weakness from your SEC auditor.[25]

The personal integrity of directors also comes into play when it comes to independence and its opposite, conflicts of interest. Board directors should be especially careful to manage conflicts of interests, which absent disclosure and recusal may lead to a violation of the duty of loyalty.

> **Andrea Bonime-Blanc**: I'm the outside ethics advisor to an oversight board involved with disaster recovery. My role is an outside chief ethics officer and board member.
>
> We have to manage conflicts of interest. Those conflicts of interest can really hurt the board if they're not handled in a proactive way.
>
> So those board members (with conflicts) know to come to me or the GC (General Counsel) to disclose real-time issues, any possible conflicts of interest that they might have, or think that they have, or that they see coming down the pike because there's a need in that particular situation to really maintain the objective, independent reputation of the board.
>
> Board members are leaning in on the conflicts of interest issue.[26]

---

22 Rules promulgated under Section 404 of the Sarbanes-Oxley Act of 2022 require internal control disclosures. https://www.sec.gov/spotlight/soxcomp.htm.

23 A material weakness may cause an error in the company's financial statements, which may have a tangible effect on a company's valuation. www.investopedia.com/terms/m/materialweakness.asp.

24 A significant deficiency is one-level less serious than a material weakness. It is a weakness in financial reporting that is significant enough to merit the scrutiny of people administering the organization's financial reporting. https://www.accountingtools.com/articles/significant-deficiency.

25 Board director/CEO interview conducted on 13 January 2021.

26 Board director interview conducted in January 2021.

Governance experts discuss integrity and ethics in the chapters: (1) "The Board and Business Ethics" in Corporate Governance: Principles, Policies, and Practices, Fourth Edition by Bob Tricker[27] and (2) "Ethics, Culture, and Conflicts" in The Private Company Board of Directors Book: What You Need to Know To Be A Director of A Private Company and What Private Company Owners Need to Know to Form and Operate a Company Board by Elizabeth Hammack.[28]

5.6 Transparency as an Organizational Value

Transparency is an organizational value because it promotes accountability, trust, and credibility. Transparency is the practice of openly and honestly disclosing information about the organization's activities, operations, and decision-making processes. When an organization is transparent, it helps to build trust with stakeholders, including employees, customers, suppliers, and shareholders. The organizational value of transparency is relevant to the audit committee's work.

> **Solange Charas**: What's going to happen in the future . . . a lot more transparency. Today quite a bit is behind closed doors . . . . The legal guys, the General Council, hates this concept of transparency. You need to be transparent. In the world of social media, everything comes out anyway. So why not embrace transparency and manage it instead of reacting to it when something bad comes out?[29]

> **"Harper"**: Companies should plan to become more and more transparent year after year. With machine learning and machine-to-machine AI, it is becoming easier to see what is happening within a company.[30]

Through transparency, the inner workings of the organization should be available to board directors.

> **"Harper"** continues: Board members should understand what is happening within the company . . . Management in particular should understand what is happening within a company and share that information as appropriate with the board members.[31]

---

27 Bob Tricker, *Corporate Governance: Principles, Policies, and Practices*, Fourth Edition, Oxford, UK: Oxford University Press, 2019.
28 Chapter "Ethics, Culture, and Conflicts," Elizabeth Hammack, *The Private Company Board of Directors Book: What You Need to Know to Be A Director of A Private Company and What Private Company Owners Need to Know to Form and Operate a Company Board*, Granite Bay, CA: BrainTrustBoard, 2019.
29 Public company board director interview conducted on 12 January 2023.
30 Board director interview conducted in July 2022.
31 Board director continues in July 2022: With increased organization transparency doesn't necessarily mean you report all findings. But it does mean you have that information available to board members.

As businesses and organizations have more stakeholders, transparency is important to customers and supply-chain partners to achieve environmental, social, and governance (ESG) goals.[32]

> **Erin Essenmacher**: In retail clothing, this idea is having a first, second, and third life. So it's not just buying clothes. It's also making the clothes and selling them—and also ensuring a long life before they end up in a landfill. The founder of a retail company where I serve as a director was the first one to have a widespread take-back program to take those clothes back and remake them into something else.[33]

Transparency between (1) the board and senior management and (2) between board directors is important to establish and build trust.

> **Anna Catalano**: It's important for a board to be transparent, honest, and open to the SLT.[34]
>
> I do not think it's healthy for a board to create camps where there's one camp that feels one way and they don't talk to the other camp and there are surprises in board meetings. I've been on boards where this has happened, and it is not good.
>
> Trust is one of the most important things and trust also comes from a lot of transparency.[35]

Finally, it is vital for board directors to be transparent

> **Hon. Carlos C. Campbell**: As a board director you have to be independent. You have to be assertive. And you have to be shareholder centric and transparent.[36]

Jill Solomon's chapter, "The Role of Transparency, Audit, Internal Control and Risk Management in Corporate Governance" in her book *Corporate Governance and Accountability*[37] links the value of transparency to internal audit, internal control, and risk.

5.7 Internal Audit, Whistleblowing, and Ethics Programs

CEOs and senior management are responsible for human resources and business practices for which the board has oversight responsibility. When there is a problem, the board directors I interviewed knew of the difficulty before audit, internal audit, and whistle blowing systems occurred. I think this is good news.

---

32 ESG is discussed in greater detail in Chapter 8, "Entire Board Topics."

33 Board director interview conducted on 20 October 2020.

34 SLT means Senior Leadership Team which includes the CEO and direct reports.

35 Public company board director interview conducted on 6 June 2021.

36 Board director interview conducted on 29 October 2020.

37 Chapter "The Role of Transparency, Audit, Internal Control and Risk Management in Corporate Governance," Jill Solomon, *Corporate Governance and Accountability*, fifth edition, Hoboken, NJ: Wiley, 2020.

But this also means that any problems board members are aware of may be significant ones that they need to tackle.

> **"Holland"**: Maintaining and reinforcing the organization values of integrity and transparency are more important than company programs. For example, if integrity is not valued in the company, then programs such as internal audit, whistle blowing, and ethic programs will be seen as short-term or ineffective.
>
> But if integrity and/or transparency is valued within a company, then such programs reinforce the values of integrity and transparency.[38]

5.7.1 Internal Audit

Internal audit is a function within a company to ensure compliance with organization policies and practices.

> **Miller Adams**: I think one of the most successful arrangements I've seen is a board that at end of the day has; (1) an executive session with the CFO, (2) an executive session with the general counsel, (3) an executive session with the executive who runs internal audit, and then (4) an executive session with the CEO.
>
> I think the executive sessions set a tone for senior management. Everyone has an opportunity to share the things that that they think would be important for the board to hear privately, particularly from those key areas.
>
> We hear from those areas during the regular board meeting of course. But it's important that the board get a chance at the end of the meeting to share anything that they think is particularly important. It happens every quarter.[39]

For more information about internal audit, see the chapter, "Internal Auditing Function" in *Corporate Governance: A Pragmatic Guide for Auditors, Directors, Investors, and Accountants* by Vasant Raval.[40] In addition, see the chapter, "Board Activities: Corporate Governance in Practice" in *Corporate Governance: Principles, Policies, and Practices*, Fourth Edition by Bob Tricker.[41]

5.7.2 Whistleblowing

Whistleblowing, in general, means notifying leaders of wrongdoing within an organization. The Securities and Exchange Commission has an Office of the Whistleblower

---

38 Board director interview conducted in July 2022.
39 Board director and general counsel interview on 21 October 2020.
40 Chapter "Internal Auditing Function," Vasant Raval, *Corporate Governance: A Pragmatic Guide for Auditors, Directors, Investors, and Accountants*, Boca Raton, FL: CRC Press, 2020.
41 Chapter "Board Activities: Corporate Governance in Practice" Bob Tricker, *Corporate Governance: Principles, Policies, and Practices*, fourth edition, Oxford, UK: Oxford University Press, 2019.

to receive tips on behavior that allegedly violates US securities law. Tipsters providing high-quality original information that leads to the collection of fines of $1 million or more may be awarded between 10 and 30 percent of the fine.

In addition, for US Federal contracts, whistleblowing means the US federal government is notified of waste or wrongdoing. For US Federal contracts, the whistleblower receives a financial reward for informing the US government of usually a percentage of the savings that the US achieves by correcting the waste or wrongdoing. The reward could be in the millions of US dollars.

Many organizations have an internal whistleblowing program in which complaints of wrongdoing is sent to a company leader. In most situations, there is no financial reward and whistleblowing is anonymous. The company leader is responsible for investigating and remedying the claim.

The process for this internal whistleblowing program may vary. I recommend reading the chapters: (1) "Developing a Robust Whistleblower Policy"[42] and (2) "Elements of a Robust Whistleblower Policy" in *Enhanced Corporate Governance: Avoiding Unpleasant Surprises* by Frederick D. Lipman.[43] The board may or may not be included in the internal whistleblower process.

> **Maureen Conners**: The board should also look at whistleblower complaints and/or the hotline calls to understand potential issues. You must protect the whistleblower, but you need to hear the language and complaints being made. It is the right of the board director to do this. Also, it is important that the board directors know the company's process for dealing with these types of issues.[44]

Employees and vendors also post their observations and feelings on websites such as Glassdoor.[45] These complaints of wrongdoing should be examined by someone in the company with remedy posted on this public website. Posting on public websites can have a significant reputation impact, which may have an adverse effect on talent recruitment and retention.

5.7.3 Ethics Programs

Some companies have developed ethics programs. If a company is considering developing an ethics program, I strongly recommend the chapter, "Ethics Programs: An-

---

42 Chapter "Developing a Robust Whistleblower Policy," Frederick D. Lipman, *Enhanced Corporate Governance: Avoiding Unpleasant Surprises,* Boulder, CO: Daniel Publishing. 2019.
43 Chapter "Elements of a Robust Whistleblower Policy," Frederick D. Lipman, *Enhanced Corporate Governance: Avoiding Unpleasant Surprise,* Boulder, CO: Daniel Publishing. 2019.
44 Public company board director interview conducted on 8 January 2021.
45 https://www.glassdoor.com/index.htm.

other Foundational Block" in the book *Governance, Risk Management, and Compliance* by Richard M. Steinberg.[46]

After talking to experienced board directors, I recommend focusing on a culture with integrity as a value. If the organization does not have a culture of integrity, then an ethics program may not be effective.

Board director Bonime-Blanc describes an ethics program at Merck, which also values personal integrity.

> **Andrea Bonime-Blanc**: I will go back to Merck, Ray Gilmartin, and my friend, Jacqueline E. Brevard, Esq. Jacqueline is a friend who I met twenty years ago. We were both on the same kind of circles and served on an ethics and compliance officer association board together . . . .
>
> She reported as a chief ethics and compliance officer directly to Ray Gilmartin. He asked her to create a robust program in 1995 before it was fashionable. Merck, to this day, has one of the best programs in the world in terms of ethics and compliance. And it's because the CEOs, not just Ray, but other CEOs over time, have really supported that, have given it resources and money, and the board listened to it.
>
> I found those who created ethics and compliance programs within their companies have all the bells and whistles of a solid program, meaning codes of conduct, policies, training, and auditing and risk assessments.
>
> Also, there's a high-level person that's overseeing the ethics program and then reporting to the Executive team and the CEO. In addition, there's a best practice of having a person also reporting to the board at least once a year. But the frequency depends on the company and the seriousness of issues. board presentations could be more often – quarterly or biannually.[47]

Ethics programs are vital to promote ethical behavior and integrity within organizations. But ethics programs can be challenged by a lack of commitment, inadequate resources, poor communication, resistance to change, lack of enforcement, and cultural differences. To be effective, ethics programs must be well-designed, adequately funded, and supported by strong leadership and enforcement mechanisms.

5.8 Regulation, Compliance, and Reporting

5.8.1 US Regulatory Compliance

The Audit Committees of public companies have numerous responsibilities; some from securities laws and some from stock exchange rules. For example, the committee over-

---

46 Chapter "Ethics Programs: Another Foundational Block," Richard M. Steinberg, *Governance, Risk Management, and Compliance*, Hoboken, NJ: John Wiley & Sons, 2011.
47 Board director interview conducted on 8 January 2021.

sees the preparation of disclosure required by SEC Regulation S-K Item 407(d)(3)(i), relating to the audit committee report to be included in the annual proxy statement. The committee must review and discuss the audited financial statements with management and recommend that they be included in the company's annual report filed with the US government.

Though board directors provide oversight and, in most cases, do not fill out or file forms, compliance details can consume their time.

Miller Adams: When students of corporate governance find out how public companies operate, they would be surprised to learn how much of public company operations is driven by the regulatory environment they work in.[48]

Christine Martin: I want to point out that in addition to the duty of fiscal oversight responsibilities and governance, the main difference for nonprofit boards is the responsibility to the State and to the Feds for upholding the charitable deductions and charitable responsibilities for the organizations that they're serving.[49]

Michael Pocalyko: A big change that I've observed in my past 28 years as a corporate director is the regulatory environment of directorship vis-à-vis executive management of the firm. Let me explain that in this way: In business in general, we tend to rail against regulation unless that regulation restricts something we want restricted, or unless it gives us an advantage that we want for our own companies or our own industries. And we ought to be honest about that.

But what's happened in corporate boards since about the mid-90s, pre-Sarbanes-Oxley,[50] is that, in the same way as government regulation, boards have become the regulators of the executive suite. Prior to the beginning of government-mandated reforms . . . in the 1980s and 1990s . . . I don't want to say that boards were exactly rubber stamps, but they were certainly much more cooperatively engaged in management.[51] Boards no longer operate that way, by and large. They take their responsibility more broadly.

So that trend is largely what I mean when I say the board has become the regulator of the executive suite. Boards have shifted, sometimes grudgingly and not all that gracefully or willingly, to provide oversight rather than managerial guidance and ultimate control. That's the major trend that I've experienced in the boardroom.[52]

"Marion": And you know how they say that a lot of your most objective regulations are developed around your five percent of bad actors. So 95 percent of organizations are doing everything right? But regulation is protecting against the five percent who are not conducting themselves perfectly. So all the regulation and all the bureaucracy is set up around this five percent.[53]

---

48 Public board director and general counsel interview conducted on 21 October 2020.

49 Board director/CEO interview conducted on 28 November 2020.

50 Sarbanes-Oxley is the name of US regulation instituted after the US financial meltdown in the 1990s.

51 Board director/CEO "Madison" says "poor performance companies still have their boards performing management. That's a trick for entrepreneurial companies to be able to move from a managerial process board to an effective oversight board. That's a big failure of many entrepreneurial companies."

52 Board director/CEO interview conducted in January 2021.

53 Board director/CEO interview conducted in September 2020.

For more information about compliance, see the chapter, "Cost-Effective Compliance Programs" in *Governance, Risk Management, and Compliance* by Richard M. Steinberg.[54]

5.8.2 International Regulatory Compliance

The legislation and the regulatory framework differ in every country.

Board directors rely on professional service providers to ensure organizations comply with regulations and legislation in other countries. The hired professional service firms should be experts in specific countries and geographic areas. Organizations and board directors should be smart enough to listen (but not always accept) the advice of an expert professional services firm.

> **Sheila Hooda**: CEOs need to leverage the board for long-term strategy development, especially in this era of rapid disruption. Changing business models dealing with new customer dynamics in the context of global nationalism.[55]

> **Julian Ha**: There are board directors here in the US who get opportunities for German companies or French companies or British companies . . . . Every country is a little bit different in this journey in terms of compliance.
> And that obviously varies if you're in a more highly regulated industry for example.[56]

Board directors and management should know that regulation and legislation also differ by industry.

> **Andrea Bonime-Blanc**: I was in senior management, reporting to the board. A board member from a mega pharmaceutical company asked me, "What are you guys doing for FCPA compliance?" I was very self-satisfied; I said, "Oh, we have a program" (because we planned ahead and did) . . . . But the point being that here I was reporting to a CEO who really got it. And to a board that really got it. And a board that was prescient that was looking forward.[57]

As noted above, professional service companies guide US companies with regulations in other countries. Some companies choose to have board directors from other countries to oversee the CEO and organization.

> **Chris Lee**: You probably have seen the internationalization of some of their boards . . . if you look at the board of directors of like Bank of America, they are 100 percent of Americans. But if

---

54 Chapter "Cost-Effective Compliance Programs," Richard M. Steinberg, Governance, Risk Management, and Compliance, Hoboken, NJ: John Wiley & Sons, 2011.
55 Public company board director interview conducted on 28 November 2020.
56 Board director interview conducted on 20 January 2021.
57 Board director interview conducted on 8 January 2021.

you look at the board of directors like a Swiss bank, I think more than twenty to thirty percent of their board members are not from that home country.[58]

5.8.3 Reporting

Reporting is important to shareholders and stakeholders. By reading audited financial reports, shareholders can track their investments. As for stakeholders, interest may lie in some of the other kinds of reports, such as sustainability reports, now produced by most US public companies (although they are not yet legally required).

Senior management is responsible for the creation of financial reports to be filed with the SEC (10-K, 10-Q, etc.). Such work is an essential part of the chief financial officer (CFO) and finance staff. The challenges of this role are growing. Reports must be filed using XBRL language and tagging and companies cannot rely on their auditors to help, due to independence rules. For these reasons, some financial reporting work is outsourced to professional service firms, with oversight from senior management and the board. Most of this oversight is conducted by the Audit Committee. Documents are then sent to the entire board for review and a vote for approval.

> **Erin Essenmacher**: If you're on a public company board, there are significant reporting responsibilities that you have from a regulatory standpoint . . . . This certainly drives a chunk of the board's agenda.[59]

Professional services firms, such as accountants, are responsible for preparing documents for regulators. But management and board directors are accountable for signing them off to confirm their accuracy. Many of these documents will be reviewed by the Audit Committee before they are sent to the full board and then the governing organization.

Because reporting is important, governance books often include substantive chapters on the topic, including "Financial Reporting and External Audit" in *Corporate Governance Matters: A Closer Look at Organizational Choices and Their Consequences* by David Larcker Brian Tayan[60] and the chapter, "Public Company Reporting Claiming Your Place at the Boardroom Table" in *The Essential Handbook for Excellence in Governance and Effective Directorship* by Thomas Bakewell and James Darazsdi.[61] By reading such material, audit committee members can strengthen their ability to oversee company reports.

---

58 Public company board director interview conducted on 8 January 2023.

59 Board director interview conducted on 20 October 2020.

60 Chapter "Financial Reporting and External Audit," David Larcker and Brian Tayan, *Corporate Governance Matters: A Closer Look at Organizational Choices and Their Consequences, Third* Edition. London, UK: Pearson, 2020.

61 Chapter "Public Company Reporting Claiming Your Place at the Boardroom Table," Thomas Bakewell and James Darazsdi, *Claiming Your Place at the Boardroom Table: The Essential Handbook for Excellence in Governance and Effective Directorship*. New York, NY: McGraw Hill, 2014.

6 Compensation Committee and Ad Hoc Committees

As noted above, most of the time and effort of board directors is spent in committees. In the past, the Compensation Committee was focused solely on CEO compensation. Owners, whom board directors represent, want additional oversight that CEOs are paid appropriately. The rationale of CEO pay is linked to organizational performance.

Today the scope of the Compensation Committee has changed significantly, specifically, broadened to human capital. This means recruiting and retaining talent to the organization and providing oversight on employee issues. For some companies, the Compensation Committee is called the Human Capital Committee or sometimes the Talent Committee.

Today, the Compensation Committee can expand to overall CEO performance management. Today, there are ad hoc committees focused on Succession Planning, CEO Recruitment and Selection, and CEO Onboarding. Alternatively these efforts may be handled by the Talent or Human Capital Committee.

> **Evelyn Dilsaver**: We don't have a Compensation Committee. We have a People and Culture Committee, which compensation is certainly a piece. But it's really much broader and intersects with that idea of a quadruple bottom line.[1]

> **Christine Martin**: Boards may have a Human Resources or Compensation Committee . . . . And honestly, that's true regardless of whether it's for profit or nonprofit. The committee has the responsibility for hiring, overseeing, providing a performance review, and managing compensation. All of those things are the responsibilities and purview of a nonprofit board and a for-profit board, typically assigned to the board chair, sometimes to the executive committee. In really large organizations, they may have a Human Resources or Compensation Committee.[2]

6.1 Compensation Committee

For public companies, the Compensation Committee must focus on CEO compensation. But at times the committee's charter expands to include oversight of executive compensation. For US public companies and nonprofits, the amount of compensation must be disclosed.

---

1 Public company board director interview conducted on 6 November 2020.
2 Board director/CEO interview conducted on 28 November 2020.

https://doi.org/10.1515/9783110689129-006

6.1.1 CEO Compensation

Public company boards often hire compensation consultants to determine the methodology for CEO compensation. Compensation consultants tie CEO performance to shareholder value. As owner shares increase in value, the CEO earns more money.[3]

> **Hon. Carlos C. Campbell**: I have tremendous respect for a compensation consultant[4] because she is a super pro. I've had the privilege to lecture with her. I will always consider her the teacher and I'm a student. I've served on panels with her, and I like the way she does everything. I like her knowledge base. I like her accessibility. And I think she's one of the stars of corporate governance.[5]

> **Anna Catalano**: There are different types of professional services . . . . We have outside consultants that are required on public boards to help us with outside auditors and the compensation advisors.
>
>   It's very important to keep a board benchmarked against best-in-class to make sure your committees understand what's going on out there in the world. What are the trends? What are the institutional investors looking at? You need to make sure you've got a finger on the pulse. And outside experts, advisors can help you with that.[6]

Obtaining metrics for the organization and compensation for CEO and senior management is key to achieving business results for owners and stakeholders.

One such metric is CEO pay versus frontline worker pay. For some organizations, CEO pay is hundreds of times greater than frontline worker pay. It may be difficult for Compensation Committees to approve CEO salaries at this high level of pay. but it may be easier for the Compensation Committee to approve if the CEO is both board chair and CEO.

Compensation consultants know CEO pay across companies and industries. Identifying "peer" CEOs is a way for CEOs to increase their pay; CEOs of high-revenue companies are usually paid more. So board directors need to confirm that the set of peers is appropriate.

> **"Lennox"**: For most of the year, we could count on the CEO for staying focused on running the business. But when "compensation season" came up, the CEO focused too much on trying to meet a personal financial target, and that played out in his attempt to influence the selection of peers.[7]

---

3 Some would say that compensation consultants are a key reason for significant salary discrepancy between CEOs and frontline workers. And as CEO salaries increase, CEO salaries increase across the board.

4 I can share name of the compensation consultant; contact https://johnhotta.academia.edu/contact.

5 Public company board director interview conducted on 29 October 2020.

6 Public company board director interview conducted on 6 June 2021.

7 Public company board director/CEO interview conducted in October 2020.

"Hunter": When you look at the rise of CEO compensation over the past decade- or decades, right? – it's because of the selection of peers. The compensation consultant analysis research that has gone up so dramatically. I mean quite frankly it's crazy, right?[8]

Likewise, CEO compensation is weighted more by incentives. The more that owners are paid, the more CEOs are paid. CEO (and senior management) compensation increases significantly If, likewise, ownership value increases significantly.

Cari Dominguez: As you know, the bulk of a CEO's earnings potential comes from long-term incentives such as performance shares, options, restricted stock . . . . Aligning executive compensation to the company's performance and to the creation of long-term shareholder value is a fiduciary responsibility of the board. So, to ensure that compensation and company performance are in sync, we have incentive awards, which are levers that can go up or down based on company and executive performance. When the market is doing poorly, we can keep executives motivated by awarding long-term incentives that, if realized, can make for very attractive gains. But all that depends, or should depend, on performance.

Of course, if the economy is in a down cycle that is affecting company value and the CEO comes to the board expressing interest in selling the company to a suitor, then the board has a different set of questions to consider. Is there alignment between the CEO's personal interests and that of the shareholders? What is the CEO's motivation for wanting to sell the company? What is behind this change of direction? Where are the CEO and executive team in their personal trajectory? If we believe the company's value is greater than the offer, how do we keep the executives motivated to ride out the economic cycle? Should the board provide additional retention incentives to motivate executives during a turnaround phase? The levers need to be applied based on situations and market conditions.[9]

Compensation between CEOs should be comparable. Compensation that is too low should not be a reason for a CEO to leave. Selecting the right CEO is critical to an organization's success, so recruiting other CEOs to fill a CEO's role is commonplace.

Dominguez continues: What is the value? How is that complementary to the culture of the organization? Will the value be different if the CEO explores other options? Do we downsize? Are there certain things that we can spin off? Can we do better on the SG&A[10]? Looking at the whole administrative overhead component can save some money and to override the financial crisis.[11]

Finally, for public company directors, proxy advisory companies advise if they believe CEO compensation is appropriate given company performance. These "say on pay" were controversial but are now commonplace.[12]

---

8 Board director interview conducted in October 2020.

9 Public company board director interview conducted on 4 September 2020.

10 SG&A is Selling, General, and Administrative expenses. https://www.investopedia.com/terms/s/sga.asp.

11 Public company board director interview conducted on 4 September 2020.

12 "Say on Pay" provisions in the US, E.U., and other countries https://en.wikipedia.org/wiki/Say_on_pay.

David Rosenblum: At the annual meeting there is significant attention to check annual compensation to ensure there are positive proxy on "say on pay" votes.[13] People pay a lot of attention to those.[14]

In addition to board directors, advisory committee members can work on CEO compensation. As described in Chapter 8, "Nominating and Governance Committee," boards can setup an advisory committee. An advisory committee usually has members with unique skills. Advisory committee members are a great pipeline for future company board directors.

Barbara Adachi: When addressing CEO compensation, the board composition and experience will influence the amount of background information required to establish reasonability and context. As most boards retain an outside compensation consultant, they provide important peer group benchmarks and industry trends. In my experience with a board that has many non-executive members (such as doctors or academics), they are not used to seeing CEOs who earn seven-figure (or multiples) compensation levels. When presenting this to the full board, it is critical to have external benchmarks representing industry-specific peers to establish reasonability and rationale for adjustments to align with their peers.[15]

Further reading on CEO compensation

There is a significant amount written about CEO compensation. I think this in part is because compensation and shareholder value are quantifiable and there is a belief that CEO compensation is a driver of shareholder value.

See chapter, "Compensating the CEO" in William G. Bowen's book, *The Board Book: An Insider's Guide for Directors and Trustees.*[16]

Chapter, "CEO Compensation" in *What is Corporate Governance?* By John L. Colley, et al.[17]

See "CEO Performance Evaluation and Executive Compensation" in Cornelis A. de Kluyver's book *A Primer on Corporate Governance.*[18]

In David Larker's and Brian Tayan's great book, *A Real Look at Real World Governance*. They have a whole section on Executive Compensation in "What is CEO Talent Worth?" "What Does It Mean to 'Make' $1 Million?" and "Netflix: Equity on Demand."[19]

See chapter, "Comp Targets That Work" in HBR's 10 Must Reads on Boards by Radhakrishnan Gopalan, John Horn, and Todd Milbourn.[20]

---

13 Public company board director interview conducted on 11 November 2020.

14 Public company board director interview conducted on 2 February 2022.

15 Past advisory committee member and current public board director interview conducted in May 2021.

16 Chapter "Compensating the CEO," William G. Bowen, *The Board Book: An Insider's Guide for Directors and Trustees,* New York, NY: Norton. 2008.

17 Chapter "CEO Compensation," John L. Colley, et al., *What is Corporate Governance?* New York, NY: McGraw-Hill, 2005.

18 Chapter "CEO Performance Evaluation and Executive Compensation," Cornelis A. de Kluyver, *A Primer on Corporate Governance,* New York, NY: Business Expert Press. 2013.

19 David Larker, Brian Tayan and Michelle E. Guttman', *A Real Look at Real World Governance,* Self-Published. 2013.

20 HBR's 10 Must Reads on Boards, Cambridge, MA: Harvard Business Review Press, 2020.

> See Mark Van Clieaf's chapter, "Designing Performance for Long-Term Value Aligning Business Strategy, Management Structure, and Incentive Design," in *The Handbook of Board Governance: A Comprehensive Guide for Public, Private, and Not-for-Profit Board Members*, Second Edition by Richard Leblanc.[21]

6.1.2 Executive Compensation

Board directors approve the compensation for many CEO direct reports. A CEO takes the lead in determining the compensation of senior executives. This means that the CEO shapes the fixed and variable compensation, hires a compensation consultant if needed, and manages the performance of direct reports. But because of internal controls, the board approves senior-executive compensation.

Board directors provide their feedback and perspective based on experience to the CEO about executive compensation.

> **Minaz Abji**: I'm on the comp[22] committee . . . . We decided compensation for the executives including the CEO; it was the biggest role of the committee, nothing else.
>
> So I went in there, I said, wait a minute, we should be approving every senior management compensation higher than their base comp, once they've elected to be a company officer, it has to come to the committee to approve the package.

> **Minaz Abji:** The CEO can hire anybody they want and give whatever compensation they want . . . . I think comp committees are not only just now approving the senior management's compensation and bonuses now, they're asking other questions.
>
> So sustainability is talking now about internal sustainability. So they're talking about equal pay based on gender, race . . . And in providing inclusion. You have diversity. And you are making these people feel good about being there. That's inclusion. That's what inclusion means.[23]

Board directors can provide their perspectives to CEOs about compensation, including their views on high compensation.

> **"Rene"**: If you don't do the right thing for your employees . . . There's increased pressure on this because there's a lot of stakeholders . . . . It's your choice between employees and shareholders to pay over market compensation to your employees in the current legal context. If you meet your fiduciary responsibilities to shareholders under Delaware law, it will stand up.[24]

---

21 Chapter "Designing Performance for Long-Term Value Aligning Business Strategy, Management Structure, and Incentive Design," Richard Leblanc, *The Handbook of Board Governance: A Comprehensive Guide for Public, Private, and Not-for-Profit Board Members*, Second Edition. Hoboken, NJ: Wiley. 2020.
22 "Comp" means compensation.
23 Public company board director interview conducted on 20 January 2021.
24 Public company board director interview conducted in November 2020.

Further reading on executive compensation

Like CEO compensation, there is much written about executive compensation. The CEO takes the lead of executive compensation and the board's role is to review and approve executive compensation.

See chapter, "Executive Compensation," in J. Robert Brown, Jr., Lisa L. Casey's book, *Corporate Governance: Cases and Materials, Second Edition*.[25]

Howard Levitt and Allyson Lee's chapter, "Lawyers' Advice to Directors on Overseeing Executive Pay" in Richard Leblanc's *The Handbook of Board Governance: A Comprehensive Guide for Public, Private, and Not-for-Profit Board Members, Second Edition*.[26]

Steven Hall and Steven Hall Jr.'s chapter, "The Effective Compensation Committee" in Richard Leblanc's, *The Handbook of Board Governance: A Comprehensive Guide for Public, Private, and Not-for-Profit Board Members, Second Edition*.[27]

Chapters "Executive Compensation and Incentives" and "Executive Equity Ownership" in David Larcker and Brian Tayan's book *Corporate Governance Matters: A Closer Look at Organizational Choices and Their Consequences*, Third Edition.[28]

Chapter "Executive Compensation" in Robert Nii Arday Clegg's book *Corporate Governance: The Boardroom, The Bottom Line, and Beyond*. United Arab Emirates.[29]

Stephen F. O'Byrne's chapter, "Measuring and Improving Pay for Performance: Board Oversight of Exeuctive Pay" and Paul Gryglewicz's "Compensation Governance and Performance-Based Executive Compensation" in Richard Leblanc's book *The Handbook of Board Governance: A Comprehensive Guide for Public, Private, and Not-for-Profit Board Members, Second Edition*.[30]

6.2 Ad Hoc Committees

As noted earlier, the scope of the Compensation Committee has been changing. Sometimes the committee focuses solely on compensation, but at times the scope is

---

25 Chapter "Executive Compensation," Robert Nii Arday Clegg, *Corporate Governance: The Boardroom, The Bottom Line, and Beyond,* United Arab Emirates: Self Published. 2019.

26 Chapter "Lawyers' Advice to Directors on Overseeing Executive Pay," Richard Leblanc, *The Handbook of Board Governance: A Comprehensive Guide for Public, Private, and Not-for-Profit Board Members*, Second Edition. Hoboken, NJ: Wiley. 2020.

27 Chapter "The Effective Compensation Committee," Richard Leblanc, *The Handbook of Board Governance: A Comprehensive Guide for Public, Private, and Not-for-Profit Board Members*, Second Edition. Hoboken, NJ: Wiley. 2020.

28 Chapter "Executive Compensation and Incentives" and "Executive Equity Ownership," David Larcker and Brian Tayan, *Corporate Governance Matters: A Closer Look at Organizational Choices and Their Consequences*, Third Edition. London, UK: Pearson, 2020.

29 Chapter "Executive Compensation," Robert Nii Arday Clegg, *Corporate Governance: The Boardroom, The Bottom Line, and Beyond,* United Arab Emirates: Self Published. 2019.

30 Chapters "Measuring and Improving Pay for Performance: Board Oversight of Executive Pay" by Stephen F. O'Byrne and "Compensation Governance and Performance-Based Executive Compensation" by Paul Gryglewicz in Richard Leblanc, *The Handbook of Board Governance: A Comprehensive Guide for Public, Private, and Not-for-Profit Board Members,* Second Edition, Hoboken, NJ: Wiley. 2020.

broader, including overall CEO performance and company-wide human capital or human resources.

Many CEO issues can be managed in ad hoc committees, usually formed by the board chair or lead director. The scope of ad hoc committees can vary greatly, but it is common to have ad hoc committees on (1) CEO succession planning; (2) CEO recruiting and selection; and (3) CEO onboarding and orientation.

Board directors work with CEOs, so experienced corporate directors have many thoughts in these areas. Working with a CEO is an art. It is not a reporting relationship.

> **"Evan"**: The biggest mistake I made when I first joined a board is thinking that the CEO reported to the board. On an org chart[31] it looks like the CEO reports to the board, but the truth is the board supports the CEO.
>
> The CEO may also be the board chair. That case is called an "Executive Chair" and that person is definitely in charge. There is a Lead Director, but not a board chair.
>
> In other cases the board chair and the CEO are separate. In this case the board chair and CEO are "equals" and the other board directors support them.
>
> That's the way it works. The directors report to the board chair and the CEO. The CEO does not report to all board directors.[32]

The median tenure for CEOs is five years[33] and seven to eight for board directors.[34,35] The likelihood is very high that a board director will be involved in succession planning, recruiting/selection, or orientation/onboarding.

6.2.1 CEO Succession Planning

There are many aspects to CEO performance management and succession planning. Some are managed in an ad hoc succession planning committee, some are held in the ongoing compensation committee, and others by the board chair or lead director.

6.2.1.1 CEO Performance
The CEO'S performance is measured by achieving or exceeding the organization's strategy. So it will be apparent if the CEO achieves results or not.

---

31 "Org chart" is organization chart, which is a graphic representation of reporting relationships.
32 Board director interview conducted in July 2022.
33 "CEO Tenure Rates," Dan Marcec, Equilar, Inc., 12 February 12, 2018, Harvard Law School Forum on Corporate Governance: https://corpgov.law.harvard.edu/2018/02/12/ceo-tenure-rates/.
34 "Director Tenure Remains a Focus of Investors and Activists," David A. Katz et al, 1 August 2016, Harvard Law School Forum on Corporate Governance: https://corpgov.law.harvard.edu/2016/08/01/director-tenure-remains-a-focus-of-investors-and-activists/.
35 The tenures of both CEOs and board directors are becoming shorter.

Managing CEO performance is unlike the supervisor-supervisee relationship or manager-subordinate interaction. Trying to replicate these kinds of models would be a mistake as CEOs have a healthy ego (and perhaps too much self-importance). CEOs don't respect board directors and therefore don't respect professional development feedback from board directors. Managing a CEO's performance is an ongoing challenge.

> **Andrea Bonime-Blanc**: All things being equal, I think a board really needs to think about their CEO . . . . in a more holistic way in terms of performance management.
>
> So it's not just about financial goals. It's also about ESG kinds of goals. How are they managing business ethics? Other core issues like health and safety, or the environment, whatever is applicable to the particular company. For a technology company, it could be AI ethics, cybersecurity, and other things like that.[36]
>
> How well are CEOs managing? And I think there's some kind of correlation between more emotionally intelligent leaders and being more willing to be holistic about these kinds of issues. Because they're thinking about their other stakeholders as well as their shareholders. So they're not just financially focused, they're also focused on some of the other core issues that affect their business. Because it's all part of that value preservation, protection, and creation, right?[37]

Boards represent owners and stakeholders, so they try to help CEOs. Board directors provide feedback to CEOs in private discussions. A CEO must be open to feedback and improvement, which is a characteristic needed when selecting a CEO. In a private discussion there must be open communication, constructive criticism, and specific examples.

> **Liane Pelletier**: I see excellent CEO performance management on a number of boards and the gauge of that is not at only a personal level – more importantly, it is how effectively the organization performs as a whole – that can only be done with the leadership of a quality CEO.[38]

The interpersonal relationship between the CEO and board directors is the focus of The Art of Director Excellence, Volume 2. Board directors become better at their jobs by helping the CEO become more effective in achieving results. This interpersonal relationship between the CEO and board directors is the focus of *The Art of Director Excellence*, Volume 2.

In addition, see the chapter, "Spotting, Catching, or Exiting a Falling CEO" in *Boards That Lead: When to Take Charge, When to Partner, and When to Stay Out of The Way* by Ram Charan, Dennis Carey, and Michael Useem.

6.2.1.2 CEO Transitions and Off-Boarding

If CEOs do not achieve results, do not enable an agreed-upon strategy, or do not behave in a way that is aligned to the organization's culture or values, the board may

---

36 Board director interview conducted on 8 January 2021.
37 Board director interview conducted on 8 January 2021.
38 CEO/Public company board director interview conducted on 6 October 2020.

need to take action to fire the CEO and transition them out of the organization. Board directors are representatives of owners and stakeholders who have a right to take action if appropriate.

"Sutton": The board is responsible for the hiring and firing of the CEOs, as well as the annual performance management and the compensation of the CEO. The board has oversight. Does the board have the check and balance on the imperial CEO[39]? Does the board that can hire and fire the CEO and compensate the CEO have the right check and balance?[40]

"Bailey": How do you fire the CEO? You talk about the risk posture of a company . . . . The risk posture is both the avoidance of risk as well as the taking of risk . . . .[41]

"Sutton": I think every board member has to understand. It is extremely likely that there's going to be a CEO transition. During his or her term right after, it's just the way things are. The board needs to be ready when there is a transition in leadership.[42]

"Rene": You have to take some tough actions. The interesting thing is that public company CEOs can't be fired right away. Even they know the contracts, they can't be fired quickly. The typical CEO contract cannot terminate without cause. And it's expensive.[43]

Anna Catalano: If the current CEO is no longer appropriate for the role it depends on the person. If the person still has a lot of runway or someone like Elon Musk and he just wants to go invent another company, you let him go. And you put someone else in the CEO role.

Sometimes it makes sense to keep the founder CEO on the board. I would caution you about the shadow that the founder CEO can cast on the next CEO. Particularly if the next CEO is an internal candidate.

If you have an external candidate as the next CEO, it's a little bit easier. But if you have an internal candidate, be careful of the founder CEO shadow can cast because they've worked for them. The founder CEO's voice is in the hallway. It's everything everywhere. You look, it's that person, it makes it tough.[44]

See the chapters, "Hiring (and Firing) the CEO – and the Board," *In How Board Work: And How They Can Work Better in a Chaotic World* by Dambisa Moyo,[45] and "Evaluating and replacing the CEO" in *The Board Book: An Insider's Guide for Directors and Trustee*s by William G. Bowen.[46]

---

39 Public company board directors "Lennox" and "Sutton" call executive CEOs as "imperial CEOs." Executive CEOs serve both as CEO and board chair.
40 Public company board director interview conducted in October 2020.
41 Public company board director interview conducted in January 2021.
42 Board director interview conducted in June 2021.
43 Public company board director interview conducted on 11 November 2020.
44 Public company board director interview conducted on 6 January 2021.
45 Chapter "Hiring (and Firing) the CEO – and the Board," Dambisa Moyo, *How Board Work: And How They Can Work Better in a Chaotic World,* New York, NY: Basic Books. 2021.
46 Chapter "Evaluating and replacing the CEO," William G. Bowen, *The Board Book: An Insider's Guide for Directors and Trustees,* New York, NY: Norton. 2008.

6.2.1.3 CEO Succession Planning Process

The CEO's health, safety and chance of changing jobs is an ever-present risk. Because this risk exists, it makes sense to have succession planning in case there is a need for someone to step into the role.

CEO succession planning is either managed by a special committee (or task force) or the Nom Gov Committee. The independent Board Chair or Lead Director is likely part of this but CEO succession planning is overall CEO performance management.

Given the median tenure of CEOs, it is wise to have an ad hoc committee for succession planning. When a new director joins a board, if an ad hoc succession planning committee does not exist, this is a discussion the new board director can have with the board chair or lead director, who must then agree and sponsor a succession planning committee.

> **"Jai":** I think that succession planning really hits a lot of buttons for boards. It touches strategy, competition, compensation . . . .[47]

When the board is developing the CEO succession planning process there must be discussion of internal and external candidates. There must be an assessment of how candidates fit the organization's culture. Board directors must evaluate the ability to create strategy with information from customers, competitors, and the workforce. And of course, there must be a track record of organizational success.

> **"Avery":** A situation that comes to mind is the public company scenario involving CEO succession planning. But that led to some rather unexpected Board reactions. The Board essentially took the position that the company ought to be auctioned off.
>
> But during the course of that, lots of odd things occurred. Friends of board members were introduced as interim executives, with associated sign-on bonuses and other unexpected sorts of financial considerations, if you will. Everyone knew that it was going to be a short-term situation, which is why I thought this was somewhat unusual.[48]

The CEO should be part of the succession process. This process with CEOs invariably runs smoothly, but as the board can encounter problems, I recommend board directors not only look at the outcome of the succession plan, but also the behaviors of the CEO, board chair, and committee chairs.

Further reading on CEO succession
I am a great fan and admirer of some of the authors below.
    See chapter, "CEO Succession and Success" in Betsy Atkins's book *Be Board Ready: The Secrets to Landing a Board Set and Being a Great Director.*[49]

---

47 Board director interview conducted in November 2020.
48 Public company board director/general counsel interview conducted in October 2020.
49 Chapter "CEO Succession and Success," Betsy Atkins, *Be Board Ready: The Secrets to Landing a Board Set and Being a Great Director.* Chicago: NEWTYPE Publishing, 2019.

See Ram Charan's chapter, "Ending the CEO Succession Crisis" in *HBR's 10 Must Reads on Boards*.[50]

See "CEO Succession: The Ultimate Decision" in Ram Charan, Dennis Carey, and Michael Useem's book *Boards That Lead: When to Take Charge, When to Partner, and When to Stay Out of the Way*.[51]

Chapter "Choose the CEO Wisely and Actively Plan for Succession" by Deborah Hick Midanek in *The Governance Revolution: What Every Board Member Needs to Know, NOW!*[52]

See "CEO Selection and Succession Planning" in Cornelis A. de Kluyver's book *A Primer on Corporate Governance*.[53]

David Larker and Brian Tayan have a great book called *A Real Look at Real World Governance*. They have a whole section on CEO Succession Planning with chapters including "Sudden Death of a CEO," "HP: The CEO Merry-Go-Round," and "Apple: Is CEO Health Public or Private."[54]

Chapter "CEO Selection, Turnover, and Succession Planning," in David Larcker and Brian Tayan's *Corporate Governance Matters: A Closer Look at Organizational Choices and Their Consequences*, Third Edition.[55]

See Gary Larkin's chapter, "CEO Succession Planning Trends and Forecast"[56] and David Larcker and Brian Tayan's chapter "CEO Succession Planning"[57] and chapters by Mark B. Nadler, "CEO Succession: Lessons from The Trenches for Directors,"[58] Richard Leblanc's "Model CEO Succession Planning Charter"[59] and Richard Leblanc's "Model CEO Position Description" in *The Handbook of Board Governance: A Comprehensive Guide for Public, Private, and Not-for-Profit Board Members, Second Edition*.

---

50 Chapter "Ending the CEO Succession Crisis," *HBR's 10 Must Reads on Boards*, Cambridge, MA: Harvard Business Review Press, 2020.

51 Chapter "CEO Succession: The Ultimate Decision," Ram Charan, Dennis Carey, and Michael Useem, *Boards That Lead: When to Take Charge, When to Partner, and When to Stay Out of the Way*, Cambridge, MA: Harvard Business Review Press, 2013.

52 Chapter "Choose the CEO Wisely and Actively Plan for Succession," Deborah Hick Midanek, *The Governance Revolution: What Every Board Member Needs to Know, NOW!* Berlin, GE: De Gruyter Press, 2018.

53 Chapter "CEO Selection and Succession Planning," Cornelis A. de Kluyver, *A Primer on Corporate Governance*, New York, NY: Business Expert Press. 2013.

54 Chapters "Sudden Death of a CEO," "HP: The CEO Merry-Go-Round," "Apple: Is CEO Health Public or Private," David Larker, Brian Tayan, and Michelle E. Guttman, *A Real Look at Real World Governance*, Self-Published: 2013.

55 Chapter "CEO Selection, Turnover, and Succession Planning," David Larcker and Brian Tayan, *Corporate Governance Matters: A Closer Look at Organizational Choices and Their Consequences*, Third Edition. London, UK: Pearson, 2020.

56 Chapter "CEO Succession Planning Trends and Forecast," Richard Leblanc, *The Handbook of Board Governance: A Comprehensive Guide for Public, Private, and Not-for-Profit Board Members*, Second Edition. Hoboken, NJ: Wiley. 2020.

57 Chapter "CEO Succession Planning," Richard Leblanc, *The Handbook of Board Governance: A Comprehensive Guide for Public, Private, and Not-for-Profit Board Members*, Second Edition. Hoboken, NJ: Wiley. 2020.

58 Chapter "CEO Succession: Lessons from The Trenches for Directors," Richard Leblanc, *The Handbook of Board Governance: A Comprehensive Guide for Public, Private, and Not-for-Profit Board Members*, Second Edition. Hoboken, NJ: Wiley, 2020.

59 Chapter "Model CEO Succession Planning Charter," and "Model CEO Position Description," Richard Leblanc, *The Handbook of Board Governance: A Comprehensive Guide for Public, Private, and Not-for-Profit Board Members*, Second Edition. Hoboken, NJ: Wiley, 2020.

6.2.1.4 CEO Succession Planning Stories

I asked board directors, "when you joined a board, what are experiences that surprised you?" I also asked, "what succession planning stories would you like to pass on to students of corporate governance?"

I received four stories of succession that I share below. As I mentioned above, the succession planning activity touches on many essential organization functions and board director experience.

> **"Darian"**: The CEO understands that lots of things are at an inflection point. The company is part of the larger environment in terms of how retail and industry are changing.
>
> As a board we have to be clear about our baseline level of responsibilities. We have to center our fiduciary responsibilities. What are the things that we need to kind of gently but firmly. There are our responsibilities as a board. There are some things that that we're going to do under those auspices. Things like putting in a more formal process around CEO succession planning.
>
> The CEO is the majority shareowner as well as the current named CEO. It is going to be the CEO's decision who the next CEO is. So that's a little bit different than some other companies.
>
> As a board it is critical to our fiduciary duties to help put a process in place to guide that decision-making. The CEO values and appreciates the perspectives that all the board members bring – and we have a highly collegial and productive discussion.
>
> We understand that part of our job is to put a clear succession process in place, to make sure that the timeline is clear, we know what all the steps are to think about. Who would be on a short list to be a successor? How are we evaluating those candidates? How are we thinking about onboarding and the unique challenges and opportunities of onboarding a new leader into a founder-led, founder-owned company?[60]

Starting with the organization's needs, board director Catalano and her board plan for the CEO appropriate for the company's place in its lifecycle.

> **Anna Catalano**: My observation is . . . . there are different types of CEOs needed for different chapters in a company's story.
>
> We're talking about CEOs . . . The founder CEO may not be the right CEO for the life of a company. Let's say the company will be around for 30 years. The founder CEO may not be the right person, he or she may be great for the first seven years. And then the board decides, we need someone else who can organically grow this organization.
>
> I think that it's really important for a board to agree on what type of CEO is needed. What do we need to run this company going forward.
>
> I've been on boards. I've been through quite a few CEO changes. I've been on one company where we're on the third CEO. Each CEO has been there for a different chapter. When you need a new CEO one of the biggest mistakes a board can make is not making a change.
>
> Who is on the board right now? We have five new directors plus two directors installed by activists. So out of 12 we are a very different board that picked the current CEO. So picking a new CEO is going to be really different.[61]

---

60 Board director interview conducted in October 2020.
61 Public company board director interview conducted on 6 June 2021.

CEOs have personal plans that may not have been shared with the board. This is another reason why boards should work on succession and compensation plans.

> **Cari Dominguez**: The CEO succession planning review process is an ongoing responsibility of the board, typically done through one or two committees, usually Nom/Governance and Human Resources/Compensation, with full board discussion. Planning for an eventuality is key. One never knows what lies ahead, whether an abrupt resignation, an accident or, suddenly, just a plain desire to move on and do something else. With a long tenured CEO, chances are that the board should be expecting a change at any moment or within a short period of time . . . one, two, three years? Of course, the board should have a sense of the CEO's plans through ongoing discussions. So, we conduct and recommend succession planning reviews at every meeting, just to be prepared.

In one particular instance, we knew that the runway of this CEO was short. One thing about most CEOs is that they "travel in packs," meaning that new CEOs want to bring their own teams—their CFO, their lawyer, and other C-suite executives. So the implication was that there would be significant turnover upon the CEO's departure, leaving the company somewhat vulnerable. For the board, this situation required extensive discussions with the CEO and use of incentives that would allow for a smooth and timely transition. Balancing the CEO's personal interests with that of the shareholders can be tricky but, in the end, there are ways to ensure a satisfactory outcome for both sides. For example, the board can approve accelerated vesting of shares in exchange for mentoring support of the incoming CEO. Or the board can buy itself a little more time with the outgoing CEO with a reallocation of responsibilities among the C-suite to make the load lighter until the change occurs. Each situation is different, requiring situational leadership on the part of the board. In our case, once the CEO retired and the new CEO took over, there were lots of changes in the executive management team, but all were accomplished without consequences to the company's value in the marketplace or its culture and employee morale. Quite a delicate but successful journey.[62]

Following the advice given by board directors, board director and CEO Christine Martin describes one organization's experience.

> **Christine Martin**: In terms of succession planning, I think too many boards get caught without any planning. I think about COVID and the fact that lots of people are getting sick and there may not be a plan and people just suddenly leave a job. So, I would say that most organizations have quickly developed a succession plan, even to the point where a new leader will come in and they'll immediately make sure that there's a succession plan.
>
> One of the best practices examples I would cite is long-term leader CEO really thinking hard about retiring the next couple of years who brought her board chair into the conversation. The CEO began a two-year planning process of training her staff of letting go of things . . . letting go of some relationships with donors or with partners in the community.

---

62 Public company board director interview conducted on 4 September 2020.

The search started six months before she was scheduled to retire. There were many people in the organization that had already established relationships and were comfortable. There was a transition plan. There's an ad hoc transition committee. That committee had been established to make sure that the CEO had a strong exit, and that the new CEO had a strong entrance.

And there's also an ad hoc search committee whose only focus is to manage a search process with an external consultant that was hired to sort of do most of the heavy lifting.

So when you think about your job as a board member it is understanding the people that are around you running that organization asking the question as if there is a succession planning . . . Asking every year that you run a CEO review process and making sure you know, if they have plans to leave or if there're concerns about how happy they are because most nonprofit leaders leave for a variety of reasons.

But a lot of times nonprofit CEOs leave because it's frustrating to work with a board that you may not be engaged with or that's overstepping boundaries. So opening up that communication and actually creating a plan together for a healthy organization because that's what most CEOs want is a healthy organization that's doing really great work in the community that they serve.

So if the CEO starts and is very transparent. The health of the organization, its people and leadership, its financial and business model, its fundraising I think you end up with an organization that can thrive even in crazy times like now in 2020.[63]

All CEO succession planning stories include defining the characteristics needed by the CEO, identifying and developing internal candidates, assessing external candidates, and selecting the new CEO. The succession planning process must include orienting the new CEO to make them productive and successful.

6.3 CEO Recruiting and Selection

CEO selection is another process that solidifies organization strategy and company values. CEO selection may be conducted by an ad hoc committee, which includes the board chair.

The board usually selects and hires a professional services firm to recruit a CEO. The firm should have an extensive network of candidates. In addition, they should provide a "high touch" experience for CEO candidates. This includes ongoing communication with candidates and an extensive background check for finalists and/or selected candidates. The executive recruiting firm should guide the board, ensuring a detailed and professional recruiting process.

Cari Dominguez: In many instances, the lead director serves as the linking pin, the conduit, between the board and the CEO. So, the discussions during executive sessions must be candid, transparent, with all the issues, concerns and expectations put on the table. When recruiting for a new CEO, this means that all board members must have a good understanding of where the CEO candidate wants to take the company, the stated vision and plans to get there. The boards I

---

63 Board director/CEO interview conducted on 28 November 2020.

have served on have always preferred to take a look at internal candidates first. They know the culture, the issues, the talent needed to move forward. But sometimes you need an outsider who is not vested to these things to make it work.

In one of my situations, this company was part of a sector that was going through a lot of dramatic changes. Unfortunately, the company was slow to respond. We had to look for a leader who showed a sense of urgency to turn it around. We had to transform the company into one that was nimble, agile, quick to respond to the competitive market. It was like turning the QE II on a dime! We needed to select a CEO who understood the challenges and had the fortitude and courage to carry out a plan of action that went against the bureaucratic grain of this company's culture.[64]

Many people, including board director R. Omar Riojas, say the board's primary role is selecting a CEO.[65] I won't argue with this popular statement.

Michael Marquardt: The board director's job is representing those shareowners that own the business. And obviously selecting the CEO; that's the most important obligation.[66]

When recruiting a CEO, the company and the executive recruiting firm must have the company strategy (reviewed by the entire board) and updated CEO compensation (confirmed during the Compensation Committee).

Marquardt continues: CEOs should largely live in the future. Where's the future of the company? As you know Jeff Bezos Amazon CEO at the time of this interview has been very outspoken about the fact that the decisions, he makes are things that you're not going to see for three years. Bezos says: I'm not living in the now. I'm spending 90 percent of my time on stuff that Amazon is not even going to announce for another year or two. Marquardt says: That was a very practical way of putting that.[67]

Andrea Bonime-Blanc: One of the areas that I've been fascinated by for years . . . . as a business ethics person, why do we have so much bad corporate behavior? Over the years, leaders that defraud or who cheat? Or who are singularly focused on their own self-aggrandizement?

So, I did some research for my book Gloom to Boom.[68] There's a chapter in it called "Leadership," and it's all about who is your leader.

I did some research on the psychology, hubris, sociopathy and all these things. And then some of the good sides including emotional intelligence. I think some of that lens has to happen at the board level.[69]

The succession planning process may have identified an internal candidate to be CEO. If that candidate has the skills and experience for the strategy needed for the forth-

---

64 Public company board director interview conducted on 4 September 2020.

65 Board director interview conducted on 25 November 2020.

66 Board director/CEO interview conducted on 4 February 2021.

67 Board director/CEO interview conducted on 4 February 2021.

68 Andrea Bonime-Blanc, *Gloom to Boom: How Leaders Transform Risk into Resilience and Value*, First Edition. New York: Routledge, Taylor and Francis Group. 2019.

69 Board director interview conducted on 8 January 2021.

coming two or three years, it makes sense to have the internal candidate as CEO. But sometimes boards like to conduct an external search too to confirm their selection.

> **Anna Catalano**: I've done both higher internal and external CEO candidates. I've done both and I've seen where both have succeeded and seen where both failed.
>
> I think the best-case scenario is the CEO gives you two- or three- years' notice that they're going to step down. Then you have the benefit of time.
>
> In that period of time, you should do an assessment of your internal, most likely candidates, and take the CEOs recommendations on who he or she thinks would potentially be candidates.
>
> But you don't limit yourself to that because you might feel that there's other people that you want to consider. Have a third party come in and do an assessment.
>
> Have your Nom Gov committee spend time with each of those internal candidates, then have a recruiter look outside and see who's available outside and compare the internal candidates with the external.
>
> I think that is a best-case situation when you have the benefit of time, and you can do that in a very transparent manner. The internal people know why they're being talked to. They also know that the board is considering external candidates. The board does its due diligence and the board is doing very good governance on picking the best process.
>
> What are the characteristics? We think our next CEO needs XX based on the strategy we want to try. And they could be significantly different than the last CEO.
>
> The CEO suddenly has to step down for one reason or another. In which case you put someone in charge to keep the lights on.[70]

6.4 CEO Orientation and Onboarding

Onboarding a new CEO is key to the CEO being productive and achieving business results. The sooner the CEO is productive, the more quickly the organization can make money.

So it is a process the board should oversee. Usually, the board chair or lead director selects board directors to assist the CEO.

Board directors can participate actively in onboarding by introducing the new CEO to customers, other owners and investors, suppliers, etc. In addition, a team of employees can onboard the CEO to many other stakeholders in a planned and systematic way.

> **Christine Martin**: Make sure the board is prepared for finding great leaders and preparing for succession in the organization. The right people on the board can help selected CEOs understand oversight governance responsibilities, which is really critical.[71]

---

70 Public company board director interview conducted on 6 January 2021.
71 Board director/CEO interview conducted on 28 November 2020.

Minaz Abji: Your board chair or your governance committee chair and certainly your staff can do a better job of orienting CEOs and giving them a social orientation. Different boards have different norms and you can make it easier for CEOs by saying, "this is how we behave."[72]

CEOs have multiple stakeholders, including the board, direct reports, employees, contractors, community members, suppliers, and customers. When CEOs start, the most important stakeholders are employees.

See the chapters "CEO Transitions" in The Board Book: An Insider's Guide for Directors and Trustees by William G. Bowen[73] and "CEO Transitions" in *Startup Boards: Getting the Most Out of Your Board of Directors* by Brad Feld and Mahendra Ramsinghani.[74]

---

72 Public company board director interview conducted in September 2020.

73 Chapter "CEO Transitions," William G. Bowen, *The Board Book: An Insider's Guide for Directors and Trustees,* New York, NY: Norton. 2008.

74 Chapter "CEO Transitions," Brad Feld and Mahendra Ramsinghani, *Startup Boards: Getting the Most Out of Your Board of Directors*, Hoboken, NJ: Wiley. 2014.

7 Board Leadership and Culture

7.1 Board Structure, CEOs, and Board Chairs

7.1.1 Board Structure

The most important roles in the boardroom are the CEO and independent chair. However, some companies have an executive chair, which combines the CEO and chair roles, and a lead director. When companies have this structure, the executive chair is the most powerful role in the organization. The executive chair role is described in the sections that follow.

The chair has the power to determine other characteristics for the board structure, including the board committees, the committee chairs, and board size. In the case of an executive chair, the lead director, who is the leader of the board, and the Nominating and Governance Committee will offer advice and guidance, but the executive chair can make the decision. The lead director, Nominating and Governance Committee, and independent chair roles are also described in the following sections.

Board directors spend most of their time and effort in committees, which is why this book starts with descriptions of committee work. Board directors spend less time in entire board meetings. There are many variations of Audit, Compensation, and Nominating and Governance Committees, as well as ad hoc committees appropriate for the organization.

Further reading on governance and board structure
See the chapters and literature below for additional perspectives on board structure and leadership.

The "Chairman and Board Structure" in Corporate Governance and Chairmanship: A Personal View by Adrian Cadbury's book.[1]

Chapter "Directors and Board Structure" in Christine Mallin's distinguished book *Corporate Governance*.[2]

Board of Directors: Structure and Consequences in Corporate Governance Matters: A Closer Look at Organizational Choices and Their Consequences, Third Edition by David Larcker and Brian Tayan.[3]

"The Formal Structure of the Board" in Startup Boards: Getting the Most Out of Your Board of Directors by Brad Feld and Mahendra Ramsinghani.[4]

---

1 Chapter "The Chairman and Board Structure," Adrian Cadbury', *Corporate Governance and Chairmanship: A Personal View*, Oxford, UK: Oxford University Press. 2002.
2 Chapter "Directors and board structure," Christine Mallin, *Corporate Governance*, Oxford, UK: Oxford University Press. 2019.
3 Chapter "Board of Directors: Structure and Consequences," David Larcker and Brian Tayan, *Corporate Governance Matters: A Closer Look at Organizational Choices and Their Consequences, Third Edition*. London, UK: Pearson. 2020.
4 Chapter "The Formal Structure of the Board," Brad Feld and Mahendra Ramsinghani, *Startup Boards: Getting the Most Out of Your Board of Directors*, Hoboken, NJ: Wiley. 2014.

https://doi.org/10.1515/9783110689129-007

> "Board Structure and Corporate Structure and Board Committees" in The Private Company Board of Directors Book: What You Need to Know to Be A Director of A Private Company and What Private Company Owners Need to Know to Form and Operate a Company Board by Elizabeth Hammack.[5]

7.1.2 Decision to Combine or Separate the CEO and Chair Roles

The first decision on whether to combine the CEO and chair roles into an executive chair may happen (1) when the company starts up and/or (2) when a private company transitions into a public company. At both times, owner and investor shareholders have significant influence on the decision. For most nonprofit organizations, the CEO and independent chair roles are not combined. In fact, in many nonprofits, the CEO is not a voting board member.

7.1.2.1 Startups

When a company is founded or starts up, one of the most important decisions is: (1) combine the CEO and chair roles (called the executive chair role) or (2) separate the CEO and chair.

A start-up has a founder, and the founder may have a strong opinion to combine the CEO and independent chair roles. For example, a serial entrepreneur[6] may have the experience of wanting more control that comes with combining the CEO and chair roles.

But investors may want a board director seat or even identify an independent chair to support the CEO. The independent chair is a CEO colleague who can offer important advice. More importantly, the CEO can divide the effort and give work to the independent board chair.

> **Michael Pocalyko**: I'm a four-time corporate chairman, but in my current company I am the CEO and a member of the board—but not the chair. We have an independent non-executive chair of the board. I'm still the majority shareholder by a significant margin. In governance terms, the non-executive chair is responsible to me as the majority shareholder. In managerial terms, I'm responsible to him as CEO to the chair. That is what we've arranged in this company, and it works for us—providing good checks and balances.[7]

---

5 Chapter "Board Structure and Corporate Structure," "Board Committees," Elizabeth Hammack, *The Private Company Board of Directors Book: What You Need to Know to Be A Director of A Private Company and What Private Company Owners Need to Know to Form and Operate a Company Board*, Granite Bay, CA: BrainTrustBoard, 2019.
6 A serial entrepreneur is someone who has founded multiple companies. See the article, World's Top 10 Serial Entrepreneurs, Shobhit Seth, 31 December, 2022 https://www.investopedia.com/articles/personal-finance/083115/worlds-top-10-serial-entrepreneurs.asp.
7 Public company board director/CEO interview conducted 13 January 2021.

7.1.2.2 Private to Public Companies

When a private company prepares to become public, it will likely have an independent Nominating and Governance Committee as required by the New York Stock Exchange. The Nasdaq does not require such a committee but requires that all new directors be approved by independent directors (which could be considered a de facto committee). When a company goes public, the Nominating and Governance Committee will give recommendations to the CEO, independent chair (or lead director) and to the entire board.

At that time, other stakeholders such as the investment banking professional services firm may guide the governance of the new public company. In the end, the CEO and the entire board make the decision to combine or separate the roles.

7.1.2.3 Public Companies

A public company Nominating and Governance Committee can recommend combining or separating the CEO and independent chair roles. Of course, the board leadership (CEO, independent chair or lead director) must agree with the recommendation and the entire board must approve.

In general, a CEO new to the role[8] may be supported and mentored by an independent chair. As a new CEO becomes more experienced, the entire board may choose to combine the roles in an executive chair and select a lead director.

7.1.2.4 Nonprofits

Most nonprofits have an independent chair. In fact, as mentioned earlier, for many nonprofits such as universities, the CEO (or President) is not even a voting director. Nonprofits work to achieve a specific charitable mission – required as a condition of their legal formation under state and federal law – and it takes more than the founder to achieve a mission. By contrast, for-profit companies can be formed for any legal purpose and may change their purpose at will. Another possible reason to keep CEOs out of nonprofit board leadership is optics. Nonprofits try to minimize the percentage of donations that go to salary. Obviously, no charity wants its public mission to be overseen by someone who is paid (and possibly overpaid) to achieve it.

7.1.2.5 Executive Chairs

The executive chair is leader of both the organization and the board. The role is powerful. But the executive chair role has even more stakeholders to manage and more work.

Being both the CEO and independent chair is difficult.

---

8 Someone who has not been a CEO in previous roles.

Anna Catalano: I think it's really difficult to be both the executive chair and CEO. It's just so hard to do.[9]

From a board director perspective, there is a preference for splitting the CEO and the independent chair roles.

"Sutton": At one of my boards, the fact that the CEO was also the chair of the board made the board explore separating the roles. . . . . I support that separation. For gosh sakes those are two very big jobs – the CEO and Independent Chair. The CEO runs the company and the Chair leads the board. By combining the roles there is a concentration of power and the independence of the board can be compromised.[10]

"Campbell": I've seen it both ways executive chair and independent chair. I've seen the executive chair work. And I've seen it not work.

I prefer to have an independent chair just because it's easier for a person to have one hat to remember.

I still think it would have been better to have an independent chair. I think independence is actually really important. Not because I don't think people are equipped to be a chair; rather because I think it is important to have that independent viewpoint, and really capitalizing on the independence of directors.

And there's no such thing as an executive session[11] when you have a combined chair and CEO. – That conversation is what you miss because the CEO is always in the room.

When you have a chair CEO you need to have a strong lead director.[12]

7.1.2.6 Lead Directors

When there is an executive chair, there is a lead director who steers the board. The experienced directors I interviewed had much to say about lead directors.

As said above, the lead director needs to be strong.

"Lennox": When a person serves the roles of both CEO and Chair (and many companies have that combined role[13]), the board must have a very strong independent lead director (LD).

Whenever I consider serving on a board with a combo CEO and Chair, my attention goes to the Lead Director and the governance principles. The LD must make sure that the conduct of the board is sound. Sometimes a LD approach may conflict with how the Chair runs the meeting, because a Chair who is also CEO may not be weighing the governance responsibilities enough.[14]

---

9 Public company board director interview conducted on 6 June 2021.
10 Public company board director interview conducted on 28 November 2020.
11 Executive sessions are meetings of board directors before or after meetings without the CEO.
12 Public company board director interview conducted in June 2021.
13 The combined roles of both CEO and Chair is an Executive Chair.
14 Public company board director/CEO interview conducted in October 2020.

Experienced corporate director Cari Dominguez has served as lead director:

> **Cari Dominguez**: On one of my boards, the lead director suddenly passed away. Being a relatively new member of the board, I did not anticipate being tapped for this role. But I was. All of a sudden, I felt the magnitude of the additional responsibilities that required broader skills. That's why governance education is so important. The message I would share with your readers is to always expect the unexpected when serving on boards. You need to be prepared at all times, you need to stay current, and anticipate that anything can happen that will require you to assume a different leadership role and tap into a different set of skills. Your ability to work effectively with others, regardless of personalities, and to be influential, will be critical to your success.
>
> There are two important things as a lead director. (1) You're the spokesperson on behalf of the other independent board members. Your feedback to the Chair of the Board should reflect the complete and balanced views and concerns of the independent directors. But (2) it also requires building trust and a good working relationship with the Chair. Chemistry is important for good teamwork between the lead director and the Chair of the Board.
>
> Another role that I took on as a lead director . . . was board evaluations. At this particular company, I used the tool of board evaluations as a way of addressing the composition of the board. And, as we looked at market and competitive trends, we asked ourselves, do we really have in place the right skill sets, backgrounds and experiences needed to go forward? So, we used our board evaluation process to do a self-assessment of what we had and what we needed to refresh the board. Many boards use outside consultants to conduct their evaluations, but for those companies that choose to do their own evaluations, the responsibility often falls on the lead independent director.[15]

The CEO and independent chair roles have equal power. When there is an executive chair and lead director, the lead director is subordinate to the executive chair.

With the lead director is subordinate to the executive chair, events can lack integrity. Morgan describes such a situation:

> **"Morgan"**: There was an ad hoc committee to hire a replacement CEO and executive chair. And the internal candidate was one of the candidates . . . . They chose the current CEO's brother who was leading the acquired management committee to become the replacement CEO.
>
> The incoming CEO made sure the lead director was on the search committee. So he always made more money. So there was a bit of I scratch your back, you scratch my back. And it didn't smell very good, right? You know?[16]
>
> I'm on the comp[17] committee . . . .we approve every senior hire compensation once they've elected . . . What happened was the CEO went and did his own thing and hired somebody. And when I questioned, why don't we know anything about the compensation package?
>
> One of the members of the compensation committee is also the lead director. The lead director is also the chair of the governance committee. He said: "the other companies I work with the CEO can hire anybody he wants and give whatever compensation he wants."[18]

---

15 Public company board director interview conducted on 4 September 2020.
16 Public company board director interview conducted on 20 January 2021.
17 Comp committee means compensation committee.
18 Public company board director interview conducted on 20 January 2021.

For insights into the lead director role, see Richard Fields and Anthony Goodman's chapter, "What's in a Name? The Lead Director Role at US Public Companies" in The *Handbook of Board Governance: A Comprehensive Guide for Public, Private, and Not-for-Profit Board Members, Second Edition* by Richard Leblanc.[19]

7.1.2.7 Independent Board Chairs

The independent board chair is sometimes called the non-executive chair. They are neither CEO nor executive chair.[20]

Both the lead director and independent chairs are the leaders of the boardroom. Like the lead director, the independent board chair must have strong leadership skills.

> **Christine Martin**: I think the best boards I know have thoughtful, strong leadership.
> The board is responsible for governing themselves. So that board chair or the vice chair is helping make sure that people are showing up, and they're participating; that they have the knowledge that they need to be successful.
> There are lots of stories where the board chair was absent, and the board was in chaos and the organization failed.[21]

Independent board chairs need to make decisions.

> **Fay Feeney**: I think the board chair's role is helping board members make big, strategic decisions that impact the well-being of the enterprise and people. So, if I set it up as that premise . . . the chair is there to help the board make informed, thoughtful decisions.
> I'll tell a story. I was chairman of a foundation and the foundation had never spent the level of resources that I was proposing to spend to do some landmark research that would not be completed during my term. My job was to take on the challenge of having the board see the value of this investment in research (R&D), that would be a long-term value to the organization and would be something that the new board chair would take on in two years.
> As board chair you have to be a colleague who helps people reach decisions and you have to be seen as an independent chair, who allows people to be seen and heard for their concerns. And be respectful of the fact that you have to move the board to a decision.[22]

When the board makes decisions, the independent chair and the board are other stakeholders for the CEO to manage. The more comprehensive and inclusive the decision process in the boardroom, the more clarity you bring to the CEO for execution.

---

19 Chapter "What's in a Name? The Lead Director Role at US Public Companies," Richard Leblanc, *The Handbook of Board Governance: A Comprehensive Guide for Public, Private, and Not-for-Profit Board Members*, Second Edition. Hoboken, NJ: Wiley. 2020.
20 Nonprofit CEOs are often called executive directors.
21 Board director/CEO interview conducted 28 November 2020.
22 Board chair interview conducted on 25 November 2020.

Liane Pelletier: I've seen many independent board chairs who are committed to making sure the board adds value to the company. Helps assure leadership and strategy and risk are managed so that the company can sustain and prosper over the long term. A good independent board chair works well with the CEO but knows that if needed, it will work with more than one CEO.[23]

Further reading on independent board chairs
See Henry D. Wolfe's chapter, "The Non-Executive Chairman: Toward a Shareholder Value Maximization Role,"[24] Elizabeth Watson and Heather Kelsall's chapter, "Great Board Don't Exist Without Great Chairs,"[25] and Richard Leblanc's "Model Independent Chair Position Description"[26] in *The Handbook of Board Governance: A Comprehensive Guide for Public, Private, and Not-for-Profit Board Members, Second Edition* by Richard Leblanc.

7.1.3 The Impact of Board Leadership

As stated earlier, the (1) executive chair and lead director and (2) CEO and independent board chair are the two most important roles in the organizations. They have a significant impact on the board and board culture. The board leadership sets the agenda and priorities.

Cari Dominguez: The role of a lead director involves working with the chair of the board i.e., executive chair and using the tools agenda setting, executive session discussions, board evaluations described below that we have in an effective manner.

The board only has just a few hours to meet and deal with a lot of issues. So, setting an agenda that hits on the critical issues for oversight is very important. We often ask ourselves, what is the CEO proposing to put on the agenda, and how relevant are those topics to the board's oversight responsibilities? Is review of strategy on the agenda? What about risk management issues? Does the agenda capture the issues raised in the executive session at the last board meeting? Much of the board's time is devoted to operational reviews and presentations. So . . . agenda setting is an important tool for boards to use to allocate time to discuss areas of concern and importance to them. What might be important to the CEO's operational focus might be less relevant to a board.

So, board evaluations, agenda setting, following up on issues raised in executive sessions . . . there are a lot of tentacles that go with the lead director's role.

---

23 CEO/Public company board director interview conducted on 6 October 2020.
24 Chapter "The Nonexecutive Chairman: Toward a Shareholder Value Maximization Role," Richard Leblanc, *The Handbook of Board Governance: A Comprehensive Guide for Public, Private, and Not-for-Profit Board Members,* Second Edition. Hoboken, NJ: Wiley. 2020.
25 Chapter "Great Board Don't Exist Without Great Chairs," Richard Leblanc, *The Handbook of Board Governance: A Comprehensive Guide for Public, Private, and Not-for-Profit Board Members,* Second Edition. Hoboken, NJ: Wiley. 2020.
26 Chapter "Model Independent chair Position Description," Richard Leblanc, *The Handbook of Board Governance: A Comprehensive Guide for Public, Private, and Not-for-Profit Board Members,* Second Edition. Hoboken, NJ: Wiley. 2020.

(Footnote: Public company board director interview conducted on 4 September 2020.)

Board leadership also ensures that issues are discussed thoroughly, and board directors contribute.

> **Michael Marquardt**: I've seen boards where you have people that have been around longest seem to get the most air time. And I've seen board chairs who have encouraged the exact opposite.
>
> Under the quote-unquote pretense of saying, "let's hear a fresh perspective from some of our directors that joined us, you know, in the last year or two." Or even, maybe their second meeting and kind of draw them out.[27]

> **Michael Pocalyko**: Depending on the culture of the company . . . depending on the culture of the board . . . I have seen the best and the worst of boardrooms.
>
> One example of best practice is where the chair or the committee chair or the lead director makes sure that everybody is heard in a discussion by formally calling on each director and requiring his or her opinion. I have also seen something creative done once, and I was skeptical at first, but it worked. We had a big decision—I mean a truly big decision like one of those betting the company decisions—and the board chair assigned different board members essentially to debate the issue, organizing opposing points of view. Sort of like a debating society . . . it was positioned as "we're just doing this as sort of a thought exercise."[28]

Board leadership conducts effective and efficiently run meetings:

> **Miller Adams**: I've been in situations where I come out of a meeting thinking that was a great meeting. The board chair really knew how to run a meeting and making it efficient. Everyone felt as though they participated. People were listened to and heard. We came out of the board meeting feeling like we've done a lot of good work. And a lot of that is the leadership of that board chair. And that comes with experience.[29]

> **Joyce Cacho**: Setting the agenda is a key role of board leadership. Board leadership shapes the bridge between "what is" and "what needs to be" to set the company up for the future.
>
> Board chairs and lead directors should focus on "what is" and "what needs to be done" for sustained growth with less volatility. If board leadership are not doing this – and not engaging board members – this is like the company board being a cart running downhill without brakes.[30]

Board leadership works with the Nominating and Governance Committee and the entire board.

---

27 Board director/CEO interview conducted on 4 February 2021.
28 Board director/CEO interview conducted on 13 January 2021.
29 Public company board director interview conducted on 21 October 2020.
30 Board director interview conducted on 16 February 2021.

"Parker": The independent chair should lead changes including "board makeup," board cul-ture,[31] and integrity / ethics.[32]

7.1.4 Board Size

In general, the number of people on a board is decreasing. This is one way for a company to decrease costs in times of increasing risk.

Corporate bylaws will give the board the flexibility to have a range of sizes. Start-up boards may have three to five board directors. Small- or medium-sized companies may have a board for five- to nine- people. A large public company may have eight- to 12- board directors.

> **Barbara Adachi**: The size of the board matters. The current boards that I serve range from six (four independent directors, two investors) to 15 independent directors. The larger board is more formal in terms of structure and procedures and most of the discussion takes place in commit-tees. The dynamics of the startup are very different from larger, long-standing organizations. De-termining the skills and industry expertise required for the board determines the frequency of board refreshment and number of members needed. Often boards will grow to acquire a certain skill set and then resize when the desired skills and experience are represented on the board.[33]

Board size depends on revenue.

> **"Morgan"**: When I joined, they had started up with seven. I was the seventh board member. Then we got eight. And then when COVID came the revenues fell like crazy. They looked at cut-ting expenses everywhere in the organization and the board looked at each other. The chair of the Nominating and Governance Committee was also the Lead Director. He and the executive chair spoke, and they said they were reducing board directors. "We're looking at expenses."[34]

There are a few factors that motivate the increase in the number of board directors. First, for nonprofits, board directors are a revenue source. So, nonprofits believe that donations will increase by increasing the number of board directors. Second, for private companies, new investors may want board seats to attend to their investments. Third, the desire to have board directors with different backgrounds and experiences.

> **"Wesley"**: For public- and private- company boards, it would be great to add gender-identity, racial-identity, sexual-identity experience. But in most cases the board size is limited. It is limited because board discussions must be productive. When the number of people on the board is too large discussions may not be productive.[35]

---

31 Board director interview conducted on 21 October 2020.
32 Board director interview conducted on 21 October 2020.
33 Public company board director interview conducted on 5 May 2021.
34 Board director interview conducted in January 2021.
35 Board director interview conducted in July 2022.

Unfortunately, the decreasing size of boards influences the goal of increasing the number of board directors from diverse backgrounds. The reader may be surprised or even offended that board size impacts board diversity. But the lack of open board seats is one of the reasons that board diversity has not had more progress. In Chapter 8, there is a discourse on why an open board seat is hard to find and why more effort must be put into board director succession planning.

> **Evelyn Dilsaver**: I think the governance books probably don't have a number. But I would say between seven and eight is ideal board size, which makes it harder to add people from the diversity point of view. But for purposes of governance getting people together and having a good discussion if you have 10 or 12 . . . 15 people, it is really hard to coordinate everybody's schedule and hear from everybody.[36]

Nonprofit boards have more of an opportunity to increase size. Most nonprofits do not compensate their board directors. In fact, as mentioned earlier, increasing the number of nonprofit board directors increases revenue streams. It is also an opportunity to increase representation of stakeholders and perspectives.

> **"Yael"**: I'm not in favor of big giant boards. I think it's just a lot of the nonprofits are very large boards. Some people are brought on to nonprofit boards for fundraising; the motivation is to bring more people on for money.
>
> Also you get an increased diversity on boards – ethnic, racial, men, women, industry, small-, medium-, large-company, tech, etc. And I think you want to get a variety of voices and the volunteer base. So sometimes you may need slightly bigger boards.
>
> Sometimes they can be unwieldy. I don't know what the magic number is.
>
> You want to have being on the board be prestigious. But I think you just have to figure out how you get that synergy with boards.[37]

Further reading on board size
"The Size of the Board" in William G. Bowen's book, *The Board Book: An Insider's Guide for Directors and Trustees.*[38]
  "Board Structure and Corporate Structure" in Elizabeth Hammack's *The Private Company Board of Directors Book: What You Need to Know to Be a Director of a Private Company and What Private Company Owners Need to Know to Form and Operate a Company Board.*[39]

---

36 Public company board director interview conducted on 6 November 2020.
37 Board director interview conducted on 7 March 2021.
38 Chapter "The Size of the Board," William G. Bowen *The Board Book: An Insider's Guide for Directors and Trustees*, New York, NY: Norton. 2008.
39 Chapter *"Board Structure and Corporate Structure,"* Elizabeth Hammack, *The Private Company Board of Directors Book: What You Need To Know to Be A Director of A Private Company and What Private Company Owners Need to Know to Form and Operate a Company Board*, Granite Bay, CA: BrainTrustBoard, 2019.

7.1.5 Advisory Committees

Boards can be augmented by advisory committees (also called advisory boards). Members of the advisory committee do not have fiduciary responsibilities. When boards want additional skills, experience, and perspectives, it may form an advisory committee to guide the board on particular topics.

Forming an advisory committee is faster than removing an existing board director and selecting a new director (see Chapter 8, "Nominating and Governance").

In the past ten years, many boards organized advisory committees on technology and/or cybersecurity. As bboard directors did not have technology or cybersecurity skills and experience, they developed an advisory committee. Members of an advisory committee can also serve as a pipeline for new board directors.

Advisory committee members are paid. So, companies trying to decrease expenses may not choose this option, though an advisory committee may be less expensive than hiring expertise from a professional-services firm.

> **"Logan"**: You could create a formal advisory committee for the company, or it can be just professional advisors. You can call up a handful of people that you know and trust to provide the needed expertise.[40]

> **Barbara Adachi**: I served on the advisory committee for several years. The reasoning behind this was the corporate by-laws required a majority percentage of scientist and engineering representation on the board, with the remaining positions filled by corporate executives, which was limited to four board members.
>
> While I was not on the board, I was asked to serve on the Compensation Committee, due to my specific skills and experience with executive compensation and succession planning. Once an opening for an executive became available, I was appointed to the board.[41]

(As book author, I will share that Barbara subsequently moved from the advisory committee to the fiduciary board.)

If an organization wants famous people at the top, an advisory committee or honorary board can be formed. An advisory committee and honorary board does not have fiduciary responsibilities.

> **Julian Ha**: I conducted a search last year for a company that was building out a global advisory board. They were looking for luminaries: former House Members, former Senators, former dignitaries because that lent credibility, cachet, gravitas, and wise counsel. These people have been around the block and have seen lots of things.[42]

---

40 Board director interview conducted in February 2021.
41 Public company board director interview conducted on 5 May 2021.
42 Board director interview conducted on 20 January 2021.

As noted above, there is a limited number of board seats available. The board leadership of the Nom Gov committee can decide to add an advisory committee; advisory committee members do not have organization fiduciary responsibilities.

> **Further reading on advisory committees**
> See "Is an Advisory Board Useful" in Brad Feld and Mahendra Ramsinghani's *Startup Boards: Getting the Most Out of Your Board of Directors.*[43]
> See also "A Board of Directors vs. Advisory Board" and "The Advisory Board" in Dennis J. Cagan's *The Board of Directors for a Private Enterprise: A comprehensive inside look at creating and managing the boards of private companies of all types.*[44]

7.2 Board Culture

Board leadership significantly impacts board culture.

> **Barbara Adachi**: Board culture varies based on who is leading the organization and the board. The CEO sets the tone for the organization and is responsible for culture. At the board level, ideally the culture is aligned with the organization, but it can be very different based on the Chair's approach.
>
> I have experienced a broad range of cultures in the boardroom. With a "command and control" type of chair, there is very little transparency or inclusion. As a board member, you can feel disconnected and question your role and contributions. A more inclusive and communicative Chair will be the opposite experience where you feel valued and part of the team.
>
> The relationship between the CEO and chair will also influence the board culture. If there is healthy communication between the CEO and board chair, the cultures will be aligned and there will be more transparency. In my experience, the CEO is often a member of the board, and this leads to a solid foundation and effective working relationship between management and the board, with the board still maintaining oversight responsibility.[45]

The experienced board directors I interviewed had much to say about board culture. In particular, new board directors were keenly observant of the other directors on the board. New board directors have the goal of "fitting in" and "being heard."

After interviewing many board directors, I think I can describe an effective board culture as (1) trust; (2) respect, and (3) disagree respectfully.

---

43 Chapter "Is an Advisory Board Useful," Brad Feld and Mahendra Ramsinghani, *Startup Boards: Getting the Most Out of Your Board of Directors*, Hoboken, NJ: Wiley. 2014.
44 Chapter, "A Board of Directors vs. Advisory Board," Dennis J. Cagan, *The Board of Directors for a Private Enterprise: A comprehensive inside look at creating and managing the boards of private companies of all types*, Bloomington, IN: AuthorHouse, 2017.
45 Public company board director interview conducted on 5 May 2021.

7.2.1 Trust and Trustworthiness

Many of the experienced corporate directors I interviewed discussed board culture. Every board has a different culture, which directly impacts board productivity.

"Trust" is a word that came up many times in interviews. It was mentioned when describing the relationship between board directors and the relationship between CEO and board directors. In addition, board directors talk about customers needing to trust the organization's products and services.

If I could suggest additional research, I would recommend focusing on trust and trustworthiness. Clearly trust is needed in the boardroom between director and with the CEO, including between the CEO and senior management team.

> **Melinda Yee Franklin**: As a board member you're not a micro-manager. You have to have a CEO in place to trust their judgment —especially in the past few years, when we had to reduce staff by half.
>
> You must have healthy conversations with the CEO – to ask probing questions . . . .to ensure "no rocks remain unturned."[46] You come to the right conclusions together.[47]

> **Andrew Chrostowski**: The CEO takes care of business and establishes trust between with board and the management team.[48]

> **Anna Catalano**: If there's no trust in the boardroom, I guarantee you there's no trust in the senior team.[49]

In particular, the CEO needs to trust each board director. Dysfunction can begin when the CEO does not trust the board or a board director.

> **Catalano continues**: I've worked with a CEO who started out being very defensive when things weren't going well – very defensive. And over time, he learned to trust the board and opened up and realized: "The board is not out to get me. They're actually here to help me."
>
> When you develop that trust, the conversation is totally different . . . totally different and more productive. It sets a very good culture in the boardroom and with senior management.[50]

When there is trust, there can be disagreement and transparency.

> **Catalano resumes**: I think trust is the most important thing in any kind of business relationship. If you don't have trust, you're not going to believe anything they say. That doesn't mean you have to agree with them. You have to trust them.

---

46 "No rocks unturned" means all options have been explored.
47 Board director interview conducted on 7 March 2021.
48 Board director/CEO interview conducted on 20 January 2021.
49 Public company board director interview conducted on 6 June 2021.
50 Public company board director interview conducted on 6 June 2021.

> So you have to understand intent. I'm a real big one on intent. What's the intent? Where are they coming from? What's the real reason why they're interested in this? And so trust is one of the most important things, and trust also comes from a lot of transparency.[51]

Trust is required to talk about difficult topics.

> **"Ridley"**: Having served on a few boards now, one of the things that I've really come to appreciate is board chemistry and how important it is. I've been on boards that the chemistry has been really, really good. I've been on boards with a chemistry has been really toxic.[52]

> **R. Omar Riojas**: You must have the courage and confidence in yourself . . . to be your authentic self in the boardroom. I've been a part of boards where you could tell that someone's just not being their real self . . . they are . . . . acting. It can result in people putting their guard up, right? Not trusting that person. Wondering "what's their angle?"[53]
>
> When people are their authentic self, people can then express their emotions, which is important. People can be angry . . . . frustrated. But those things are healthy, you know.
>
> When the door closes, the board makes important decisions. So that chemistry is a very important thing for me from a board perspective.[54]
>
> It is important for the board culture to be good because there were a lot of difficult discussions, especially when the doors shut and you're in an executive session.[55]

Trust is also important when selecting new board directors. A candidate will not be selected for the boardroom unless the candidate is trusted.

> **"Tristan"**: For candidates to be invited to be on the board you must have confidence and trust in the candidate. If you don't trust a candidate, you don't want to serve with them on a company board.[56]

7.2.1.1 Board Director Conflicts

When private, public, and nonprofit directors benefit from a company, directors must be transparent about any financial gain. Private company directors are likely to be partial owners of the company. If a director is a supplier to the company, the director must be transparent to other directors.

Just as board directors need to know what motivates the CEO, they need to understand what motivates other board directors. Not knowing creates a risk, but this risk can be mitigated with transparency and discussions of the right actions for the company.

---

51 Public company board director interview conducted on 6 June 2021.
52 Board director interview conducted in November 2020.
53 Executive session is described in Chapter 10, "The Board Agenda."
54 Board director interview conducted on 25 November 2020.
55 Board director interview conducted on 25 November 2020.
56 Board director interview conducted in September 2020.

"Kyle": It was easier for our accounting firm to ask the questions to understand how board directors benefit. The third-party firm could ask more nuanced questions about directors and their families. It was easier for accounting firms to ask and document . . . .

Then the independent board chair, nominating committee chair, and lead directors get involved in how to manage the board director participation on the board. At a minimum, board members should not vote on issues in which they have conflicts.[57]

7.2.2 Respect for Different Opinions and Experiences is a Boardroom Value

A core value for the board, and a well-functioning organization, is respect for different opinions and experiences. Board directors need to respect the other board directors and the organization's senior management.

Minaz Abji: We all got along. You have to have a relationship and cordial relationship with all board members. You have to respect them when they say something. Not argue with them. Listen to what they're saying. I think you learn by listening to what others say and contribute. You have to get along with people.

You cannot be a person to join a board and criticize. You can suggest. You can ask questions. But not to criticize anybody and be in a proper relationship. Otherwise, you won't have a collegial relationship.[58]

Board directors must appreciate everyone in the boardroom.

Anna Catalano: One thing that's really important is that directors in the board room respect and trust. There has to be a great deal of respect for one another's experiences, talents, wisdom, and knowledge. There has to be a great deal of trust that everyone is doing it for the right reason. Board directors must believe in what the company is doing.[59]

Ryan Patel: You have to be a real well-oiled machine. That means you got to trust everybody. You have to understand everybody. You got to actually truly listen . . . . They're going to do their homework. They're going to actually listen.

This is not about themselves. This is not about their perspective. It's about adding their own experience and perspective . . . they're prepared to talk about their differences.[60]

There must be appreciation for experiences.

Michael Marquardt: We have a 22-member board, which is pretty large. But we have the CFO of a private equity firm on the board. We have the number three guy at XX Air Lines on our board. We also have a long-time volunteer who's a basketball coach.

At a very high level, you have to have an environment where those people can talk to each other respectfully. And not say, "look you've never run a multi-billion-dollar company. I'm not

---

57 Board director interview conducted in July 2022.
58 Public company board director interview conducted on 20 January 2021.
59 Public company board director interview conducted by 6 June 2021.
60 Board director interview conducted on 30 October 2020.

going to listen to you." An environment where every person may have some insights on the senior-leadership team dynamic that nobody else observed.

You want to have cognitive diversity in the boardroom. Of course, you want to achieve actual diversity in the board room (racial gender, age diversity, gender diversity . . . .). But when you don't have actual diversity there's a way to get cognitive diversity by getting people to speak up and offer slightly different points of view (as opposed to going around the room). Otherwise you have groupthink setting in . . . . People are in their own echo chamber.[61]

Actual diversity ensures cognitive diversity.

Solange Charas:[62] We know that cognitive diversity generates cognitive conflict which generates high-quality governance. And the only way you get cognitive diversity is if you have physical, gender, ethnic, racial diversity that comes with the package, right? I cannot possibly think like a black man . . . I can't. A black man cannot think like a white woman. It's impossible.

The only way you can have that thought represented in the room is by having that person represented in the room. That's why diversity is so important. Not because we're trying to check the box. Because we're trying to enhance cognitive diversity, cognitive conflict, and board governance quality, which is an outshoot of that cognitive conflict.[63]

How do these different skills and experiences add to the company?

"Logan" Everyone brings their skillset and experience to the board and offers an interesting hodgepodge.

I have my own opinion. I hear your perspective. This helps the company strategy which helps the company.[64]

7.2.3 It's Okay to Disagree – in a Respectful Manner

A healthy board culture includes trust and respect. This culture allows board directors to have candid discussions, which includes disagreements.

Being able to discuss different perspectives is linked to trust.

R. Omar Riojas: In order to have those kinds of discussions, you have to be able to have your trust in your fellow board member and it's okay to disagree. It's okay to talk about something that's very difficult. There's got to be that element of trust that it's okay to express your view . . . without being judged.

In order to have those kinds of discussions, you have to be able to have your trust in your fellow board member. It's okay to disagree.

And I think it's also important to have this sort of relationship with management.[65]

---

61 Board director/CEO/independent chair interview conducted on.
62 Charas is a white woman.
63 Public company board director interview conducted on 8 December 2020.
64 Board director interview conducted in February 2021.
65 Board director interview conducted on 25 November 2020.

Andrew Chrostowski: You need to build that open, trusting relationship on a board to be successful . . . . You don't want people who think like you and act like you. You need to trust to say that when you disagree on something. It's this ability to be highly professional, yet disagree, and explore a topic in a way that adds value . . . .

There's just too much of that groupthink. I think establishing trust becomes an absolutely vital part of an effective and functioning board. Trust makes it easier to explore disagreements in a professional and positive way.[66]

Board directors need to disagree without being disagreeable.

Erin Essenmacher: Best practices for boards are having healthy dissent, dialogue, and conversation. You have to disagree without being disagreeable, to challenge each other. So I think there should be a healthy amount of disagreement . . . . A culture where we can have that healthy back and forth.[67]

The ability to disagree respectfully is a factor in recruiting new board directors.

Barbara Adachi: Board culture will influence open discussions in the boardroom, including the decision process and ability to disagree in a respectful manner. A broader lens around diversity will bring members who have different skills and experiences. Consequently, the board must have a culture of being able to have respectful debates, questioning and even disagreement with the understanding it is acceptable to "agree to disagree." The key objective is to be respectful in all discussions and ensure that all voices are heard.[68]

Michael Marquardt: One of the things frankly is one of the biggest tests to me for when interviewing a potential director is whether they have a personality that allows them to disagree agreeably.[69]

Board leadership and structure impact board culture, which in turn impact boardroom discussions and decisions, which influences the organization. This discussion on board leadership and culture is critical to the work of the Nominating and Governance Committee, described in the next chapter.

---

66 Board director/CEO interview conducted on 20 January 2021.
67 Board director/Independent chair interview conducted on 20 October 2020.
68 Public company board director interview conducted on 5 May 2021.
69 Board director/CEO interview conducted on 4 February 2021.

8 Nominating and Governance Committee

Most board directors use the term "Nom Gov committee" rather than Nominating and Governance committee, so I will use Nom Gov for the remainder of this book.

The Nom Gov committee works closely with board leadership, even if the executive chair, lead director or independent board chair is not a member of the committee. While board composition is important, board leadership is arguably more so. As described above, board leadership sets the agenda, the board structure, and has significant impact on choosing board directors. I recommend research to verify my hypothesis.

After board leadership is the composition of board talent. Remember back to the opening quote of this book, the CEO, board leadership, and board directors can work together to further the organization to "achieve the unachievable,"[1] So, the membership of the board matters.

Per Chapter 6 on compensation and ad hoc committees, the board works on CEO performance management, CEO succession planning, and CEO selection. And per the upcoming Chapter 9 on entire board responsibilities, the board influences company strategy, organization culture, and company purpose. All this takes talented people on board.

The Nom Gov committee, as its name suggests, influences director nominations and general governance. This committee leads board director succession planning, recruits new board directors, and works on board director orientation. It also works on general governance issues, including board size, the separation or combination of the CEO and chair roles, and committee structure.

Decisions made by the Nom Gov committee come in the form of recommendations that need to be confirmed by board leadership and the entire board.

8.1 Board Composition

In the past, boards may have been rubber stamps[2] or people with big names[3] and titles rather than a group responsible for the CEO's actions and the company's strategy and results.

> **Joyce Cacho**: When I talk about boards . . . . oversight is about seeing around the corner. You need "others" in the room because "others" will be your markets in the future. Markets will be defined by embedding their norms, their expectations, into your product and service.[4]

---

1 Board director/CEO interview conducted on 4 February 2021.
2 "Rubber stamp" means giving automatic approval without proper consideration.
3 "Big name" means someone who is famous.
4 Board director interview conducted on 12 January 2023.

https://doi.org/10.1515/9783110689129-008

"Sutton" (Nom Gov committee chair of two different organizations): I will share an interview that I did recently when recruiting a director to my board. The candidate had spent 40 years in the boardroom. He was a more experienced gentleman. He said prior board directors were old school.[5] They were rubber-stamp, country-club and golf-course types doing whatever the CEO wanted. He noted that the current breed of board directors are involved, they are engaged, and they are constantly learning![6]

Andrea Bonime-Blanc: I'm Nom Gov chair of one of the Boards that I serve on. And one of the jobs of Nom Gov is to bring in new board members and to do the skills matrix and the self-evaluation and all these good things that are supposed to cater to having the right people on the board and having the right kind of onboarding and off-boarding.

Who's on our board? What's our skills mix? What are we missing? That is really the fundamental piece of the puzzle. When it comes to having the right kind of diversity, are we being proactive at the board level to make sure that we have the right skills, matrix, and backgrounds and the right people?[7]

8.1.1 Independent Directors

The experienced corporate directors interviewed for this book are independent directors, i.e., board members who do not have material or financial relationships with the organization prior to becoming a board member. Independent directors are not employees and are not involved in the daily operations of the company.

Solange Charas: One of the things I learned is that if you want to enhance board governance, you recruit strangers onto your board.

If you bring me onto your board because I'm doing a deal with you someplace else, I'm not willing to disagree with you on the board because I don't want to screw up that deal.[8]

In addition to the formal definition of independent directors, there are relationships between board directors that decrease independence.

Rich Horan: If a board has – supposedly – independent directors, but when you look closely, there are multiple people serving on multiple boards together – that's not independent.

Also look at personal relationships. If someone tells you "Oh, yeah. I knew John from back when we were in college or worked together." That's an indication of not being an independent board member. The resume may look like it is. But the actual relationship is not.[9]

This section is about independent directors, but readers should understand that board directors can be investors, members of the management team (e.g., Chief Finan-

---

5 "Old school" means out-of-date.
6 Public company board director interview conducted on 28 November 2020.
7 Board director interview conducted on 8 January 2021.
8 Public company board director interview conducted on 8 December 2020.
9 Board director interview conducted on 16 February 2021.

cial Officers), and employees, etc. When considering board composition, the CEO and board chair need to determine board size and the number of independent directors.

8.1.2 Some Board Directors Are Appointed by Investors and Owners

In Chapters 2 and 3, experienced corporate directors shared that they represent owners of public and private companies. Owners – also called shareholders or investors – are primary stakeholders who at times take a lead role in deciding board composition.

In some cases, investors require a seat on the board as a requirement for their investment.

The board meets frequently when under activist investor attack.

> **Bala Iyer:** Activist attacks are becoming more frequent. When a high-performing, local company was under attack, the board met more than 50 times.[10]

> **Sheila Hooda**: When you think about the board . . . and when there's an activist . . . . maybe a small number of board directors are supported by the activists. Even a small number has a big impact on the overall boardroom.[11]

Because activist investors are tireless, experienced board directors, public company directors must learn how to "think like an activist." A director may have their board seat thanks to an activist investor, but it is a "best practice" for directors to represent all investors, including activists.

> **Evelyn Dilsaver**: Think like an activist if you will. This means knowing the weak points of your business . . . . You can think from the standpoint of the company's customers as well as look at those products that contribute the most to the company revenue.[12]

> **Further reading on activists and governance**
> *See* "Activist Shareholders and Their Role in Governance" in Thomas Bakewell and James Darazsdi' book *Claiming Your Place at the Boardroom Table: The Essential Handbook for Excellence in Governance and Effective Directorship.*[13]

---

10 Public company board director interview conducted on 8 January 2021.
11 Public company board director interview conducted on 28 November 2020.
12 Public company board director interview conducted on 6 November 2020.
13 Chapter "Activist Shareholders and Their Role in Governance," Thomas Bakewell and James Darazsdi, *Claiming Your Place at the Boardroom Table: The Essential Handbook for Excellence in Governance and Effective Directorship*. New York, NY: McGraw Hill, 2014.

See "In Search of the Activist Investor" in Ira M. Millstein's book *The Activist Director: Lessons from the Boardroom and the Future of the Boardroom.*[14]

See also "The Rise of Hedge Funds and Emergence of Aggressive Activism" in Deborah Hick Midanek's book, *The Governance Revolution: What Every Board Member Needs to Know, NOW!*[15]

8.1.3 Board Director Skills, Knowledge, and Experience

Even though some board directors are selected by activist investors (or elected by shareholders thanks to activist campaigns), no director should be on a board simply because of a powerful connection. The Nom Gov committee should be continually appraising the skills, knowledge, and experience of board directors individually and the board overall.

The Nom Gov committee put together a matrix of skills, knowledge, and experience needed by the company on the x-axis.[16] And because diversity is important, on the y-axis[17] there can dimensions of diversity including gender, race, sexual identity, and other intrinsic personal characteristics. As described in Chapter 7 "Board Culture," board director diversity will help the board see strategy characteristics that other board directors may not see.

> **Andrea Bonime-Blanc**: Diversity is like a Rashomon[18] kind of situation. Diversity helps see the world in a more complete way. To me that means creating company value. There is a direct connection back to the purpose of a corporation. For me, diversity of the boardroom is incredibly important.[19]

The experienced board directors I interviewed had much to say about professional and personal diversity.

Everyone has a combination of skills, knowledge, experience, and personal differences. Today when thinking about a board, the Nom Gov committee looks at a matrix of skills, knowledge, experiences, and dimensions of diversity. The skills matrix identifies the board's assets and what the organization needs to fulfill its purpose and strategy.

---

14 Chapter "In Search of the Activist Investor" in Ira M. Millstein. *The Activist Director: Lessons from the Boardroom and the Future of the Boardroom.* New York, NY: Columbia Business School Publishing. 2016.

15 Chapter "The Rise of Hedge Funds and Emergence of Aggressive Activism," Deborah Hick Midanek, *The Governance Revolution: What Every Board Member Needs to Know, NOW!* Berlin, GE: De Gruyter Press, 2018.

16 The x-axis on a graph is the horizontal line.

17 The y-axis on a graph is the vertical line.

18 "Rashomon" is a movie in which the same situation is seen differently by each character https://en.wikipedia.org/wiki/Rashomon.

19 Board director and Nom Gov chair interview conducted on 8 January 2021.

There is a need to have institutional memory. Institutional memory is the director's knowledge, experiences, and historical information that accumulates within an organization over time. It includes the shared understanding of the organization's culture, values, procedures, successes, and failures.

> **"Skylar"** We need institutional memory, especially since the founder was no longer part of the board. He was "interesting," so I want to be careful about what's disclosed. There was no lead director and there was no chairman.[20]

Many investors also believe that board directors with technology, cybersecurity, and ESG experience will lead to better business results. As investors believe this kind of expertise on the board leads to better financial results, the SEC may require specific expertise on the board.

Following passage of the Sarbanes-Oxley Act of 2002, the SEC required public companies to have financial expertise on the board, specifically an "audit committee financial expert" serving on the audit committee.[21] In addition, NYSE listing requirements require all audit committee members to be or to become "financially literate," as defined by the board within a reasonable period of time. Nasdaq requires all audit committee members to be financially literate at the time of appointment, defining this as "the ability to read and understand financial statements."[22] These requirements make sense. It seems hard to imagine a board with no board directors with financial expertise. Without board-level financial expertise, on some nonprofit boards for example, the board cannot challenge financial information from the company.

Also crucial for the board is technology expertise. Having such on the board allows the board to push back on management's technology plans. Likewise, having environmental, social, and governance (ESG) experience on the board allows the board to provide guidance and push back on management's plans in these domains.

Based on the content of educational programs being offered to directors today,[23] in the early 2020s, it appears that the skills, knowledge, and experience needed by boards are primarily in the domains of technology and ESG. These programs address trends of digitization, cyber risk, climate change, and diversity. In the future, other expertise may be required to help the organization move forward profitably.

To fill the gap in skills, knowledge, and experience, Nom Gov organizes training, sets up advisory committees and recruits new board directors.

---

20 Board director Interview conducted in December 2020.
21 "Standards Relating to Listed Company Audit Committees," US Securities and Exchange Commission https://www.sec.gov/rules/final/33-8220.htm.
22 "Audit Committee Requirements," See this discussion from Deloitte: https://www2.deloitte.com/us/en/pages/center-for-board-effectiveness/articles/audit-committee-requirements.html.
23 See, for example, nacdonline.org.

8.1.3.1 Technology

Michael Marquardt: As a board we're doing a cybersecurity course . . . . We're having our CISO[24] come in and we're going to do . . . . a basic catchup on technology. On the recruiting side, I still don't see technology being prioritized in recruiting new directors. I'm sure it's happening. I don't see enough of it.[25]

See Dr. Elizabeth Valentine, Dr. Steve De Haes, and Dr. Anant Joshi's chapter, "Responsive governance in a Digital World: The Need to Up-Skill" in Richard Leblanc, *The Handbook of Board Governance: A Comprehensive Guide for Public, Private, and Not-for-Profit Board Members, Second Edition.*[26]

8.1.3.2 International

One expertise that experienced corporate directors discuss is international expertise which is skill-based as well as a dimension of diversity.

Maureen Conners: The future requires a global mindset. It also means being more aware of how global trends and issues can impact your business. Tracking what is happening at CES and the World Economic Forum annually is also helpful for keeping a global perspective.[27]

Michael Marquardt who was born and spent his youth in Germany: What do I bring to the table? I love serving on a board especially because of my international background.

When the company is discussing a situation with a German regulator, the CEO already looks in my direction.[28]

Larry Taylor: I've always been international. I was involved with ISO[29] in the late eighties and early nineties where I . . . helped write the international standard for environmental management ISO 14001. I was tasked to go around the world to train lead auditors because this was the auditing process. I went to Japan, Switzerland, and India . . . . I had offices in those places. I had to learn the corporate governance of those places just to operate in those places . . . .

I think that was kind of unique. I did a lot of work with USAID, giving aid to disadvantaged countries . . . . US ETI Environmental Training Institute . . . IP3 the public-private partnership, which is an international organization out of Switzerland . . . . The United Nations . . . . The World Bank. It's always been international for me.[30]

---

24 "CISO" is a Chief Information Security Officer who is responsible for the organization's digital security.

25 Board director/CEO interview conducted on 4 February 2021.

26 Chapter "Responsive governance in a Digital World: The Need to Up-Skill," Richard Leblanc, *The Handbook of Board Governance: A Comprehensive Guide for Public, Private, and Not-for-Profit Board Members, Second Edition.* Hoboken, NJ: Wiley, 2020.

27 Public company board director interview conducted on 8 January 2021.

28 Board director/CEO interview conducted on 4 February 2021.

29 ISO is the International Organization for Standardization https://en.wikipedia.org/wiki/International_Organization_for_Standardization.

30 Board director interview conducted on 27 October 2020.

Chris Lee: If you take a company public in the US like a China-based company operating in the US in which I served on the board . . . . The founders were engineers from China and then they became an international company.

It was listed domestically in China. They were also listed in Hong Kong; it was . . . . only a ten-year-old company. Given the growth rate, the founders were very cognizant of the fact that they needed to have experienced board directors who had international capital markets experience.[31]

8.1.4 Dimensions of Diversity

In addition to different skills, knowledge, and experience, board directors also represented other dimensions of diversity. There are many dimensions of diversity including gender, race, age, sexual orientation, physical ability, and socioeconomic status. As noted throughout this book are the findings that organizational performance improves with diversity.

Financial performance improves because the organization strategy is more robust. When both the board and senior management are diverse, it is easier to identify risks and new opportunities which can create a better strategy. Likewise, diverse boards and senior management can also find more opportunities and risks in operations that can be improved.

For these reasons some institutional investors and private equity look for gender and racial diversity on boards. Some investors, including BlackRock, has said they will not fund a company unless there is board diversity. Proxy advisors may not recommend election of specific public-company directors if the board director is not from a diverse background.

In addition, some governments require board directors from diverse communities. For example, the EU requires that 40% or more of independent board seats are taken by women.[32] The State of California has legislated that 30% or more of board seats are taken by diverse board directors representing gender, racial, and sexual orientation diversity, though the California State Supreme Court benched this legislation.

CEOs, board chairs, and board directors are responsible for board and organization diversity.

Diversity is important, but the inclusion of diverse leaders in the strategy and operations of the organization is even more important. As stated earlier in Chapter 7 of Board Leadership and Culture the organization should have a culture that respects the experience, skills, and knowledge of all workers including diverse board directors.

"Tristan" I have been working on board diversity almost as long as I've been a board director. It's a never-ending challenge.

---

31 Public company board director interview conducted on 7 December 2020.
32 "EU revives plans for mandatory quotas of women on company boards" *The Guardian*. 5 March 2020.

It takes some time to get the CEO, the board chair, and the Nom Gov chair to work together to increase the diversity of board. Fortunately there are plenty of great diverse candidates.

Usually it's a surprise to other board members how great the candidates are. But it just goes to show you the small bubbles that each of us live in.[33]

Boards of directors oversee but do not manage nor operate companies. But there are many things that CEOs, board chairs, and board directors can do to encourage and support diversity:

– Monitor and track HR metrics: The CEO and senior management set diversity goals and the board can monitor progress towards those goals.
– Hold executives accountable: CEO and officer compensation can be tied to achieving diversity goals. For example, a percentage of variable pay may be tied to diversity goals. Or variable compensation can be withheld if diversity goals are not achieved.
– CEOS, senior management, and HR leaders can decide to recruit diverse candidates from pools of diverse candidates. Unconscious bias training may be provided to company leaders and employees. Employee resources groups for women, LGBTQ+, veterans, people of color, and other dimensions of diversity can be supported to encourage and enable employees.
– CEOs, board chairs, and board directors can create an inclusive culture by creating policies and monitoring practices

"Sam": To increase board diversity quite frankly you need to create seats on the board. That means transitioning directors off the board, which is very challenging. It's incredibly hard to move someone off the board. But you look at the skills matrix and if you are diligent year-after-year you can open new board seats and find great candidates.

That's how you change the board, board culture, and board composition.[34]

8.1.4.1 Gender

Maureen Conners: I was the first woman on a public board. I came from a global company Gillette that was marketing driven . . . . I'm a strong believer in marketing to build your business; that also influenced my Board decisions for investments in growing a business.[35]

Andrea Bonime-Blanc: I happen to be a woman. I'm white. So, I'm part of the white privileged class . . . . But I'm a woman. So, I understand the issues from a gender standpoint. I've learned, I think, to really be much more sensitive to some of the challenges that non-white people have in the boardroom. That serves as a fundamental sort of lens for me about why diversity is so important on the board.

Here we are. I was at that place from 1995 to 2002 and we're almost two decades later and the whole issue of diversity has been so slow. And so hard won.

---

33 Board director interview conducted in September 2020.
34 Board director interview conducted in November 2020.
35 Public company board director interview conducted on 8 January 2021.

I think it is starting to be turbocharged a little bit in the last couple of years . . . . But now especially with the last year i.e., 2020, the pandemic and the social justice issues and the need for diversity on boards.

And I spent a good chunk of my career, both as a board member, an executive, and now as a consultant . . . . Pushing hard for people to think about diversity in a broader sense the importance of how diversity creates value.

It could be people with diverse backgrounds, whether it's gender, ethnicity race, geographical location and functional expertise . . . . any of those things . . . . I think, especially in this country US is so important, right?

We've had a few years of people becoming more sensitive to the gender issue. And now in the last year, I think finally the US is starting to think about race and about corporate racism.[36]

Michael Marquardt: We certainly understand the drive for greater diversity, both in terms of gender and racial diversity on boards because that helps advance the kind of diverse thinking the company needs to be successful.[37]

Joyce Cacho: I think this book – The Art of Director Excellence – needs to make it plain that diversity is not theory anymore. It's about bringing stakeholders who aren't in the room, into the room, and by doing so creating value in the boardroom and in the company.[38]

"Cassidy": We've got to take this whole notion of diversity out of the mental space of being decoration: "Oh, we've got the Black viewpoint." "We've got the Asian viewpoint." We need to increase the numbers of non-white males and non-white females on the board.[39]

Julian Ha: Our Nom Gov committee wanted to have both regional balance, industry balance, gender balance . . . . Also we're thinking if this person would be a good member for the Finance Committee. Would he or she be a good member for the Comp Committee? Or Nom Gov? Do they have those skill sets? . . . . Could they be in the pipeline for future committee service?[40]

Lisa Chin: I think we're going to see a shift in the types of directors that are being tapped . . . . It's going to be an interesting time in corporate governance.[41]

You may be reading this book at a time and place when there are regulatory requirements to disclose gender, racial identity, sexual identity or other dimensions of diversity. In addition, even if there is no regulation, there is a belief that boards should reflect the diversity of the organization's customers and employees. Many investors believe that increased diversity on boards lead to better financial results.[42]

---

36 Board director interview conducted on 8 January 2021.

37 Public company board director/CEO interview conducted on 20 January 2021.

38 Board director interview conducted on 16 February 2021.

39 Board director interview conducted in February 2021.

40 Board director interview conducted on 20 January 2021.

41 Board director/CEO interview conducted on 30 September 2020.

42 "How and Where Diversity Drives Financial Performance," Rocio Lorenzo and Martin Reeves, 30 January 2018, https://hbr.org/2018/01/how-and-where-diversity-drives-financial-performance.

Further reading on board diversity
There are several chapters on diversity, in particular gender diversity.

See chapter "4-D Diversity – When Is Board Diversity Actually Diverse?" in Dennis J. Cagan's *The Board of Directors for a Private Enterprise: A comprehensive inside look at creating and managing the boards of private companies of all types.*[43]

See chapter "Diversity and Independence" in Elizabeth Hammack's *The Private Company Board of Directors Book: What You Need to Know to Be a Director of a Private Company and What Private Company Owners Need to Know to Form and Operate a Company Board.*[44]

See Dr. Mary Halton's chapter, "Board Behaviors: How Women Directors Influence Decision Outcomes"[45] and Dr. Nancy Gianni Herbert's chapter, "The State of Gender Diversity in Boardrooms"[46] in Richard Leblanc, *The Handbook of Board Governance: A Comprehensive Guide for Public, Private, and Not-for-Profit Board Members, Second Edition*

8.1.5 Boardrooms Were Once Filled with CEOs

There was a time when boardrooms were filled with CEOs. The belief was that only other CEOs could help a current CEO or that only CEOs understood the difference between governance and management; in other words, stay out of the way of the CEO and approve the CEO's decisions.

CEOs may appreciate having other CEOs on the board because the CEO role is unique and CEOs may think that only other CEOs understand the role. Also, they may want a "rubber stamp" board, which a board of CEOs may provide.

Today's CEOs understand their strengths and weaknesses and are willing to accept assistance from board directors.

> **"Blake"**: You have to choose people who can leave their ego at the door. If you choose people who are CEOs, there is a lot of egos and there is an inevitable clash of egos, which does not serve the organization.[47]

---

43 Chapter "4-D Diversity – When Is Board Diversity Actually Diverse?" Dennis J. Cagan, *The Board of Directors for a Private Enterprise*, Bloomington, IN: AuthorHouse, 2017.

44 Chapter "Diversity and Independence" and "Board Committees," Elizabeth Hammack, *The Private Company Board of Directors Book: What You Need To Know To Be A Director of A Private Company and What Private Company Owners Need to Know to Form and Operate a Company Board*, Granite Bay, CA: BrainTrustBoard, 2019.

45 Chapter "Board Behaviors: How Women Directors Influence Decision Outcomes," Richard Leblanc, *The Handbook of Board Governance: A Comprehensive Guide for Public, Private, and Not-for-Profit Board Members, Second Edition*. Hoboken, NJ: Wiley. 2020.

46 Chapter "The State of Gender Diversity in Boardrooms," Richard Leblanc, *The Handbook of Board Governance: A Comprehensive Guide for Public, Private, and Not-for-Profit Board Members, Second Edition*. Hoboken, NJ: Wiley. 2020.

47 Board director interview conducted on 11 September 2020.

See the chapter, "Are CEOs the Best Directors?" in David Larker, Brian Tayan, and Michelle E. Guttman's book *A Real Look at Real World Governance.*[48]

Further reading on board composition
There is a great deal written about board composition.

See the Chapters "Building a Board" and *"Board Refreshment"* in Betsy Atkins's book *Be Board Ready: The Secrets to Landing a Board Set and Being a Great Director.*[49]

See Chapter "Building the Board" in William G. Bowen's book, T*he Board Book: An Insider's Guide for Directors and Trustees.*[50]

See Chapter "The Board of Directors" in Robert Nii Arday Clegg in *Corporate Governance: The Boardroom, The Bottom Line, and Beyond.*[51]

See Chapter David A. Nadler's "Building Better Boards" in *HBR's 10 Must Reads on Boards.*[52]

See "When to Create, or Recreate Your Board," in Mark A. Pfister's *Across the Board: The Modern Architecture Behind an Effective Board of Directors.*[53]

See Chapter "Board Membership" in Adrian Cadbury's book, *Corporate Governance and Chairmanship: A Personal View.*[54]

See the Chapter "Who Should Be on The Board" in Elizabeth Hammack's *The Private Company Board of Directors Book: What You Need To Know to Be A Director of A Private Company and What Private Company Owners Need to Know to Form and Operate a Company Board.*[55]

See *"The Board: Role and Composition"* in Cornelis A. de Kluyver's book *A Primer on Corporate Governance.*[56]

See Estelle Metayer's Chapter "Strategic Blindspots in the Boardroom" in Richard Leblanc's book, *The Handbook of Board Governance: A Comprehensive Guide for Public, Private, and Not-for-Profit Board Members, Second Edition.*[57]

---

48 Chapter "Are CEOs the Best Directors?" David Larker, Brian Tayan, and Michelle E. Guttman, *A Real Look at Real World Governance*. Self-Published. 2013.

49 Chapter *"Building a Board"* and *"Board Refreshment,"* Betsy Atkins, *Be Board Ready: The Secrets to Landing a Board Set and Being a Great Director*. Chicago: NEWTYPE Publishing, 2019.

50 Chapter *"Building the Board,"* William G. Bowen, T*he Board Book: An Insider's Guide for Directors and Trustees*, New York, NY: Norton. 2008.

51 Chapter "The Board of Directors," Robert Nii Arday Clegg in *Corporate Governance: The Boardroom, The Bottom Line, and Beyond,* United Arab Emirates: Self Published. 2019.

52 Chapter "Building Better Boards," *HBR's 10 Must Reads on Boards,* Cambridge, MA: Harvard Business Review Press, 2020.

53 Chapter *"When to Create, or Recreate Your Board,"* Mark A. Pfister, *Across the Board: The Modern Architecture Behind an Effective Board of Directors,* Port Jefferson, NY: Pfister Strategy Group, 2018.

54 Chapter *"Board Membership,"* Adrian Cadbury, *Corporate Governance and Chairmanship: A Personal View*. Oxford, UK: Oxford University Press, 2002.

55 Chapter "Who Should Be on The Board," Elizabeth Hammack, *The Private Company Board of Directors Book: What You Need to Know To Be A Director of A Private Company and What Private Company Owners Need to Know to Form and Operate a Company Board,* Granite Bay, CA: BrainTrustBoard, 2019.

56 Chapter "The Board: Role and Composition," Cornelis A. de Kluyver, *A Primer on Corporate Governance*. New York, NY: Business Expert Press. 2013.

57 Chapter "Strategic Blindspots in the Boardroom," Richard Leblanc, *The Handbook of Board Governance: A Comprehensive Guide for Public, Private, and Not-for-Profit Board Members, Second Edition.* Hoboken, NJ: Wiley. 2020.

See "Creating a High-Performance Board" in Cornelis A. de Kluyver's book *A Primer on Corporate Governance.*[58]

See Chapter "Creating Your Board" in Brad Feld and Mahendra Ramsinghani's *Startup Boards: Getting the Most Out of Your Board of Directors.*[59]

See Chapters "Building a Board" and "Board Refreshment" in Betsy Atkins book *Be Board Ready: The Secrets to Landing a Board Set and Being a Great Director.*[60]

See the Chapter "The Public Company Board" in J. Robert Brown, Jr., Lisa L. Casey, *Corporate Governance: Cases and Materials, Second Edition.*[61]

8.2 Board Director Evaluation

In Chapter 6, we covered the importance of CEO succession planning. Because of the frequency of CEO turnover, and that it makes sense to have discussion about CEO succession planning in many executive sessions (Chapter 10, "The Entire Board Agenda") and ad hoc committees.

Likewise, board director succession planning is an ongoing process. At a minimum, board director succession planning is completed annually by the Nom Gov committee.

The skills matrix described earlier is a starting point into the board director succession planning process including the behaviors needed for the agreed-upon board culture.

Then there are board director evaluations, including self-evaluation, peer evaluations, and entire-board evaluations. Even with these evaluations, transitioning a board director off the board is a very difficult task. It is much more difficult than transitioning an employee out of the company. Hence many boards use term limits to transition board directors off the board directors rather than evaluation findings.

Key questions are: Should the board directors go through evaluations if board leadership and the Nom Gov committee rely on term limits (rather than evaluation results) to transition directors off the board? Will evaluation results lead to improved board performance?

---

58 Chapter "Creating a High-Performance Board," Cornelis A. de Kluyver, *A Primer on Corporate Governance*. New York, NY: Business Expert Press. 2013.

59 Chapter "Creating Your Board," Brad Feld and Mahendra Ramsinghani, *Startup Boards: Getting the Most Out of Your Board of Directors*, Hoboken, NJ: Wiley. 2014.

60 Chapters "Building a Board" and "Board Refreshment," Betsy Atkins, *Be Board Ready: The Secrets to Landing a Board Set and Being a Great Director*. Chicago: NEWTYPE Publishing, 2019.

61 Chapter "The Public Company Board," J. Robert Brown, Jr. and Lisa L. Casey, *Corporate Governance: Cases and Materials, Second Edition*, Durham, NC: Carolina Academic Press, 2016.

8.2.1 Individual Evaluations

For an employee in an organization, there is a role description. For board directors, there is a role description which is used primarily when recruiting new board directors.

When an employee does not fulfill the role description, the employee is offered feedback and training to improve. If employees do not improve, then they are fired.

One can argue that the board directors should be treated like employees. But experienced corporate directors do not report much feedback or consequences from evaluations.

> **Solange Charas**: One of the things that boards are not very good at – based on my PhD research – is identifying quality standards, measuring against those standards, and then taking action to correct. Boards inherently think they're doing a good job because they don't measure themselves. I think that's the Achilles heel.[62]

> **"Skylar"** When you've got a group of people who are leaders in their field who have been successful, that's why they're selected to be on boards. They have a blind spot about their own performance.[63]

There is much written about board evaluation. Board evaluations should link to open seats in the boardroom, and the selection of new board directors. See chapters "Board Member Evaluation and Selection" and "Board Assessments, Tools, and Insurance" in Mark A. Pfister's *Across the Board: The Modern Architecture Behind an Effective Board of Directors*.[64] But board evaluations do not necessarily lead to open board seats.

> **David Rosenblum**: You want a level of experience and institutional memory on boards.[65] On the other hand issues change. For example getting a company to scale.
> So you're making sure that the board has the people on it who are able to address forward challenges. Do boards have succession plans just as we have succession plans for management?
> We hired a professional services firm to do our self-assessment . . . . Online performance assessment is the basis for performance assessment . . . .[66]

For peer feedback, there is an assessment tool that board directors fill out regarding each other.[67] Then feedback is given to the independent board chair, lead director, Nom Gov chair, or other board leader. After reading this feedback, a board leader should have individual discussions with directors to improve performance.

---

62 Public company board director interview conducted on 8 December 2020.
63 Board director interview conducted in December 2020.
64 Chapter "Board Member Evaluation and Selection" and "Board Assessments, Tools, and Insurance," Mark A. Pfister, *Across the Board: The Modern Architecture Behind an Effective Board of Directors*, Port Jefferson, NY: Pfister Strategy Group, 2018.
65 Company institutional memory should be captured in the skill, knowledge, and experience matrix described in Chapter 8.
66 Public company board director interview conducted on 11 November 2020.
67 One example of a board assessment tool is from BoardSource: https://boardsource.org/board-support/assessing-performance/board-self-assessment/.

Phil Haas: We had performance evaluations for board members. It was very meaningful, useful, and well done. When the board chair's term ran out her successor was the perfect person for this undertaking.[68]

Lead directors works closely with executive chairs. In this association, the lead director reads the board evaluations.

Cari Dominguez: Board evaluations are critical. So, all of a sudden as the lead director . . . . I'm cast in a role where I'm evaluating individuals or providing feedback to the individuals that have been around for a long time. So, you have to tap into your skills, your fortitude, your diplomacy, and your ability to convey a message in a constructive positive manner to prevent an individual from feeling stigmatized.

I'm reading peer evaluations, committee, and board evaluations. It generates a whole different set of action items. In terms of feedback – which is all anonymous – you see how the board members are ranked by their peers. And at some point, you're going to have to address improvement areas. At one of my boards, we had one-on-one meetings with each board member to provide some summary feedback. As a result of those evaluations – not because a board member was not qualified or capable – the direction that the company was taking required a different set of skills, needing to offboard members and recruit new ones. Boards are shrinking in size. We used to have 12–15 member size boards. Now, you're down to 9–10 or 9–12 that type of thing. So, how do you maximize the opportunities that you have? And board evaluations are critical for that.[69]

There are good books on board evaluations. See "Director Evaluation" in Ram Charan, Dennis Carey, and Michael Useem in *Boards That Lead: When to Take Charge, When to Partner, and When to Stay Out of the Way*,[70] and the chapter, "Board Evaluation: Reviewing Directors and Boards" Bob Tricker's *Corporate Governance: Principles, Policies, and Practices, Fourth Edition*.[71]

8.2.2 Entire Board Evaluations

For entire board evaluations, the Nom Gov[72] committee selects a professional service consultant to interview all board directors. The consultant then writes up their assessment of individual board directors and the entire board.

---

68 Board director interview conducted by 6 May 2021.

69 Public company board director interview conducted on 4 September 2020.

70 See the Appendix "Director Evaluation," Ram Charan, Dennis Carey, and Michael Useem, *Boards That Lead: When to Take Charge, When to Partner, and When to Stay Out of the Way*, Cambridge, MA: Harvard Business Review Press, 2013.

71 Chapter "Board Evaluation: Reviewing Directors and Boards," Bob Tricker, *Corporate Governance: Principles, Policies, and Practices, Fourth Edition*, Oxford, UK: Oxford University Press, 2019.

72 Nom Gov means Nominating and Governance Committee.

David Rosenblum: Our board does regular board assessments. So there are general comments or observations about the board assessment . . . . It's actually fairly common to have a consultant come in the board room and do the assessment.

The assessment is online, and it covers select officers . . . . There's a set of questions that are relevant. You can supplement it with questions although one of the things that you need to be careful about is not changing the questions every year because then you don't have a good baseline . . . .

I think most boards are using these kinds of techniques where they are using software provided by someone.[73]

Further reading on board evaluations
See "Root Out Dysfunction" by Ram Charan, Dennis Carey, and Michael Useem in *Boards That Lead: When to Take Charge, When to Partner, and When to Stay Out of the Way*.[74]
See also chapter "Actively Evaluate Board Performance to Constantly Improve" by Deborah Hick Midanek in *The Governance Revolution: What Every Board Member Needs to Know, NOW!*.[75]

8.3 Succession Planning and Transitioning Directors off the Board

The (1) skills matrix and (2) board evaluation results are fed into board director succession planning.

A succession plan can also be as simple as knowing when board directors will term off[76] and the skills, knowledge, experience, and diversity needed for the board.

David Rosenblum: When a board director hits their term limit, unless there's something very special about the board director that we can't easily replace with a new board director, we'll give you another two- or three-years, whatever the term it is.[77]

For public companies, there may be investors or external pressure to remove a board director.

"Rene": There can be the extraordinarily unusual shareholders "no" vote . . . . And unless there was egregiously bad – outrageously bad behavior – transitioning a director off the board is not something the board does frequently.[78]

---

73 Public company board director interview conducted on 11 November 2020.
74 Chapter "Root Out Dysfunction," Ram Charan, Dennis Carey, and Michael Useem, *Boards That Lead: When to Take Charge, When to Partner, and When to Stay Out of the Way*, Cambridge, MA: Harvard Business Review Press, 2013.
75 Deborah Hick Midanek, *The Governance Revolution: What Every Board Member Needs to Know, NOW!* Berlin, GE: De Gruyter Press, 2018.
76 "Term off" means when a director has a term on the board and the term has ended.
77 Public company board director interview conducted on 11 November 2020.
78 Public company board director interview conducted in 2020.

Assessing board directors and transitioning a director off the board is the way to bring new skills, experience, and diversity to the board. It is possible to add new skills, experience, and diversity on the board by expanding board size. But the likelihood of increasing board size is small.

It is more likely to add needed skills and experience to an advisory committee.

> **"Sam"**: It's raising the question is to make a tough call pushing people off the board to get ideas with a small number – and even dwindling number – of board seats down to 7–8.
>
> To be brutally frank, I think the performance gets better when you're pushing directors off the board more quickly due to performance.[79]

> **Solange Charas**: If the board has a board director who's ready to be refreshed[80] and he's the only board director you have on the board that knows something about the industry, or has something that is unique about what they bring to the board that is not going to be easily replaced, then maybe you extend that board director for another term, right?
>
> I was relatively new on this particular board – a good sized company – and came to realize that there really was no clear succession plan.
>
> This gives us the opportunity to say if we didn't do succession planning the right way, it gives us another period of time to actually find somebody that could replicate that skill set vacuum that the departing board member is creating.[81]

Regarding Charas's situation above, the skills matrix described earlier in this chapter should balance the needs of having company- and industry-specific knowledge and experience versus new skills and diversity needed for the board and company. This situation can also be mitigated by temporarily increasing board size.

When directors leave the board, they can continue to serve the organization. Former directors can continue to advise the CEO and the board without fiduciary responsibilities. A former director can also join an advisory committee if one is formed.

Transitioning directors off the board is much easier when you have a pipeline of new directors. I discuss assessing board directors first because having an opening on the board is prerequisite to new board directors.

> **Further reading on board director succession**
> For more information, see Jakob Stengel's chapter "Board Succession, Evaluation, and Recruitment: A Global Perspective" in Richard Leblanc, *The Handbook of Board Governance: A Comprehensive Guide for Public, Private, and Not-for-Profit Board Members, Second Edition*[82] and the chapter, "Company to Director, You're Fired!" *The Board of Directors for a Private Enterprise: A comprehensive inside look at creating*

---

79 Board director interview conducted in November 2020.
80 "Refreshed" means transitioned off the board.
81 Public company board director interview conducted on 8 December 2020.
82 Chapter "Board Succession, Evaluation, and Recruitment: A Global Perspective," Richard Leblanc, *The Handbook of Board Governance: A Comprehensive Guide for Public, Private, and Not-for-Profit Board Members, Second Edition.* Hoboken, NJ: Wiley. 2020.

and managing the boards of private companies of all types by Dennis J. Cagan, *The Board of Directors for a Private Enterprise.*[83]

8.4 Board Director Recruiting

The Nom Gov committee takes the lead in recruiting new board directors.

8.4.1 Role Description

Many boards hire a professional services firm to assist in recruiting and selecting board directors.

One of the first things that a professional services firm will ask for is a role description. The skills matrix described earlier in this chapter and an agreed upon board culture (described in Chapter 7). The Nom Gov committee takes the lead in creating a job description.

Some of the unique characteristics of the board director role description include strategy oversight, representation and interaction with shareholders and stakeholders, fiscal responsibility of an organization, risk management and compliance, and collaborative problem solving. For a sample role description and more information, you can see Richard Leblanc's "Model Individual Director Position Description" in Richard Leblanc's *The Handbook of Board Governance: A Comprehensive Guide for Public, Private, and Not-for-Profit Board Members, Second Edition.*[84]

8.4.2 Board Director Compensation

When recruiting a board director, it is likely that candidates will ask about compensation and D&O insurance.[85] When recruiting board directors a few things are needed; a role description and board director compensation and D&O insurance, which are usually reviewed annually.

---

83 Chapter: "Company to Director, You're Fired! The Board of Directors for a Private Enterprise: A comprehensive inside look at creating and managing the boards of private companies of all types," Dennis J. Cagan, *The Board of Directors for a Private Enterprise*, Bloomington, IN: AuthorHouse, 2017.
84 Chapter, "Model Individual Director Position Description," Richard Leblanc, *The Handbook of Board Governance: A Comprehensive Guide for Public, Private, and Not-for-Profit Board Members, Second Edition*. Hoboken, NJ: Wiley. 2020.
85 "D&O insurance" is director and officer insurance, which covers individual board directors and company officers when a plaintiff bring a case against the company. https://www.investopedia.com/terms/d/directors-and-officers-liability-insurance.asp.

Board director compensation differs for public, private, and nonprofit organizations.

8.4.2.1 Director Pay at Public Companies

Public company directors are compensated primarily in stock. This is to incentivize board directors to act on behalf of shareholders. In general, public company directors hire compensation consultants to set director compensation. In addition, there are associations who publish compensation reports, so directors know the range in which board directors at comparable companies are paid.[86]

Because public company directors are paid mostly in stock, it is possible that board directors may not gain much financially if the organization does not do well.

8.4.2.2 Director Pay at Private Companies

Private company directors are usually owners of the organization. Research conducted over decades suggests that the rate of pay is less than half of what public companies are paid for service on companies of similar size.[87] When the company becomes more profitable and there is an exit, private company directors who hold stock may be paid an additional amount.

8.4.2.3 Director Pay at Nonprofit Organizations

Nonprofit company directors are usually unpaid. The resources that could be paid to directors are used to assist the stakeholders that the nonprofit serves. Nonprofit directors represent the community, including the stakeholders that the organization serve.

The tax documents for nonprofits (such as Form 99) are online and in general the compensation for senior management and board directors are posted. This disclosure of compensation is accessible to donors, philanthropists, and the people served by nonprofits. When there is significant compensation for management and board directors, there is less funding for people who benefit from the nonprofit.

The experienced directors I interviewed had much to say about compensation:

Anna Catalano: Most directors are people who have had successful careers. So, we don't necessarily become board directors for the money. We are directors because we believe our experience can help a board.

I think it's really important for readers to understand we become board directors because we care about the company.

We also have skin in the game because half – or more than half – of our pay is via equity. So, it is in our own best interest to make sure that the company does well.[88]

---

86 "2021–2022 Director Compensation Report" Pearl Meyer and NACD, https://www.nacdonline.org/insights/publications.cfm?ItemNumber=73431.

87 Source: Surveys of private company pay conducted periodically by the National Association of Corporate Directors. https://www.nacdonline.org/.

88 Public company board director interview conducted by 6 June 2021.

Board chairs and committee leaders do more work and have additional responsibilities, so they have higher compensation.

Board directors may be underpaid in many situations.

"Madison": Simply stated, we're under-compensated as corporate directors. Many persons hold the erroneous belief that for four or five meetings a year, I get paid two or three hundred thousand dollars in cash. People just don't know how corporate directors are compensated. They don't know what we do, or what we are responsible for. There is a prevailing opinion—and this includes people who are in mid ranks in large corporations—that we do little but nod our heads when management briefs us.

We are not well served by the reporting of big numbers that appear on the Forbes website without any of the many nuances of director compensation. If I am able carefully to explain how that number is arrived at, the mechanics of how we actually get paid, our long delay in compensation, the chance of us getting very little, and the unglamorous work of directorship, they're shocked and think I'm lying. It's much sexier in the age of social media manufactured outrage to perpetuate the myth of the no-work overcompensated director. The public at large also doesn't understand that the gross compensation of a director is a highly risk-valued number. When they see that it's in the $200,000 range—which is probably the range of a publicly traded company that's reported online—they don't comprehend what it takes to get to the boardroom, or the number of professional hours that we put in. If our compensation was reported on the basis of billable hours, I'd estimate that directors are getting $70 or $80 an hour. That's far less than a consultant who works out of his spare bedroom. Less than a coder in Silicon Valley. It's severely risk valued.

I was once on a corporate board where I worked for four years for options. I paid taxes on the valuation of those options when I received them. The tax was paid with cash that came out of my pocket. Then my options ended up valueless when the company was acquired and the new private equity owners destroyed its substantial value. My experience is not unique. I took a risk, I knew what I was getting into, and I could afford it. Exorbitant compensation is certainly a problem, but directors are for the most part not part of that problem. It's in the executive suite, not often in the boardroom. The number of people that are exorbitantly and unconscionably compensated isn't a systemic problem; it's because a contract was written a certain way and events played out a certain way.[89]

"Bailey": One of the reasons we're so poorly compensated as directors is here are so many people who want to be corporate directors.

The best corporate directors are being well compensated. They stovepipe themselves into companies where they can have effective compensation.

"Jai": There is a large pool of people who want your job. It's like public school teachers. There's so many that I don't need to compensate board directors more . . . .

Yes, board directors need to be better compensated, but so do public school teachers.[90]

Compensation consultants, a specialized professional services firm, guide board compensation.

---

89 Board director/CEO interview conducted in January 2021.
90 Public company board director interview conducted in 2023.

"Bailey": We have a compensation problem on board and an enabler of that problem. The trend that you never hear talked about is the movement to compensation consultants to become as indispensable to public company compensation committees, just as the SEC auditor is indispensable to public company audit committees. I've worked with a number of compensation consultants. Some of them are the best in the world . . . .

Many of them will provide objective advice. At the same there are others who will take guidance from the Compensation Committee Chair or CEO and try to provide analytical support for the conclusion that the CEO or Comp Chair wants to get to.[91]

Further reading on board director compensation
See "Directors' performance and remuneration" in Christine Mallin's great book *Corporate Governance*.[92]

Chapter "Compensation Models and Metrics: It's about More than Money" in Dennis J. Cagan's book *The Board of Directors for a Private Enterprise: A comprehensive inside look at creating and managing the boards of private companies of all types*.[93]

Chapter "Board Membership: Director's Appointment, Roles, and Renumeration" in Bob Tricker's book *Corporate Governance: Principles, Policies, and Practices, Fourth Edition*.[94]

8.4.2.4 Directors and Officers (D&O) Liability Insurance

Most directors would consider being covered by D&O insurance (i.e., Directors and Officers Liability Insurance) an essential part of their compensation package. D&O insurance is bought by the organization to protect directors and company officers from legal actions.

Investors closely watch board director activities and will file lawsuits if they believe board directors are not acting on behalf of the shareholders. The cost of D&O insurance has increased significantly because the number of lawsuits are on the rise.

Joyce Cacho: There is a reason there is D&O insurance. The board is part of the legal system. D&O insurance services to protect a director's personal assets from litigation liability and to support a director to thoroughly commit to the fiduciary duties of the board director role.[95]

---

91 Public company board director interview conducted in January 2021.

92 Chapter "Directors' performance and remuneration," Christine Mallin, *Corporate Governance* Oxford, UK: Oxford University Press, 2019.

93 Chapter "Compensation Models and Metrics: It's about More than Money" The Board of Directors for a Private Enterprise: A comprehensive inside look at creating and managing the boards of private companies of all types by Dennis J. Cagan, *The Board of Directors for a Private Enterprise*, Bloomington, IN: AuthorHouse, 2017.

94 Chapter "Board Membership: Director's Appointment, Roles, and Renumeration," Bob Tricker, *Corporate Governance: Principles, Policies, and Practices*, Fourth Edition, Oxford, UK: Oxford University Press, 2019.

95 Board director interview conducted on 16 February 2021.

Minaz Abji: I've been asked to go on a private company board . . . . My first response was, "I'm open to it. But do you have D&O insurance?" They said no we don't. I said, "Sorry, I can be an advisor, but I will not be a board member." The risks are much higher.[96]

"Lennox": Each year I sit through the D&O price increases. I keep thinking "Well, holy cow. We're must now be at a whole new plateau." But it keeps going up. This last cycle has seen a 40 percent and that increase is untenable.[97]

Nonprofit board directors also need D&O insurance too as they have fiduciary responsibility for the organization. See "The Liability of Board Members" in Michael E. Batts, *Board Member Orientation: The Concise and Complete Guide to Nonprofit Board Service.*[98]

8.5 Selecting Board Candidates

Public, private, and nonprofit boards source board-director candidates from different places.

Public companies know that investors will examine the skills, knowledge, and experience of board directors and will hire professional recruitment firms to assist in the recruiting process. Recruiting board directors is a high-touch, high-interaction experience, so executive recruiting firms are hired. The executive recruiting firm will also research the candidate's background.

Experienced directors and the CEO provide the requirements for new board directors. They provide these requirements to executive search firms who will sort through candidates and make recommendations to the Nom Gov committee.

If the Nom Gov committee does not like the slate of candidates that the recruiting firms create, the Nom Gov committee can return the slate of candidates to the professional services firm. For example, for many years, slates included few candidates from diverse gender, racial, and sexual backgrounds. By returning the slate to recruiting firms, the firms needed to form more relationships with diverse candidates.

Public companies also source board candidates from advisory committees. Advisory committee members provide needed expertise to the board, so they are natural candidates for the board.

Private companies source board candidates primarily from investors. As private companies are motivated primarily by investment, many consider investment more important than governance.

---

96 Public company board director interview conducted on 20 January 2021.
97 Public company board director/CEO interview conducted in October 2020.
98 Chapter "The Liability of Board Members," Michael E. Batts, *Board Member Orientation: The Concise and Complete Guide to Nonprofit Board Service.* Orlando, FL: Accountability Press. 2011.

Private company directors need to take an active role in the company – in particular directors look for other investors for the company. Upon the CEO's request, a private company director may take on other responsibilities.

Nonprofit directors are identified by other board director volunteers, and other people identified by nonprofit staff. They may also use executive recruiters to expand the board.

> **Ryan Patel**: I think knowledge is very important, to find and surround yourself with people who are knowledgeable around different topics.
>
> For example, if we have cybersecurity hacks in hospitals, I don't know what all that stuff means. I know how it happens, but I can go to a couple of people who are rated top 10 on any list of cybersecurity threats. I can go and ask, "What does this mean?"
>
> I think having those people built in your network for a long period of time or you can have a real open conversation . . . I trust you. I built the relationship of who fits this bill.[99]

> **Patel** continues: But if you don't have diverse candidates in a Rolodex. So, what does that mean? That means you've got to go look for candidates that embody what you're looking for . . . .
>
> My whole point is, go find these people. They're not in the traditional process . . . . If you want diversity you have to search all kinds of backgrounds and understand the interconnectedness between Industries. Because it's important that the skills do transfer to the company.[100]

CEOs may also invite board director candidates. They may contact candidates directly or submit names to the executive search firms.

> **Liane Pelletier**: One of my board director opportunities was through the CEO versus a recruiter. When you don't have a recruiter as an intermediary, it can be easier and quicker to assess if there is a mutual fit. The more experienced director will be able to ask about the artifacts of boardroom culture for example and that is not something the recruiter can necessarily know.[101]

There are many great candidates for a board director role. If you ever hear "we just can't find someone" to join the board, this is simply not true. "We can't find someone" says more about the limitations of the person saying this and probably the small circle of people that the person lives in.

Further reading on selecting board candidates
For sourcing and recruiting directors, see the chapters:
   "Recruit Directors Who Build Value" in Ram Charan, Dennis Carey, and Michael Useem's book in *Boards That Lead: When to Take Charge, When to Partner, and When to Stay Out of the Way.*[102]

---

99 Board director interview conducted on 30 October 2020.
100 Board director interview conducted on 6 February 2023.
101 CEO/Public company board director interview conducted on 6 October 2020.
102 Chapter "Recruit Directors Who Build Value," Ram Charan, Dennis Carey, and Michael Useem, *Boards That Lead: When to Take Charge, When to Partner, and When to Stay Out of the Way*, Cambridge, MA: Harvard Business Review Press, 2013.

Dennis Cagan's chapter "Finding Directors" in his book *The Board of Directors for a Private Enterprise: A comprehensive inside look at creating and managing the boards of private companies of all types.*[103]

Chapter "Recruiting Board Members" in Brad Feld and Mahindra Ramsinghani's book *Startup Boards: Getting the Most Out of Your Board of Directors.*[104]

Mark A. Pfister, *Across the Board: The Modern Architecture Behind an Effective Board of Directors.*[105]

8.5.1 Interviewing Candidates

The process for interviewing and selecting candidates is the same for public, private, and nonprofit organizations. Nom Gov committee members interview candidates, as well as lead directors, independent board, and executive chairs. The CEO, corporate secretary, and others may also interview these candidates.

These interviews are rigorous. Board directors and CEOs are very experienced and will ask a wide range of questions. If board candidates fit the skills matrix and the board culture, then many board directors and senior management will continue the interview.

Barbara Adachi: I serve on several Governance and Nominating committees and one of the best practices we have implemented is developing selection criteria. When interviewing potential new board members, the criteria is used to evaluate key attributes, experience and "fit" with the board. The criteria include culture fit, communication style, leadership, industry knowledge, strategic thinking, etc. Each criterion is weighted based on importance to the Committee. In one scenario, culture fit represents nearly 50% of the weighting.

In terms of "fit" we examine if we can picture the individual in the boardroom with the current members. Will he/she engage in heathy debate? What unique perspective and value will they bring? In one organization, we use similar criteria for the annual board evaluation – are you demonstrating value, leadership and helping the organization succeed? Overall, having specific criteria has encouraged more objectivity and alignment with the organization's culture and values.[106]

---

103 Chapter "Finding Directors" in The Board of Directors for a Private Enterprise: A comprehensive inside look at creating and managing the boards of private companies of all types, Dennis J. Cagan, *The Board of Directors for a Private Enterprise*, Bloomington, IN: AuthorHouse, 2017.

104 Chapter "Recruiting Board Members" in Brad Feld and Mahendra Ramsinghani's *Startup Boards: Getting the Most Out of Your Board of Directors*, Hoboken, NJ: Wiley. 2014.

105 Chapter "Available Options and Services to Build Your Board", Mark A. Pfister, *Across The Board: The Modern Architecture Behind an Effective Board of Directors*, Port Jefferson, NY: Pfister Strategy Group, 2018.

106 Public company board director interview conducted on 5 May 2021.

8.6 Board Director Orientation and Onboarding

There is a significant amount of effort in identifying gaps in skills, diversity and recruiting and selecting a board director. Identifying a new board director is an accomplishment.

The organization benefits from a new board director; it makes sense to enable the new board director to become productive quickly.

> **"Morgan"**: Prior to my first meeting I read all the documents that they had. What they do. What are all the committees they have. How they onboard a board member and their philosophy. It sounded very good. And it read very good.
>
> My first board meeting they were acquiring this large portfolio of assets. Of course, the company had been working on the acquisition and bought this portfolio. I didn't disagree with it. I didn't know anything about it, but I was there.
>
> It was interesting what transpired. And there were some red flags. But at that moment, I didn't know that.[107]

The Nom Gov committee is responsible for orientation and onboarding. Many committees do not follow through to make board directors productive.

> **Julian Ha**: I was the rookie board director and trying to always figure out what was happening or learning the history. I found you have to ask a lot of questions and figure out who to go to for these questions . . . .
>
> The onboarding process was not as well-developed given that it was a private company and did not often add new board members. So I found that I had to push a little bit more to say, "hey could I look at the minutes from a year ago." "Or can I have the previous org chart" because I don't have that sense of history.
>
> It's hard to be parachuted in and then try to come up with a good opinion or good point of view when you don't have that historical knowledge.
>
> There was a little bit of catch-up of what I had to do in the first year. And then, working with the other independent board members just trying to understand who's in the driving seat. What is their goal here?[108]

The Nom Gov committee should take the lead in orienting and onboarding new board directors.

> **"Morgan"**: I asked, "when am I doing my on boarding?" The response "When would you like to." So I gave them a date. I went there. And when I went to my onboarding, it was very clear they were not prepared for the onboarding. The onboarding that they talked about during recruiting was on paper. In reality there was not a process.
>
> So that was my first red flag: "Gosh it's interesting." But I said, maybe it's a small cap. Small caps don't have the diligence that large companies have. I said: "I should just be patient" . . . .

---

107 Public company board director interview conducted in January 2021.
108 Board director interview conducted on 20 January 2021.

Every start-up should have a few things. And the onboarding process is a "must have" and should be a good process.

The red flag was the nom and governance committee should run at it. The nom and governance committee should ask how was it? What did you learn? Any questions?[109]

Assigning a board buddy is the most common way for a new director to be productive on a board. The experienced "board buddy's" responsibility is to share information about board traditions, organizational culture and values, and other information to help the new director be more productive. New board directors can ask questions privately from experienced board directors.

What board members should know at the beginning:

Miller Adams: In general, I have really found that it's important for board members to get a good sense of the organization's vision and mission.

I've been in some situations where it's been pretty slipshod to tell you the truth. And you had to kind of dig around to figure out what's going on with the company. And I've been in other situations where it's very straightforward, including sitting down with the corporate secretary and going through board minutes for the last year. Some of that information was sent in advance. Some of it was presented and talked through together.

I think it's important to have a formal onboarding process for new board members particularly in companies that are complex. I mean some board orientation packages are hundreds of pages long when they arrive. Even if it's electronic, you still have to read it.

As for board meeting materials, we no longer get the big books delivered our homes of offices. We still have the material to review before the board meetings. It is important to know the format is going to be used for board communications. Board members need to be prepared.[110]

Boards are composed of people who are very successful in their companies. A board director can be intimidating. But it is important that every board director contributes to discussions, especially in discussions of strategy, risks, and opportunities. (See Chapter 9 "Entire Board Responsibilities.")

In addition to orientation and onboarding, the board director needs to change their behavior in board meetings to have an impact.

R. Omar Riojas: I say to myself there's nothing special about that person. Sometimes personalities can drive certain things. But what's unique about being on a board is understanding that you are there representing other stakeholders.

For example, in my situation . . . the decision that we're going to be making will be impacting folks. The decision is not about me . . . . My point is that . . . there is a lot of human dynamics in the board room. But you need to understand how the process plays out.[111]

---

109 Public company board director interview conducted in January 2021.
110 Public company board director/general counsel interview conducted on 21 October 2020.
111 Board director interview conducted on 11 January 2023.

Further reading on board director orientation

There are some chapters about board director orientation.

See "Welcome Aboard to Your 'Youngster' on the Board," *The Board of Directors for a Private Enterprise: A comprehensive inside look at creating and managing the boards of private companies of all types* in Dennis J. Cagan's book, *The Board of Directors for a Private Enterprise.*[112]

Chapter "Completing the Orientation Process by Providing Organization-Specific Information to Board Members" in Michael E. Batts's book, *Board Member Orientation: The Concise and Complete Guide to Nonprofit Board Service.*[113]

Chapter "Director Onboarding, Education, and Pay" in Elizabeth Hammack's book, *The Private Company Board of Directors Book: What You Need to Know to Be A Director of A Private Company and What Private Company Owners Need to Know to Form and Operate a Company Board.*[114]

---

112 Chapter "Welcome Aboard to Your 'Youngster' on the Board" in Dennis J. Cagan, *The Board of Directors for a Private Enterprise*, Bloomington, IN: AuthorHouse, 2017.

113 Chapter, "Completing the Orientation Process by Providing Organization-Specific Information to Board Members," Michael E. Batts, *Board Member Orientation: The Concise and Complete Guide to Nonprofit Board Service.* Orlando, FL: Accountability Press. 2011.

114 Chapter "Director Onboarding, Education, and Pay," Elizabeth Hammack's *The Private Company Board of Directors Book: What You Need To Know to Be A Director of A Private Company and What Private Company Owners Need to Know to Form and Operate a Company Board*, Granite Bay, CA: BrainTrustBoard, 2019.

9 Entire Board Responsibilities

9.1 Purpose, Values, and Culture

9.1.1 Shareholder Primacy and Stakeholder Capitalism

In the early 2010s and decades before, shareholder primacy was the prevailing belief. Shareholder primacy[1] is the belief that providing returns to shareholders — whether through dividends or share price appreciation — is the main goal of a company. Even today, when discussing corporate performance, the presumption is that it must be correlated to shareholder returns. The SEC's new rule on pay versus performance defines performance as total shareholder returns (TSR). Since there can be no returns without profits, there are many board directors who continue to believe that ensuring profit maximization is their main goal.

But since the last 2010s, there has been shift in this idea about the purpose of the organization, from the focus on shareholders to a broader emphasis on stakeholders.

> **Solange Charas**: There is a new definition of the purpose of the corporation. This gets really tricky, because when shareholder primacy was the focus of the board, it was really easy to make decisions.
>
> So now board directors actually need to balance the interests of multiple stakeholders . . . . The Business Roundtable,[2] Davos,[3] and World Economic Forum[4] identified the new purpose of the corporation as many ESG (environmental, social, governance) indicators.
>
> We need to find a new way of measuring governance quality, not just as a financial indicator. And I hope that we come up with something that's more objective than subjective. Because right now, it's all subjective.[5]

Another experienced corporate director adds his thoughts on the shift from shareholder primary.

> **Hon. Carlos C. Campbell**: Rightfully, directors have been criticized for not being assertive in the ESG space. The Business Roundtable in August 2019 came out and basically countered what Milton Friedman said back in the 70s that the purpose of the corporation is to create wealth with shareholders, basically profit. I love that as a capitalist.

---

1 A Legal Theory of Shareholder Primacy, Robert J. Rhee, 11 April 11, 2017 https://corpgov.law.harvard.edu/2017/04/11/a-legal-theory-of-shareholder-primacy/.

2 The Business Roundtable is an association of US businesses https://www.businessroundtable.org/.

3 Davos is a shorthand to describe the meeting of global businesses https://www.weforum.org/agenda/.

4 The World Economic Forum is an international association of Nonprofit and government organizations https://www.weforum.org/.

5 Public company board director interview conducted on 8 December 2020.

https://doi.org/10.1515/9783110689129-009

But in point of fact, the Business Roundtable made statements saying that businesses are more than that. We have to look at all of the stakeholders, the community at large, the suppliers, the employees, etc., the way business used to be early in the 20th century.[6]

To summarize, from the 1970s to early 2010s, there was a belief in shareholder primacy.

"Tennyson": The purpose of the corporation is to make a profit. That's why the shareholders get their profit. And that's just something you accepted because you're new.[7]

In the late 2010s, there has been a shift to more stakeholders.

Anna Catalano: What's the purpose of the organization? It's not something for personal material gain.[8]

So as the purpose of the business changes, what does this mean for the organization?

Sheila Hooda: What is the purpose of the company? What is the mission, the vision, and the strategy? How are you dealing with the human capital and the innovation and the disruption. What are your key risks?[9]

"Sage": A board member can very seriously talk about mission, values, strategic plan, and focus.[10]

Solange Charas: Boards should review the business model for relevancy. We've seen a shift in business model focus from production to technology to customer.

I think the next evolution is employee-centric business models. We can't have a business unless we're paying attention to our employees . . . . Who, by the way, are our customers and community as well. So you basically hit three of the stakeholders when you're treating your employees well, you're treating your customers well and you're treating your community well.

So I think there's going to be an evolution in the focus of the business model. And then, we need to think about supply chain . . . . So I think board composition needs to change, so the focus of boards needs to change. When you bring on the right people, it's easier to do better governance.[11]

As the book's author, I recommend that boards determine the purpose of their organization. Is it profit maximization or is the business purpose something in the ESG area? CEOs and their organizations must decide the purpose of the business. Boards can oversee this action and offer perspectives from their knowledge and experience.

---

6 Public company board director interview conducted on 29 October 2020.
7 Board director interview conducted in October 2020.
8 Public company board director interview conducted on 20 October 2020.
9 Public company board director interview conducted on 28 November 2020.
10 Board director interview conducted on 11 September 2020.
11 Public company board director interview conducted on 12 January 2023.

9.1.2 Values

A friend and colleague who was a board director at one of the ten largest global companies in the world recommended my co-founder and I focus on values when we started our business. Values are fundamental to all aspects of the company and organization.

When there is a conflict between organizational values and purpose, there is a problem. When there is a conflict between values and human capital practices, employees notice.

Earlier in this book, experienced corporate directors discussed the values of (1) integrity and (2) transparency; see Chapter 5 "Audit Committee." In Chapter 8, "Nominating and Governance Committee," I described the board value of respect for different perspectives and experiences; this board value can be expanded to an organization's value.

Organizations can choose to select other organizational values, such as innovation and reinvention. Other organizational values include diversity and inclusion, customer focus, sustainability, collaboration and teamwork, and continuous improvement. Board directors can oversee this action and offer perspective and experience.

When the organization does not have values, there can be a loss of productivity. Or if there is a lack of respect for different perspectives and experiences, there can be workers and advisors who are not part of key decisions.

> **"Asa"**: Working with private equity has been a wake-up call in many respects, particularly around diversity. As a sector, private equity is still male dominated with very few women or people of color in leadership roles. When I first joined a PE-sponsored webinar in 2021, there were 25 participants, but no other women on the call. For me, it felt like the 1980s again. During the call, one of speakers compared sharing financial information to a woman in a bikini by saying "you don't need to see everything." I was shocked and dropped off the call. It was a clear reminder of how far we still must go to make meaningful progress in diversity, equity, and inclusion.[12]

There has been a shift in the organizations that workers want to join. Maybe this shift is because of significant income inequities or enormous stress caused by the pandemic. Workers align themselves to people who have similar values.

> **Ryan Patel**: Corporate governance matters. Its leadership matters. You want to align yourself with people who believe in the things that you do and have values. That's how you'll be successful. Don't get caught up into hey, I gotta get on one board and see what happens again. I feel like I've learned in my experience. You know, what? Forget that because that's not going to help my journey in this perspective.[13]

---

12 Public company board director interview conducted in May 2021.
13 Board director interview conducted by 30 October 2020.

9.1.3 Purpose

Purpose and values are organizational tissue and glue. They bind employees and management together to a common goal. Directors use different words for "purpose" including "mission" and "vision."

Lisa Chin: Directors are ultimately responsible for the overall health, profitability, wellbeing, and the mission purpose of the organization.[16]

Hon. Carlos C. Campbell: Leadership requires vision purpose, and the ability to motivate. It also requires the willingness to assess and take risks. The big thing is to inspire, motivate, and have a vision that you can quantify.[17]

Andrea Bonime-Blanc: There is a distinct connection back to the purpose of a corporation, which is to make money right without treading on the stakeholders.[18]

---

14 Chapter "Evaluating Values, Vision, and Mission," Mark A. Pfister, *Across the Board: The Modern Architecture Behind an Effective Board of Directors*, Port Jefferson, NY: Pfister Strategy Group, 2018.

15 Chapter "Controlling Ethics and Prudence: What's Not OK, Even if It Works," John Carver, *Boards That Make a Difference: A New Design for Leadership of Nonprofit and Public Organizations. Third Edition.* San Francisco, CA: Jossey-Bass, 2006.

16 Board director/CEO interview conducted on 30 September 2020.

17 Public company board director interview conducted on 29 October 2020.

18 Board director interview conducted in January 2021.

19 Chapter "Focus on Results: The Power of Purpose," John Carver, *Boards That Make a Difference: A New Design for Leadership in Nonprofit and Public Organizations, Third Edition.* San Francisco, CA: Jossey-Bass. 2006.

9.1.3.1 Nonprofits Are Mission- and Purpose-Driven Organizations

Most nonprofits are organizations in which board directors, management, and employees are aligned to a common service. Everyone is aligned to purpose serving a specific community need.

Board directors, management, employees, donors, and the community have a passion for the organization's purpose and mission.

Board director and CEO Christine Martin describes the purpose-driven alignment from donors' contributions to the organization to the service provided to the community.

> **Christine Martin**: It's a pretty significant difference between a for-profit and nonprofit because there's a duty for serving the charitable purpose of a nonprofit, whether it's the Red Cross or the YMCA or your school's PTA. The charitable donation being made are being done appropriately, recorded appropriately, and the money that is coming in is being used in the way that it is intended. And there's not anything going on that shouldn't be. Again, that's the main difference.
>
> The board cares a lot about the mission.
>
> And I would argue that in the for-profit space, the mission is sort of synonymous with making money. For private and public companies it's very clear that that's how you make decisions for profit maximization.[20]

Because nonprofit board directors know the organization's purpose "a board member can very seriously talk about mission, values, strategic plan, and focus."[21]

The board's role is to enable the mission:

> **Anne Hamilton**: For us, the green line what board directors should do and not the role of management is our involvement in forward looking and thinking "do we have the right policies and procedures for the college to fulfill its mission?" Do we have the right mission and purpose for the college?[22]

When a nonprofit board recruits and selects a new executive director CEO, the passion for an organization's mission and purpose is the first priority.

> **Erin Essenmacher**: Our executive director passed away suddenly. The board had to go through an executive director[23] search and bring in somebody completely new. The mission of the organization didn't change but working with a brand-new executive director, especially under those circumstances, it changes the dynamics.
>
> What helped us was staying rooted in a passion for the organization, the mission. At a company that might mean the product or the customers, but you need to have a purpose that keeps you focused and engaged in wanting you to help move that entity forward from a board standpoint.[24]

---

20 Board director/CEO interview conducted on 28 November 2020.
21 Board director interview conducted on 11 September 2020.
22 Trustee interview conducted on 6 June 2021.
23 An executive director is a CEO of a nonprofit.
24 Board director interview conducted on 20 October 2020.

9.1.3.2 Many Private Companies Are Aligned by Purpose

Many start-ups and SMEs[25] are aligned to a purpose. Board directors, senior management, and employees are aligned to the company's product and service.

> **Andrew Chrostowski**: There was a vision of the founders of Realwear to talk about the importance of the frontline worker and the frontline professional . . . . How to make the frontline, worker, inherently safer and more productive.
>
> We think of ourselves as a knowledge transfer company to frontline people. We would add value to enterprises from field service to maintenance to manufacturing, etc. . . . First- and frontline workers have been left out primarily for the technical connection changes that office workers take for granted.[26]

People and board directors in family-owned businesses may also be aligned by purpose, products, and services.

> **"Channing"**: My loyalty as a board director was to the family members that brought me in. They were shaping what they believed the company values were . . . .
>
> Whatever you're selling, whatever the product or services, the director's involvement has to reflect the values or the objectives of what the company is trying to serve.[27]

9.1.3.3 B Corporations Are Aligned in Their Social and Environmental Impact

> **Erin Essenmacher**: Eileen Fisher is a B Corp.[28] Social and environmental impact are built into the DNA of the company.
>
> We don't have an audit committee, we have a quadruple bottom line committee, because they're looking at the whole ecosystem of value creation. We've made commitments to things like supply chain, transparency, sustainability, the culture and the company, and how we treat employees.
>
> We don't have a compensation committee. We have a people and culture committee, of which compensation is certainly a piece, but it's really much broader and intersects with the idea of a quadruple bottom line and people as one of those key aspects.[29]

---

25 SMEs are small-to-medium sized enterprises and businesses.
26 Public company board director/CEO interview conducted on 20 January 2021.
27 Board director/CEO interview conducted in September 2020.
28 B Corporations are for-profit companies that have social and environmental impact https://www.bcorporation.net/en-us.
29 Board director interview conducted by 20 October 2020.

9.1.4 Culture Is More Important Than Strategy

Peter Drucker said that "culture eats strategy for breakfast."[30] This suggests that organizational culture is responsible for company success more than strategy. This is why there is a focus on culture in this book.

Organizational culture is formed by company purpose and values, the behaviors of the CEO and management, and human resource practices. The CEO and their management team are responsible for organization culture, and board directors can offer perspectives and expertise.

Experienced corporate directors have expertise in culture:

> **Hon. Carlos C. Campbell:** I've been in three cultures. I was in the military, I was in the government, and I was in the corporate Community; three very different cultures.[31]

Culture is critical for founder-led firms.

> **Chris Lee**: One public company I served had a board led by a founder who had a very dominant personality, which shaped the firm's culture.[32]

It is important for directors to understand their company's culture.

> **Anna Catalano**: I think it's really important for directors to get a feel for the culture of the company. That means spending time with people other than the people making presentations in board meetings.
>
> So, in all of the boards that I sit on, we make it a habit – a routine – the night before the board meeting, we have a dinner with a wider group of employees. We also visit plants and refineries and chemical plants. We go to visit call centers in our consumer services company. You sit with the organization. You talk to the real people. You get a feel what it's like to work there. You get a sense of culture. I think that that's really important.[33]

CEOs and senior management are responsible for organizational culture. Senior management must take action to change the culture.

Because changing culture is difficult, there is a tendency for management to not take on the challenge to make those changes.

> **Ryan Patel**: Being on the ET[34] team on occasion it's easy for the leadership team to say: "We'll bring 'culture' up at the next meeting."

---

30 "What does culture eats strategy for breakfast mean?" Stephen Conmey, 4 May 2022, Corporate Governance Institute: https://www.thecorporategovernanceinstitute.com/insights/lexicon/what-does-culture-eats-strategy-for-breakfast-mean/.
31 Public company board director interview conducted on 29 October 2020.
32 Public company board director interview conducted on 7 December 2020.
33 Public company board director interview conducted on 6 June 2021.
34 ET is an abbreviation for executive team.

The board governance culture can oversee the executive team, so it does to say "we'll put that off to address culture next time." It should be addressed now.[35]

Rich Horan: It's a very strategic move by the board to reinforce morale and culture. The board should know what's going on. Is there alignment? Maybe there is something to address . . .

We had the CEO of a Fortune 50 company as a guest lecturer. During a Q&A session, I asked "As keeper of your culture, how do you keep a finger on it and assess your culture?" At first, he gives a short answer "It's hard" and is about to go to the next question . . . I raise my hand again. "I know it's hard to assess the culture. But what is it specifically that you're doing?" After a long pause he goes into detail about how the C-suite thought the company culture was great. After the company did an internal climate assessment, they found the culture was not as good as they thought and needed to be addressed. At that point culture issues were reported at the C-suite level on a quarterly basis. With continued focus, the company turned the culture around. It got much better with visibility from the CEO.[36]

With many office workers operating from home, board directors were concerned about organizational culture. Board directors knew that culture would be hard to grow with office workers operating from home.

Evelyn Dilsaver: I really worry about how do you do two things: (1) make the culture live in organization when people don't see each other. If you don't see how things get done from the way people interact – that's culture.

(2) The second big piece is mentoring and observing other people's behaviors as leaders. You don't see that behavior anymore. And you don't get invited into the rooms where those decisions get made because you're not part of that mentorship anymore. I think a zoom mentorship is a very different than: "Hey John come to this meeting that I'm having with these executives and just sit in and listen to what we talked about. How we ask each other questions how we behave?" It doesn't happen. It can't happen quite as easily and spontaneously.[37]

Culture is important to CEO selection.

Cari Dominguez: We identified a couple of other potential CEO successors coming from within. There was a preference – and there is always a preference for internal candidates – because of understanding of the culture and understanding of the institutional knowledge. The results of research show that the more successful CEOs come from within a company.[38]

> **Further reading on culture**
> There are many good chapters on governance and culture.
>   See chapter: "A Culture Revolution Enters the Boardroom" in Dambisa Moyo's book *How Board Work: And How They Can Work Better in a Chaotic World.*[39]

---

35 Board director interview conducted by 30 October 2020.
36 Board director interview conducted on 16 February 2021.
37 Public company board director interview conducted by 6 November 2020.
38 Public company board director interview conducted on 4 September 2020.
39 Chapter "A Culture Revolution Enters the Boardroom," Dambisa Moyo, *How Board Work: And How They Can Work Better in a Chaotic World.* New York, NY: Basic Books. 2021.

Chapter "Culture, the Critical Driver" by Richard M. Steinberg in *Governance, Risk Management, and Compliance*.[40]

Chapter "The Character of the Company" in Adrian Cadbury's book, *Corporate Governance and Chairmanship: A Personal View*.[41]

Chapter "Organizational Culture" in Frederick D. Lipman's *Enhanced Corporate Governance: Avoiding Unpleasant Surprises*.[42]

Chapter "Corporate Governance and Culture" in J. Robert Brown, Jr. and Lisa L. Casey's book *Corporate Governance: Cases and Materials, Second Edition*.[43]

Chapter "Establish the Appropriate Tone at the Top" by Deborah Hick Midanek in *The Governance Revolution: What Every Board Member Needs to Know, NOW!*[44]

9.2 Risk, Opportunity, Strategy, and Metrics

The entire board is responsible for reviewing and approving company strategy and risk. Some boards ask the audit committee to monitor risk. Like other audit committee documents reviewed in detail, after the audit committee approves these documents, they are reviewed and approved by the entire board.

> **Erin Essenmacher**: The board's job is oversight of strategy and risk. This is to help ensure the long-term health of the enterprise, right? If the world has changed around us then to create value the enterprise must change too, right? This means challenging old assumptions of how we view create value.[45]

9.2.1 Risks

The CEO and senior management are responsible for managing organizational risk. The CEO and senior management should be looking around corners to look at consumers and competitors for insights and opportunities. Because the board represents owners and stakeholders, the board should provide oversight of the CEO and senior management.

---

40 Chapter "Culture, the Critical Driver," Richard M. Steinberg, *Governance, Risk Management, and Compliance*. Hoboken, NJ: John Wiley & Sons, 2011.
41 Chapter "The Character of the Company," Adrian Cadbury, *Corporate Governance and Chairmanship: A Personal View*. Oxford, UK: Oxford University Press, 2002.
42 Chapter "Organizational Culture" in Frederick D. Lipman's *Enhanced Corporate Governance: Avoiding Unpleasant Surprises*. Boulder, CO: Daniel Publishing. 2019.
43 Chapter "Corporate Governance and Culture," J. Robert Brown, Jr., Lisa L. Casey, *Corporate Governance: Cases and Materials, Second Edition*, Durham, NC: Carolina Academic Press, 2016.
44 Chapter "Establish the Appropriate Tone at the Top," Deborah Hick Midanek, *The Governance Revolution: What Every Board Member Needs to Know, NOW!* Berlin, GE: De Gruyter Press, 2018.
45 Board director interview conducted on 20 October 2020.

An experienced corporate director learns to determine between low- and high-risk items regardless of management guidance.

A board director needs to identify problems:

Michael Pocalyko: I call this the Osama bin Laden 9/11 problem . . .

In reading the 9/11 Report it is very clear that, when looking backwards, the United States Intelligence Community had within its massive stores of data and signals intelligence the basic building blocks of information about the attacks. If it had been possible to assemble that information coherently into intelligence, to analyze it with a high degree of confidence, and then to make the right judgments, we could have had an effective risk management of the threat and discovered something about the plot for 9/11. But how are you going to know? The raw data was enormous and amorphous. Going backwards, however, knowing what did happen, it's very easy to find.

A similar situation is when you consider the cumulative causes of the Great Depression. Every economist I know can tell me exactly how every recession since 1863 occurred. We've had 32 major recessionary events since the Civil War, counting what happened with Covid-19. Every economist who studies this stuff can tell you what the factors were that brought about each recession. Yet no economist I know can tell you when the next recession is going to occur.

Only retrospection and knowledge of what already happened will get you there—knowing the problem, challenge, and risk with clarity. That's the Osama bin Laden 9/11 problem. And that's what we get in corporate boards. You have massive volumes of information, often with insufficient clarity.

You can't blame the executives. They can say "I gave you the information and you didn't give me any guidance." Well, the problem is, you gave us so much information that we were not able to reconcile and analyze it.

It's the opposite of the problem where the executive only gives you one analytical pathway in an attempt to drive the board to one pre-determined conclusion. How to present the board with information—that's an art. That's not science. And unfortunately, you only get good at that art after seeing a lot of mistakes made in the boardroom.[46]

When a board director identifies a risk, it should be brought to other board directors. It is possible that other board directors will not share the same perspective.

"Lennox" The Chair/CEO[47] arranged a call among the board directors. The chair said "this is a low, low risk item." Actually, it was a very high-risk area which turned out poorly. I tried to put light on the risks during and after the call, but the other board directors were following the Chair/CEO's assessment. They had been carrying water for the CEO for quite some time.[48]

9.2.1.1 Enterprise Risk Management (ERM)

In addition to identifying risks, board directors can work to ensure there is a systematic enterprise risk management (ERM) program. Risk management is the process of identifying, assessing

---

46 Board director/CEO interview conducted by 13 January 2021.
47 A combined Chair/CEO is an Executive Chair.
48 CEO/Public company board director interview conducted in October 2020.

and controlling financial, legal, strategic and security risks to an organization's capital and earnings.[49]

The CEO and senior management can implement an ERM (Enterprise Risk Management) program to identify and mitigate risks. These ERM programs usually work with a board committee, such as the audit committee or an ad hoc committee to inform the board of risks and mitigations.

ERM programs include components including reputational risks, financial risks, human capital risks, etc. As senior management handle risks identified by the ERM process, a profile of the company's risk tolerance[50] (described below) will develop. Likewise, when risks and mitigations are presented to the board, the board will develop its risk tolerance.

Larry Taylor: I chair the University Audit and Risk Committee. We have a risk matrix that I developed. Right now, 30 items are on there. And you know what a risk matrix looks like.

Is there a social media impact? Is there social injustice? How are we responding? What's the likelihood of those things happening?

It's on the board agenda because it's part of the Audit and Risk report that I give at every board meeting. What we look for is color coded. We look at a particular risk item and see if it's right.

The University CFO is in charge of collecting all this information from all the different departments about risk and how they think it's changing. The board gets the ERM report which reflects: (1) students and the student views on these issues; (2) equity perspectives on these issues; and (3) then the administration's opinions on these issues. Then the board expresses our opinion on the report . . . .

So I met with other schools. They "asked what are you doing?" All the schools now adopted the one that we have.[51]

9.2.1.2 Risk Appetite of the Company

After reviewing risks, over time the board will identify its risk appetite.

Bala Iyer: It's always possible to come up with 15 reasons why you don't do something. A management team can become risk averse. The board is the only group that says "hey we shouldn't be doing this?" and challenge management's thinking.

So, you have to question the risk posture of the company. When you hire a CEO, when you manage the performance of the CEO and when you fire the CEO, you talk about the risk posture of a company.[52]

---

49 "Why is risk management important?" IBM, https://www.ibm.com/topics/risk-management.

50 Risk tolerance is the degree of risk that an organization is willing to endure given the volatility in the value of the situation. See the article, "What Is Risk Tolerance, and Why Does It Matter?" Alexandra Twin, 7 July 2022, https://www.investopedia.com/terms/r/risktolerance.

51 Board director interview conducted on 27 October 2020.

52 Public company board director interview conducted on 8 January 2021.

Further reading on risk management and risk appetite

See chapter "Implementing ERM" and "Risk Management and the Financial System's Near Meltdown" in Richard M. Steinberg's book, *Governance, Risk Management, and Compliance*.[53]

See chapter "Managing Risk Effectively" in Deborah Hick Midanek's book, *The Governance Revolution: What Every Board Member Needs to Know, NOW!*[54]

See chapter "The Board's Expanding Role in Managing Risk" by Brian Stafford and Dottie Schindlinger in *Governance in the Digital Age: A Guide for the Modern Corporate Board Director*.[55]

See Norm Keith's chapter, "Board Risk and Responsibility Under Regulate and Criminal Law" in Richard Leblanc's book, *The Handbook of Board Governance: A Comprehensive Guide for Public, Private, and Not-for-Profit Board Members, Second Edition*.[56]

See chapter "The Board's Role in Risk Management" in Michael E. Batts's book, *Board Member Orientation: The Concise and Complete Guide to Nonprofit Board Service*.[57]

See Michael Useem's chapter, "Governing Boards, Risk Management, and Deliberative Thinking,"[58] F. Edward "Te" Price's chapter, "100 Questions Directors Should Ask When Assessing the Effectiveness of Risk Systems"[59] Stephen J. Mallory's chapter, *"Risk Oversight for Directors: A Practical Guide*"[60] and Ingrid Robinson's chapter, "Risk Governance"[61] in Richard Leblanc's book, *The Handbook of Board Governance: A Comprehensive Guide for Public, Private, and Not-for-Profit Board Members, Second Edition*.

See chapter "What is Risk Management About?" *in Richard* M. Steinberg's book, *Governance, Risk Management, and Compliance*.[62]

See chapter "The Governance of Corporate Risk" in Bob Tricker's book, *Corporate Governance: Principles, Policies, and Practices, Fourth Edition*.[63]

---

53 Chapter "Implementing ERM," Richard M. Steinberg, *Governance, Risk Management, and Compliance*. Hoboken, NJ: John Wiley & Son, 2011.

54 Chapter "Managing Risk Effectively," Deborah Hick Midanek, *The Governance Revolution: What Every Board Member Needs to Know, NOW!* Berlin, GE: De Gruyter Press, 2018.

55 Chapter "The Board's Expanding Role in Managing Risk," Brian Stafford and Dottie Schindlinger, *Governance in the Digital Age: A Guide for the Modern Corporate Board Director*. Hoboken, NJ: Wiley. 2019.

56 Chapter *"Board Risk and Responsibility Under Regulate and Criminal Law,"* Richard Leblanc, *The Handbook of Board Governance: A Comprehensive Guide for Public, Private, and Not-for-Profit Board Members, Second Edition*. Hoboken, NJ: Wiley. 2020.

57 Chapter "The Board's Role in Risk Management," Michael E. Batts, *Board Member Orientation: The Concise and Complete Guide to Nonprofit Board Service*. Orlando, FL: Accountability Press. 2011.

58 Chapter "Governing Boards, Risk Management, and Deliberative Thinking," Richard Leblanc, *The Handbook of Board Governance: A Comprehensive Guide for Public, Private, and Not-for-Profit Board Members, Second Edition*. Hoboken, NJ: Wiley. 2020.

59 Chapter "100 Questions Directors Should Ask When Assessing the Effectiveness of Risk Systems," Richard Leblanc, *The Handbook of Board Governance: A Comprehensive Guide for Public, Private, and Not-for-Profit Board Members, Second Edition*. Hoboken, NJ: Wiley. 2020.

60 Chapter "Risk Oversight for Directors: A Practical Guide," Richard Leblanc, *The Handbook of Board Governance: A Comprehensive Guide for Public, Private, and Not-for-Profit Board Members, Second Edition*. Hoboken, NJ: Wiley. 2020.

61 Chapter "Risk Governance" in Richard Leblanc, *The Handbook of Board Governance: A Comprehensive Guide for Public, Private, and Not-for-Profit Board Members, Second Edition*. Hoboken, NJ: Wiley. 2020.

62 Chapter "What is Risk Management About?" in Richard M. Steinberg, *Governance, Risk Management, and Compliance*. Hoboken, NJ: John Wiley & Son, 2011.

63 Chapter "The Governance of Corporate Risk," Bob Tricker, *Corporate Governance: Principles, Policies, and Practices, Fourth Edition*, Oxford, UK: Oxford University Press, 2019.

9.2.2 Risks and Opportunities

Experienced corporate directors look not only at risks, but also at opportunities.

> **"Harper"**: A friend of mine who is a risk expert – he has a business that's focused simply on enterprise risk – always reminds me that it's not only about risks with negative consequences . . . but also opportunities.
>
> When you're doing the environmental scan, it's important and easy to look at both what our risks are as well as opportunities which include opportunities for improvement and opportunities for new businesses.[64]

Board directors talk about the limits of a matrix that looks at risks only.

> **Maureen Conners**: I was talking to the CFO and said that the Enterprise Risk Management Report is not robust enough to capture new opportunities, new business models that are growing. AI, new contactless technologies, new payment systems which are on the horizon Buy Now, Pay Later (BNPL), biometrics, etc. and the probability about what is going to happen within the next two years . . . .
>
> Someone who's on top of those, who's tracking it should be incorporated in the quarterly ERM so you know then you could drill down further quantifying different scenarios about new technologies, the business model changes and the potential financial impacts.[65]

Rather than look at weakness only, you look at opportunities too.

> **Bala Iyer**: Look at information that is publicly available and very interesting and how that does impact thinking and possible strategy for the company. I guess that fits into an overall risk and opportunities framework for the company.
>
> When you look at a framework of both opportunities as well as weaknesses that you know you could kind of take all these different pieces and put it into that framework . . .
>
> Everyone talks about risk management and the board's role in risk management. It is also the case that sometimes CEOs and management teams are too risk averse. And it is important for boards to challenge management's thinking.
>
> I have experienced this personally in an industry with significant consolidation activity, where the management team was overly conservative and lost out on a number of attractive M&A opportunities, which could have improved their competitive position.
>
> The team had to be challenged on their thinking by the board before they stepped up and prevailed in their acquisition strategy.[66]

---

64 Board director interview conducted in October 2020.
65 Public company board director interview conducted on 8 January 2021.
66 Public company board director interview conducted on 8 January 2021.

9.2.3 Risk (and Opportunities) Matrix and SWOT Analysis

Along with strategy, the CEO and management are responsible for identifying risks and opportunities, external and internal, to the organization. Board directors may also be asked to review SWOT (strengths, weaknesses, opportunities, and threats) analysis.

> **Phil Haas**: If this was part of the SWOT, an opportunity may arise. Is there a company willing and able to acquire our company with the right mission, vision, values, and price? Is a win-win deal on the horizon?[67]

The board calendar should include an entire board discussion of a risk and opportunities matrix and SWOT analysis with strategy implications. The same process to identify risks and challenges are used to determine strategic opportunities.

See "Turning Risk into Opportunity" in Ram Charan, Dennis Carey, and Michael Useem's *Boards That Lead: When to Take Charge, When to Partner, and When to Stay Out of the Way.*[68]

9.2.4 Board Directors Should Always Look for (and Learn About) Opportunities

Board directors are good sources of new opportunities for the organization. Possible new opportunities can be fed into a SWOT matrix that is the basis for company strategy.

The best ways for directors to identify new opportunities are to (1) look globally, (2) look at different industries, and (3) learn continually.

> **"Kyle"**: One way for board directors to identify new opportunities for the company to look at global markets and similar companies, different industries or identify opportunities.[69]

> **Maureen Conners**: A board director has to have a much broader scope. You're looking. You're being aware of what's influencing the environment in which you're competing . . . . One example was BNPL (Buy Now Pay Later).
>
> I did not think it was anything exciting . . . yet some of the Gen Z and Millennials customers did and there was much faster adoption than I ever expected. Other alternative payment approaches, using crypto, BNPL, digital wallets are standards of doing business, as is BNPL. Additionally, social media and the use of buy button has disrupted some traditional channels.
>
> For example, I might have blown off Bitcoin because personally I would never buy it; it's too risky. Yet I see a lot of my consumers are Gen Z. They have a different attitude . . . . Bitcoin is

---

67 Board director interview conducted on 6 May 2021.

68 Chapter "Turning Risk into Opportunity," Ram Charan, Dennis Carey, and Michael Useem, *Boards That Lead: When to Take Charge, When to Partner, and When to Stay Out of the Way*, Cambridge, MA: Harvard Business Review Press, 2013.

69 Board director interview conducted in July 2022.

going to be bigger so how you put it on the corporate treasurer's radar screen . . . . You say the whole payments relationship between payments and other industries, and it could become the standard . . . . And if you want to do business in China you gotta be willing to learn. You've seen the influence of Alibaba and using Alipay. It's a whole different life. It is a financial approach for people who use social media.[70]

"Kyle": Good board directors are learning constantly . . . . I always learned something from different presentations. Continuous learning is a great way for board directors to get a sense of new opportunities for the company.[71]

9.2.5 Strategy

The company should have an annual strategy process that includes board review and input.

> **David Rosenblum**: Boards need to be part of the strategy development process and strategy incorporates looking out, three or four or five years into the future.[72]

One of the board's responsibilities is to oversee strategy. Assuming the board has determined the organization's purpose, the company strategy is to increase value.

> **Paul Chan**: The role of the Board has expanded beyond the traditional governance responsibilities to include, in response to the rapid rate of market changes, strategic resources for the company. The Board's oversight role on mere financial performance, although critical, is grossly inadequate without integrating the intangible non-financial values of the company into the company's strategies.
>
> The non-financial values may include the values of its brand, reputation, intellectual capital, human capital . . . extending to elements of Environment, Social and Governance (ESG), Social Development Goals (SDG), Climate Risks/Opportunities, Carbon Neutral, etc.
>
> The market demands a paradigm shift in the Board's thinking to focus on creating value for the company – including non-financial values, which are a significant and integral part of the total value of the company. The Board may embrace the strategies in integrated thinking and integrated value creation to chart the path of the company toward sustainable growth and corporate values.[73]

Board directors should look for new opportunities to make a positive impact on the organizations they serve. They should be aware of the new opportunities that company competitors are pursuing. Board directors can attend industry conferences or meetings in different, but similar, sectors. Keeping up to date is crucial.

---

70 Public company board director interview conducted on 8 January 2021.
71 Board director interview conducted in July 2022.
72 Public company board director interview conducted on 11 November 2020.
73 Board director interview conducted on 1 October 2020.

"Dana": We had a customer that contributed thirty percent of our revenue stream. The margins of the company were much lower than everybody else because they were able to negotiate a big discount because of the size of the revenue. When this company got acquired (and taken private) they came after us for more margin.

In other words. They wanted more of our profit margin and the CEO of the company realized that might have to be a possibility. So as a board, we spent time thinking through what if this customer left and so from a governance point of view, I think the lessons learned for anybody is if you have a customer that has more than 25 percent for those responsible for more than twenty-five percent of your revenue.

You should go through a financial analysis to understand what would happen to you, our revenue and our margins if this comforter company were to leave. And if that were to happen, what would be Plan A or Plan B (or maybe we don't have a plan) to recover that revenue from other sources or find new sources of growth?[74]

Board directors help their companies think through many options.

"Dana" continues: It was a risk to the company. But it was also strategic because they were our largest customer base, where there was a lot of growth. An important part of what we needed to understand is where is the growth coming from? Can it last? They strategically did not want us to move into the direct consumer space. But we made baby steps into it. We shouldn't be held hostage to that.[75]

Another board director helped their company prepare for acquisition.

"Dylan": The board and certain committees looked at many acquisition opportunities as well as the possibility of being acquired ourselves. You know, you either grow in revenue organically or via acquisition. There are two main levers to consider when a company's market shares drop significantly. You either cut down on expenses, mostly involving layoffs, closing offices, deferring on certain investments or buying back shares. Or you can figure out how to diversify and grow revenues differently. Those are the two main levers. We decided, because we did have good reserves to really start investing more in digital transformation and diversification of services.

But most importantly, the opportunity to either grow revenues wherever they existed, whether nationally or globally, and the opportunity to cut down on costs and eliminate unnecessary expenses became our primary strategic focus. All that review was being addressed by the various committees as well as by the full board. That's what you do as a board member when a company hits a snag, starts losing market share, or becomes vulnerable to an acquisition or hostile takeover. Review of strategy, market trends, and other opportunities become top of mind.[76]

Board directors know the business and help the company make strategic decisions.

Further reading on the board's role in strategy
See the chapter "The Board's Role in Strategy Development" in Cornelis A. de Kluyver's book *A Primer on Corporate Governance*.

---

74 Public company board director interview conducted in November 2020.
75 Public company board director interview conducted in November 2020.
76 Public company board director interview conducted on 4 September 2020.

Chapter "The Role of Strategy," Mark A. Pfister, *Across the Board: The Modern Architecture Behind an Effective Board of Directors.*[77]
Chapter "Setting the Company Strategy," Dambisa Moyo, *How Board Work: And How They Can Work Better in a Chaotic World.*[78]

9.2.6 Metrics

When a strategy is being developed, board directors should ask, how will the board and management know that the strategy is working? For example, what are leading indicators that market share is increasing? Is the profit margin increasing?

Solange Charas: Nobody runs companies with their gut feelings anymore.[79]

"Blake": Fortunately or unfortunately, there is always discussions about metrics at every board meeting. How can metrics be improved? What are better metrics?
Metrics and results are ways in which board directors can ask how the company is doing without getting into the weeds of what management is doing.
Having good metrics is essential to understanding what's happening within the company.[80]

Board books include PowerPoint slides on strategy and corresponding metrics. They review metrics and results, then write questions and notes to management and other directors in the board books. Discussions about metrics can occur in executive sessions or board meetings, as described above.

"Jackie": Results metrics which are aligned to strategy are the same metrics that are used for CEO performance and compensation. So believe me, the CEO is very focused on those metrics.
It's important for directors to review the results in the board book before board meetings. And to really ask questions, you know, in the board book itself as well as have discussions within the executive committee meeting that may be held before the meeting starts or during the board meeting.[81]
I think it's important to look at metrics from the outside. Look at it from a Wall Street perspective; look from an activist perspective. Look from a proxy advisor perspective. Unfortunately, the metrics provided by the company are not always too insightful. They tend to be favorable towards management.
But if you look at results with a clear eye, you can see how the company is really performing relative to other companies and industries.[82]

---

77 Chapter "The Role of Strategy," Mark A. Pfister, *Across the Board: The Modern Architecture Behind an Effective Board of Directors*, Port Jefferson, NY: Pfister Strategy Group, 2018.
78 Chapter "Setting the Company Strategy," Dambisa Moyo, *How Board Work: And How They Can Work Better in a Chaotic World.* New York, NY: Basic Books. 2021.
79 Public company board director interview conducted on 8 December 2020.
80 Board director interview conducted in September 2020.
81 Board director interview conducted in July 2022.
82 Board director interview conducted in July 2022.

An experienced corporate director suggests one metric to watch, that of CEO pay and frontline-worker pay:

"Murphy": One metric that board directors should look at is the difference between CEO pay and frontline-worker pay. This metric is something that is usually not presented on a regular basis by management. But I think it's something that board directors should keep in mind because employees certainly are looking that metric and are making their own personal calculations.

I realize that CEO pay is published. But it's becoming more and more apparent as we move forward in the future. It's something that can be found on the Internet with some searching.

So, I think the difference in pay inequality is something that's growing in the past 30+ years. It's something that the board directors should keep in mind.[83]

A technology savvy board director said:

"Carter": When you think about now and in the future there should be real time data coming. The idea of having PowerPoints which are stale within a day (or a week). The results are stale when they printed. In the future we will get real-time or near real-time data to gauge the performance of companies.[84]

Board director Charas suggests convincingly measuring HR metric.

Solange Charas: HR is key to most organizations. I think most boards recognized that during the pandemic, HR became the key issue.

It's interesting to me that boards are still resisting recruiting CHROs (Chief Human Resource Officers) – although this trend is changing slowly. Boards are still focused on recruiting CFOs, CEOs, CTOs. What's surprising to me is that most organizations spend more than 50% of total expense on human capital – yet they don't have someone on their board that represents the function. If a company spent more than 50% of total expense on real estate, you would expect at least one board director to know something about real estate.

It's logical until you get to HR.

Based on the last several CEO surveys, talent acquisition and management are among the top five challenges or issues for companies, yet the board doesn't typically have a director who is an HR subject matter expert.

Many board directors are now claiming they have HR experience. But being a manager of people does not qualify you to be a subject matter expert in the full range of HR programs.

In addition to knowing the function, an HR SME must understand how human capital has a material impact on the enterprise and can understand human capital metrics like HCROI (Human Capital Return on Investment), HCVA (Human Capital Value Add), HEVA (Human Economic Value Add), HCMV (Human Capital Market Value) and other efficiency metrics. These metrics determine if companies are getting a return on investment in human capital and their relative performance to peer companies.

I just did a talk with about 350 board directors. I asked them, how many of you have heard of HCROI? About five people raised their hands. How is that possible? That's the first thing you should be measuring. Is it going up or down?[85]

---

83 Board director interview conducted in July 2022.
84 Board director interview conducted in July 2022.
85 Public company board director interview conducted on 12 January 2023.

9.3 Unexpected Events and Crisis

A resilient organization has a robust risk process. During a six- or nine-year board director tenure, it is reasonable for a board director to expect a crisis.

> **Hon. Carlos C. Campbell**: I've served on the better boards that are very aware, alert, and prepared for crisis. Most boards are not prepared for crisis. And that's the weakness of governance, the lack of awareness and ability to respond.
>
> In the Navy – and that's unique about the military – we go through every drill you could imagine. We go to camps for prisoner of war indoctrination . . . . We have to tread water in the middle of the ocean where you can't see land and get a helicopter pick up. When you're flying the airplane, you go through engine out procedures, losing your electrical system, all that sort of stuff, because as a pilot is an exercise in crisis management.[86]

But many good organizations did not foresee the challenges posed by COVID-19. Fortunately, many insurances (and reinsurance companies) planned for a global pandemic. But even those companies did not foresee employee work from home or employee dissatisfaction.

These interviews were conducted when there was limited information about COVID and no vaccine. The following are two stories from (1) a nonprofit director and (2) a public company director operating during the early months of COVID.

This first story is from a college board director in the same city as the initial US COVID outbreak.

> **Anne Hamilton**: The initial impact came from the front line from the staff in the college . . . . Nobody in the U.S. knew about COVID. Nobody in the country here, except for one case in Everett Washington State until the infection hit the college. We have both the staff and students who worked at that senior care center in Kirkland. So we had to instantly figure out, what do we do
>
> So we had people have to self-quarantine. What if they did not have the resources? Let's get the foundation involved. We got them hotel rooms and groceries, and anything they needed to responsibly self-quarantine. There is nothing that I wouldn't say publicly about what the college did.
>
> So, Amy the college president was on it. She was snapped in instantly. There were initial things about getting those who are affected quarantined. And then there was a period of time where we scrubbed the school down every hour, you know, every four hours or whatever. We hired vendors and people to scrub the school down to keep students and faculty safe while they were on campus.
>
> And then we quickly went into lockdown and being right on top of that. The college president was holed up in the City of Kirkland bunker essentially. The college was connected with the local government to deploy in a very holistic way the right solutions for the college, based on everything that was going on in the community. We were deeply connected with the mayor, the chief of police. So there was a lot of forethought for things we didn't think of.[87]

---

86 Public company board director interview conducted on 29 October 2020.
87 Trustee interview conducted on 6 June 2021.

This second story is from a public company director of a global company.

> **"Avery"**: The most interesting, most challenging, and most instructive challenge is a board to work through some sort of crisis. For example, a crisis of leadership; crisis within management of the company. A crisis when one of the products fails.
>
> I find myself rising to the occasion in those situations getting into a situation where I have to help management and the board navigate a pathway out of those scenarios. And of course, we're facing a crisis now with the pandemic; a crisis that's associated with COVID-19.
>
> All of them seem to have similar themes. I made some notes for myself to reflect on this. Most of the pathways out of these situations seem to be centered around communications.
>
> What is the management team telling the board? What is the board hearing, which is not necessarily what management is telling the board. You pick up on many conversations. When you have side conversations with board members you realize that they don't really understand the message that they were getting from management . . . .
>
> So (1) how can the board help itself and then (2) how can the board help management in the current crisis that they're facing . . . .
>
> Remember, the board is not running the company. The board is there to essentially work on behalf of the stakeholders of the company. Nowadays stakeholders are more than just the shareholders.
>
> So, you have to ask some very pointed questions – and at times some challenging questions – of management. And you need to give them the opportunity to respond. If they aren't responding in a way that is informative, you need to let them know. And work on a communications plan that is consistent and appropriate for the situation.
>
> Everyone has to keep their wits about them. There needs to be an analysis of the crisis. Is this a crisis of the day? Is it a crisis of the week? Of the month? Of the year? Is it a crisis with no end point in sight? This makes things particularly challenging.
>
> It is different if you have a building that catches on fire. The crisis happens and you know how to react appropriately for that situation and get through it. In the age of the pandemic, we don't know when this is going to end which leads to a different sort of approach to managing the crisis.[88]

When developing a skills matrix of experiences needed by the board, perhaps a Nom Gov committee should consider what experience candidates have had with crises.

> **Evelyn Dilsaver**: When considering crisis, we talk about experience. We have board members who have perspective and experience in crisis. It's a good balance with those who don't.
>
> The other lesson in the crisis is you need calm board members. There is enough stress in the organization that you don't need somebody yelling at you at the top.[89]

Because an unexpected situation or crisis is likely to occur during the tenure of a board director, it is an experience that bonds board directors together.

> **Melinda Yee Franklin**: Some of the issues that happen through crisis create strong bonds between the board and staff. That is invaluable.[90]

---

88 Public company board director interview conducted in October 2020.

89 Public company board director interview conducted on 6 November 2020.

90 Board director interview conducted on 7 March 2021.

> **Liane Pelletier**: How does the board work together? Has the board ever had to engage in a crisis? How did that go? The answer to that adds color to the culture of the boardroom.[91]

9.4 Stakeholder Communication

During uncertain times, employees want to hear from company leadership. The interviews in this book were collected during a time when little was known about COVID, and employees were asked to be productive from home.

> **Miller Adams**: My public company management team has just done a masterful job of advising us the board on what is happening. Company leadership was almost over-communicating early at this very large, global company.
>
> How is COVID going to impact the workforce of several hundred thousand employees spread across the world. There were different COVID-related situations unfolding from continent-to-continent, based on how governments and other forces were reacting to the pandemic.
>
> So the communication early on was very dramatic, very heavy communication again. Management was not seeking approval from the board, just telling the board what they were we're doing. Management asked us – the board – if we had any questions.
>
> We had one or two special board meetings, which I thought was appropriate . . . . Businesses started to close their doors and go to a remote work environment, overnight essentially. And then things tapered off to more steady communications, which has continued until today.[93]

Wall Street is a very important audience for public and private companies. For public companies, owners want to optimize shareholder value. Creating and maintaining the story about the company is essential to Wall Street to project value.

> **Miller Adams**: Board service is hard work, particularly public company boards where there are a lot of issues around governance. And a lot of issues around communications and SEC reporting . . . . So it's very important for board members to be prepared.[94]

See Stephen Erlichman's "Director/Shareholder Meetings" and James McRitchie's "Proxy Scorecards Will Empower Investors" in Richard Leblanc, *The Handbook of Board Governance: A Comprehensive Guide for Public, Private, and Not-for-Profit Board Members, Second Edition.*

---

91 CEO/Public company board director interview conducted on 6 October 2020.
92 Cornelis A. de Kluyver, *A Primer on Corporate Governance*. New York, NY: Business Expert Press. 2013.
93 Public company board director/general counsel interview conducted on 21 October 2020.
94 Public company board director/general counsel interview conducted on 21 October 2020.

Bala Iyer: Sometimes the crisis can involve, for instance, activists who have their own timeline who don't have any restrictions on when and what they can communicate. While the company has all the restrictive levels of communication based on regulators. Sometimes the attacks get personal. Activists have no problem putting up the names of the directors, so you know you really earn your pay.[95]

In the COVID and election years in the US, many employees asked their CEOs and senior management to make public statements about social issues. This is a decision that each CEO should make for themselves. But it is likely that CEOs will seek or receive feedback from board chairs and directors.

Michael Pocalyko: If you're a CEO in socially conscious Silicon Valley you had better be available to and aligned with your people . . . . Your sense of social justice and your political views are going to matter.

However, if you're in Washington, D.C. and you're running a company like mine (a government contractor) you had better be out of politics. You need to stay away from partisan political matters entirely, as a matter of personal integrity and neutrality.

We have a rule in this company that you may not make a political donation if you're on the board. And you may not endorse any candidate.[96]

Board directors are very careful about what they communicate. This is why approximately half of my board friends and colleagues asked to be anonymous for this book. This also means social media posts, presentations at conferences, publications, etc.

"Skylar": I know that your book is not coming out for you know a year or so. Hopefully, by then this whole thing the situation described to the author will be over. But I still don't want to put myself in risk. I do not want risk exposure.[97]

Board directors are careful to be accurate. Communication is concise and directors will refer to management frequently.

Phil Haas: And particularly in communications with the [organization], she can tell you pieces to which I was not as close.[98]

Further reading on stakeholder communication

For more information about stakeholder communication. See:

Chapter "Communicate, Clearly, Consistently, and Constantly" in Deborah Hick Midanek's book, *The Governance Revolution: What Every Board Member Needs to Know, NOW!*.[99]

Chapter "Shareholder Communication and Engagement" in Vasant Raval's book Corporate Governance: A Pragmatic Guide for Auditors, Directors, Investors, and Accountants.[100]

---

95 Public company board director interview conducted on 8 January 2021.
96 Board director/CEO interview conducted on 13 January 2021.
97 Board director interview conducted in December 2020.
98 Board director conducted on 6 May 2021.
99 Deborah Hick Midanek, *The Governance Revolution: What Every Board Member Needs to Know, NOW!* Berlin, GE: De Gruyter Press, 2018.
100 Vasant Raval, *Corporate Governance: A Pragmatic Guide for Auditors, Directors, Investors, and Accountants*. Boca Raton, FL: CRC Press, 2020.

10 Entire Board Agenda and Learning Topics

The lead director or independent board chair, with the CEO, sets the agenda and priorities for the entire board. As described in Chapter 7, on board leadership, this is why these roles are the most important roles in the board and organization.

The independent board chair, lead director, and CEO usually discuss and review the agenda for entire board meetings multiple times before sending to the entire board. There are two important drivers of board meetings, (1) the board book, described below, and (2) the meetings themselves.

10.1 Board Books and Corporate Secretaries

The board book is the name for what used to be a physical notebook full of documents. Today these documents are typically contained via an electronic portal. The portal can contain several hundred pages of solid content. Content can include: (1) minutes from all the committee and board meetings, (2) strategy PowerPoints with quarterly metrics and results, (3) financial statements, and much more. Contents of the board book should be reviewed thoroughly by the appropriate committees.

Board directors should be expected to read the entire board before the board meeting. The material is presented to the entire board for review and approval.

> **"Piper"**: I think it's common courtesy to other board directors and the organization staff to read the board book before the board meeting. There's a lot of work in those board books. First, it makes me feel prepared to ask appropriate questions that I want to ask the CEO and senior management. Second, it helps me understand what value I can add to the company.[1]

> **"Wesley"**: Reviewing PowerPoint presentations at the meeting is a waste of time. PowerPoints are something that can be included in the board book and digested before the meeting begins.
> Board meeting time is for real discussion of significant issues, including the company's strategy. Routine information should be captured in the board book containing key topics to be covered within board meeting discussions.[2]

As mentioned earlier, committee meetings and board meeting minutes are captured in the board book. Minutes are important documents.

> **"Vic"**: I learned the importance of minutes when I captured my objection to a certain issue. I made sure my objection – with reasons – were added to the minutes.
> I'm sure my addition to the meeting minutes helped me avoid being investigated by the DOJ.[3] The other board members, and the company, were investigated after I left that board.

---

1 Board director interview conducted in July 2022.
2 Board director interview conducted in July 2022.
3 "DOJ" is the Department of Justice which is the US federal criminal investigation department.

https://doi.org/10.1515/9783110689129-010

To this day, I make sure I read the meeting minutes in detail, and I add in my personal vote on controversial issues. I think I avoided a bullet by having my thoughts and votes documented in meeting minutes, so I read them carefully . . .

I think people misunderstand the importance of minutes. The minutes can't be too detailed and they can't be too high level. I think there's an art to writing minutes. I feel fortunate that I am not the person who has to write the minutes. But I am a person who read the minutes in detail. These are legal documents.[4]

The board secretary or the corporate counsel has the role of taking meeting minutes and making sure the meeting minutes are written appropriately. The board secretary is also responsible for ensuring all parts of the board book are completed with quality.

"Lane": Corporate secretaries oftentimes do administrative activities such as organizing meetings, board books and minutes. Often, they stay in their administrative role.

But the board secretary can make sure all the legal documents for the board are reviewed and approved by the full board. They could also work on other activities to ensure the full functioning of the board, which is something that better corporate secretaries do.[5]

Further reading on board documents

There are a few good chapters on board books, minutes, and board documents. See:

"Board Machinery" in William G. Bowen's book, *The Board Book: An Insider's Guide for Directors and Trustees.*[6]

"Governing and Policy Documents" in Michael E. Batts, *Board Member Orientation: The Concise and Complete Guide to Nonprofit Board Service.*[7]

10.2 Executive Sessions

The most important part of the entire board meetings are the executive sessions. An executive session is when the CEO and board directors meet to discuss issues without senior management, corporate secretaries or notetakers. This is a time for candid discussions.

Most agendas have one executive session, but best practice is to have two sessions:
1. The first executive session is at the beginning of the entire board meeting with the CEO. It is a time to discuss information in the board book, including company strategy and results.

---

4 Board director interview conducted in July 2022.
5 Board director interview conducted in July 2022.
6 Chapter "Board Machinery," William G. Bowen, *The Board Book: An Insider's Guide for Directors and Trustees*, New York, NY: Norton. 2008.
7 Chapter "Governing and Policy Documents," Michael E. Batts, *Board Member Orientation: The Concise and Complete Guide to Nonprofit Board Service*. Orlando, FL: Accountability Press. 2011.

2. The second executive session is at the end of a board meeting without the CEO. This is when the board chair discusses the CEO's performance with the entire board, including CEO succession.

As discussed in Chapter 7, "Board Leadership," when there is an Executive Chair, executive sessions are held without the CEO present. To make the session independent, the lead or presiding director presides over the meeting. NYSE Section 303A requires that the independent (non-management) directors of each listed company must meet at regularly scheduled executive sessions without management. The rule further states that an independent director must "preside over each executive session of the independent directors." The board may rotate this position, but this is not considered best practice. Best practice suggests that boards appoint a lead director to preside over executive sessions. Because there are few entire board meetings, time on the board meeting agenda is at a premium and why for most boards, there is only one executive session.

> **Evelyn Dilsaver**: The first story I want to talk about is that relationship with the CEO and how it gets developed. This is an area of trust I'm sure the governance books don't talk about. Board directors have many executive sessions with the CEO . . . Executive sessions are where relationships are developed.[8]

Executive sessions are when there are discussions whether the company has the right CEO.

> **Dilsaver** continues: The board has the fiduciary responsibility to make sure they have the right CEO to execute the strategy. It's really much more of a partnership than a manager-subordinate hierarchy. The one thing I want to emphasize to readers is the need for executive sessions.
>
> All of my boards now have moved to executive sessions prior to a board meeting and after a Board meeting and many of my board chairs send an email to the board prior to the meeting to set the stage.
>
> The executive sessions are like two hours before a board meeting, and we really talk about what's on the CEOs mind. It's a discussion. It's not a PowerPoint presentation. It's really a discussion to "summarize the three things that are going well and three things that are not."
>
> The board has read the board book is prepped for what to talk about at the board meeting. We can get a lot of our questions out of the way in the executive session including sensitive topics around people and how they're doing. Who's doing well, who's not. Succession planning can be discussed.
>
> I will tell you, the executive session is probably the best part of the board meeting. You get open and honest discussions. You get the CEO talking about what they are really worried about. You don't always get that in the more formal session.[9]

---

8 Public company board director interview conducted on 6 November 2020.
9 Public company board director interview conducted on 6 November 2020.

Anna Catalano: Executive sessions are for board directors and the CEO. First, we talk about issues without any of the executives in. Executive sessions can be about some succession issues. It can be about things to keep the CEO up to date that they don't want to share with everyone else.

In executive sessions – without the CEO with just the directors – we talk how we feel the company is going. Do we feel we have the right person to lead? Do we think we have the right team? How is this team developing over time? Is the CEO growing? Is he doing better? Is she doing worse?

I think executive sessions are really important. The board meeting is the primary meeting with the CEO and the senior team to utilize the board in a more effective way. One of the real challenges is understanding the risk that the enterprise has – what can go wrong?[10]

10.3 Board Calendar and Learning Topics

The tool most used by board directors is the calendar. The board calendar identifies the dates of board and committee meetings. In my experience, board meetings are arranged one year in advance because board directors are busy people.

David Rosenblum: In public companies, there's a calendar up on my wall and I have meetings through the end of the following calendar year . . . . There's a quarterly reporting cycle. There's a cadence . . . . for example, there are quarterly financial filings that the SEC requires.[11]

"Morgan": I was on the audit committee. We met four times a year. However, the Nom and Governance committee did not meet more than once a year. The comp committee met only twice a year. I was also on the comp committee.

I just felt that it was not a very public company. It was not a well-run board because the chairman and the CEO knew what they wanted, and the board was a "rubber stamp" board.[12]

In addition to the quarterly (or more frequent) meetings, there are additional meetings scheduled to cover issues such as unexpected situations and CEO succession planning.

At least one of the four meetings is used to cover identified risks, opportunities and updated annual strategy. Other entire board meetings may be used to cover organizational values and purpose; topics that require entire board discussion and approval.

Other meetings may include learning topics, including those mentioned below. They change frequently and at least annually. I have included links in other governance books to these topics, but I highly recommend getting up-to-date information.

Maureen Conners: Today, business is much more complex. So many more areas that must be considered – climate, ESG, human capital . . . . Your core asset has changed. How are you doing work? . . . What we are facing now is so much more in 2023 than in 2020.

---

10 Public company board director interview conducted on 6 June 2021.
11 Public company board director interview conducted on 11 November 2020.
12 Public board director interview conducted in January 2021.

> The core principles remain the same: ethics, visions, and the ability and flexibility to meet objectives.[13]

Board directors continue to learn to be able to contribute to the organization they serve. Board directors must keep up-to-date and continue to learn to help their CEO and their organization.

> **Subash Anbu:** I've seen a lot of board members attending a lot of conferences through PDA (Private Directors Association) and other organizations. Board directors ask to bring in experts and are asking questions. Board directors say "I want to learn about Meta . . . . I want to learn about Chat GPT" right? "I want to learn about cybersecurity."
> I think boards have gotten a lot smarter. They have education through organizations. Board directors are asking their CIOs and other senior executives a lot of questions.[14]

These topics can be covered by board directors as a group or as individuals. Board directors continue to represent the interests of owners and stakeholders. So, the learning areas should further the interests of owners and stakeholders.

10.3.1 Mergers and Acquisitions (M&A)

Boards should accomplish many annual activities before discussing mergers and acquisitions. The organization strategy should be updated annually. The key question is organic growth or growth via acquisition. For significant growth, most companies choose growth via acquisition.

When acquiring a company, organizations will be highly dependent on investment bankers and other specialized advisors. When a company is acquiring another organization, there will be many committee and entire board meetings to discuss – before approving – the acquisition. Investment bankers, specialized professional service advisors, and company management will be leading the discussion.

The general readings below will be helpful to understanding acquisitions. But when considering board composition and the skills/experience matrix, it is better to have board directors that have significant M&A knowledge and experience.

Board discussions about acquisitions should include:
- Strategic fit: Is the target company a good fit to be acquired. Can the target company be integrated successfully into the company to achieve financial targets?
- Due diligence: With the experience of board directors, management, and professional advisors what are the areas to be examined in target companies? And after examination, are findings within acceptable range to approve the acquisition?
- Valuation: Is the target company priced appropriately? After the findings of due diligence and risks are mitigated, is the price appropriate?

---

13 Public company board director interview conducted on 9 February 2023.
14 Board director interview conducted on 18 March 2023.

– Regulation: What are the regulations that the acquisition will face? Will there be any local, state, or federal regulation the acquisition will need to overcome?
– Stakeholder communication: When appropriate, what will the company communicate to investors, employees, suppliers, and community members? Who is appropriate to communicate the message?

Further reading on Mergers and Acquisitions

It is likely that during a board director's term, a company will be a target of an acquisition, or the company will want to acquire an organization as part of its strategy. Fortunately, many board directors come with M&A skills, knowledge, and experience.

See "Selling a Company" and "Going Out of Business" in Brad Feld and Mahendra Ramsinghani's book *Startup Boards: Getting the Most Out of Your Board of Directors.*[15]

See "*The Market for Corporate Control: Hostile Tender Offers and Proxy Contests*" in J. Robert Brown, Jr. and Lisa L. Casey's book. *Corporate Governance: Cases and Materials, Second Edition.*[16]

For overall guidance on M&A, there is the "Art of M&A" series at McGraw-Hill, including *The Art of M&A: A Merger, Acquisition, and Buyout Guide, by Alexandra R. Lajoux and Capital Expert Services, LLC*[17] I am one of the experts interviewed for this book.

10.3.2 Human Capital

The entire board can have a board meeting to learn more about the human resources or human capital of the organization. In such a meeting, board directors may need to be reminded that their role is to govern, rather than manage or operate. The CEO and senior management are responsible for people resources.

But in such a meeting, the board can discuss:
– Culture: The board's and CEO's role is setting the organization's culture. Many leaders believe that "culture eats strategy for breakfast"[18] therefore having a discussion of culture and organizational values is worthwhile. Do performance management systems align with the desired culture and values? Do management and board behaviors align with desired culture and values?
– Does the desired culture include diversity and inclusion efforts? Does the desired culture engage workers?

---

15 Chapters "Selling a Company" and "Going Out of Business," Brad Feld and Mahendra Ramsinghani, *Startup Boards: Getting the Most Out of Your Board of Directors*, Hoboken, NJ: Wiley. 2014.

16 Chapters "The Market for Corporate Control: Hostile Tender Offers and Proxy Contests," J. Robert Brown, Jr. and Lisa L. Casey *Corporate Governance: Cases and Materials, Second Edition*, Durham, NC: Carolina Academic Press, 2016.

17 Alexandra Reed Lajoux and Capital Expert Services, LLC *The Art of M&A. Fifth Edition: A Merger, Acquisition, and Buyout Guide*, New York, NY: McGraw Hill, 2019.

18 Peter Drucker, Work and Tools. *Technology and Culture*, p.28, 1959.

- Metrics: The board should review human capital metrics. What is employee satisfaction? Retention rates? Diversity and inclusion efforts? Employee engagement? What story do these metrics tell to drive business success?
- Risks: Is the organization violating any labor laws or regulations? And if there are any violations how are these problems being mitigated? Are there any areas (such as sales, product development, etc.) which are having human capital problems?
- Opportunities: Is there any human resource areas that need further financial investment? Does compensation need to be increased to be competitive? Are these changes captured in annual strategy plans?

The reading below provide background information on human capital. But is best to get current information from management and professional advisors. For example, the books and chapters below do not yet include all the learning from the COVID pandemic years.

In the past few years, with the many workforce changes, discussions with experts in human capital have been needed. Of course, organizations have their experts employed in the organization to guide boards. But sometimes, board leadership and board directors want additional expertise and perspectives.

See Solange Charas and Stela Lupushor's book, *Humanizing Human Capital: Invest in Your People for Optimal Business Returns.*[19]

See also Solange Charas and Michael Young's chapter, "Winter is Coming: The Approaching Human Capital Management Storm," Jay A Conger and Edward E. Lawler III's chapter, "Mind the Gap: How Human Resource Can Become More Integral to the Corporate Boardroom Agenda" in Richard Leblanc, *The Handbook of Board Governance: A Comprehensive Guide for Public, Private, and Not-for-Profit Board Members, Second Edition.*[20]

10.3.3 Technology and Cybersecurity

Board directors provide oversight and do not manage nor operate in most situations. I note this again because the CEO and senior management are responsible for implementing technology throughout operations, as well as ensuring that the organization prevent and is resilient to cybersecurity problems.

Technology and security challenges change so frequently that boards should be updated by management and advisors to have the most current information. Governance

---

19 Solange Charas and Stela Lupushar, *Humanizing Human Capital: Invest in Your People for Optimal Business Returns*, Dallas, TX: BenBella Books, Inc. 2022.
20 Chapter "Winter is Coming: The Approaching Human Capital Management Storm," Jay A Conger and Edward E. Lawler III, *Mind the Gap: How Human Resource Can Become More Integral to the Corporate Boardroom Agenda in Richard Leblanc, The Handbook of Board Governance: A Comprehensive Guide for Public, Private, and Not-for-Profit Board Members, Second Edition.* Hoboken, NJ: Wiley. 2020.

books and the reading below are helpful guides but are not current. This chapter describes the entire board agenda. But I want to remind the reader about board composition described in Chapter 8. For the board to provide oversight on technology, it is critical for at least three directors to be technology savvy. A finance expert or a human resource expert or another domain expert can also be technology savvy. It is only when three or more directors are technology savvy that the board provides oversight.[21]

The board can provide oversight to ensure the organization has:

- Company strategy uses technology to provide a better product or service to customers. For example, artificial intelligence can be used to improve operations. Most companies are on a journey of digital transformation.
- The EU has consumer and employee data privacy regulations. Consumers increasingly understand the importance of data privacy, so organizations must change business processes and technology tools to protect data.
- Emerging technologies are always changing. A few years ago, 5G, the Internet of Things, and artificial intelligence were emerging technologies. But now those technologies are well baked into products, services, and operations.
- Since I am a technology effort, with over 25 years of professional technology leadership roles, I will identify quantum computing is an emerging technology that will break encryption and many cybersecurity technologies. But this increased processing power will enable new business models, new collaboration between the customers, your organization, and the supply chain, and new competitors.

There will be new emerging technologies that I cannot anticipate at this time that will create new risks and opportunities. See Dr. Gary L. Evans's chapter, "Technology and the Corporate Board 2020 and Beyond" in Richard Leblanc's book, *The Handbook of Board Governance: A Comprehensive Guide for Public, Private, and Not-for-Profit Board Members, Second Edition.*[22]

Chapter "Cybersecurity Responsibility" in Dennis J. Cagan's book *The Board of Directors for a Private Enterprise.*[23]

See also Jack J. Bensimon's chapter, "The Impact of Blockchain Technology for Corporate Governance," Dr. Elizabeth Valentine, Dr. Greg Timbrell, Lachlan Feeney, and Dr. John Puttick's chapter, "Blockchain: An Introduction for Boards of Directors" in *Richard Leblanc's book, The Handbook of Board Governance: A Comprehensive Guide for Public, Private, and Not-for-Profit Board Members, Second Edition.*[24]

---

21 MIT CISR (Center for Information Systems Research) https://cisr.mit.edu/

22 Chapter "Technology and the Corporate Board 2020 and Beyond," Richard Leblanc, *The Handbook of Board Governance: A Comprehensive Guide for Public, Private, and Not-for-Profit Board Members, Second Edition.* Hoboken, NJ: Wiley. 2020.

23 Chapter "Cybersecurity Responsibility," Dennis J. Cagan, *The Board of Directors for a Private Enterprise,* Bloomington, IN: AuthorHouse, 2017.

24 Chapters "The Impact of Blockchain Technology for Corporate Governance," "Blockchain: An Introduction for Boards of Directors," Richard Leblanc, *The Handbook of Board Governance: A Comprehen-*

10.3.4 Innovation and Disruption

Innovation is the process of creating and implementing new ideas, products, and services. Innovation can be incremental with small improvements or disruptive with entire new products or services that fundamentally change the market.

Disruption is a specific type of innovation; it fundamentally changes an industry or market.

For an organization to be innovative or create disruption it requires a culture that rewards agility, collaboration, and constructive competition. It is the CEO's, board chair's, and board's role to set the tone and create the culture for risk-taking and experimentation. This means learning from failure and taking calculated risks should be rewarded.

The CEO and board must plan for financial investment in new technology, research and development, and professional development programs to promote creativity and problem solving. There also should be a financial investment in diversity, thought, experience, and background. A diverse team is more likely to generate new and innovative ideas.

Emerging trends and competitive threats should be included in every board book preparation. These emerging trends and competitive threats can be discussed in executive sessions or in entire board meetings.

The further reading below can provide general background information. An entire board meeting on innovation and disruption should not be general, but specific to the company's industry and competitors. In addition, specific company employees or teams can present new innovations to the board.

Innovation and disruption may be a change in the business model or finding a new market niche. Innovation may be enabled by technology but may also be from the opportunities uncovered by a risk and market scan.

See Linda A. Hill and George Davis's chapter, "The Board's New Innovation Imperative" *in HBR's 10 Must Reads on Boards.*[25]

See "Innovate or Die: The Existential Crisis of the Twenty-First-Century Board" in Dambisa Moyo's book *How Boards Work: And How They Can Work Better in a Chaotic World.*[26]

---

sive Guide for Public, Private, and Not-for-Profit Board Members, Second Edition. Hoboken, NJ: Wiley. 2020.

25 Chapter "The Board's New Innovation Imperative," *HBR's 10 Must Reads on Boards*, Cambridge, MA: Harvard Business Review Press, 2020.

26 Chapter, "Innovate or Die: The Existential Crisis of the Twenty-First-Century Board," Dambisa Moyo, *How Boards Work: And How They Can Work Better in a Chaotic World.* New York, NY: Basic Books. 2021.

10.3.5 Corporate Social Responsibility (CSR), Environmental, Social, and Governance (ESG)

ESG (Environmental, Social, and Governance) was mentioned in a United Nations report in 2005. It has been a concept that has existed for a few decades, but it has been discussed frequently in US boardrooms since the 2020s.

ESG is a way in which organization and company performance can be reported to investors and stakeholders. It is also an area that continues to be discussed in new ways. Though the books and articles below have good ESG information, I highly recommend receiving current information from management or company advisors.

It is important to discuss ESG in the context of your company's risks, opportunities, and strategy. Financial performance and organization growth continues to be the highest priorities. Also, it is critical for the board to discuss the organization's purpose and where it sits on the continuum between shareholder primacy and stakeholder capitalism.

Many investors believe that companies increase their long-term value by increasing their CSR ratings. In addition, companies are working to identify purpose and reasons to motivate employees beyond shareholder value. See the chapter, *"Corporate Governance and ESG Ratings"* in David Larcker and Brian Tayan's book, Corporate Governance Matters: A Closer Look at Organizational Choices and Their Consequences, Third Edition.[27]

See "Corporate Governance: The Link Between Corporations and Society" in Cornelis A. de Kluyver's book A Primer on Corporate Governance.[28]

10.3.5.1 Corporate Social Responsibility

If management and board decide the company is on the side of shareholder primacy, then the company may work on corporate social responsibility (CSR) initiatives. There is a significant different between CSR and ESG efforts: (1) CSR are voluntary actions and initiatives, while (2) ESG is a framework to evaluate the company's performance on environmental sustainability, social responsibility, and corporate governance.

CSR initiatives are voluntary. This may include company philanthropy. Or they may be efforts to improve the company's reputation or position the organization within regulatory compliance.

---

[27] Chapter "Corporate Governance and ESG Ratings," David Larcker and Brian Tayan, *Corporate Governance Matters: A Closer Look at Organizational Choices and Their Consequences, Third Edition.* London, UK: Pearson, 2020.

[28] Chapter "Corporate Governance: The Link Between Corporations and Society," Cornelis A. de Kluyver, *Primer on Corporate Governance.* New York, NY: Business Expert Press. 2013.

ESG is a framework to evaluate the organization's framework. ESG factors should be integrated into the company's strategy. Companies should assess their environmental risks, labor practices, executive compensation, and board diversity. Likewise companies can find opportunities to reduce energy costs, increase customer loyalty from a solid social responsibility record and good governance. Customers, employees, suppliers, community members, and investors should be engaged. And the company should report these efforts using the SASB[29] or GRI[30] frameworks.

> **Further reading on Corporate Social Responsibility**
> See chapter, "Corporate Social Responsibility" in Adrian Cadbury's book, *Corporate Governance and Chairmanship: A Personal View.*[31]
> See "Philanthropy, Social Responsibility, and Stakeholder Rights" in J. Robert Brown, Jr. and Lisa L. Casey's *Corporate Governance: Cases and Materials*, Second Edition.[32]
> See chapters, "Corporate Governance and Stakeholder Accountability" and "Responsible Investment" in Jill Solomon's book in *Corporate Governance and Accountability*, Fifth Edition,[33] with sections about environmental reporting and CSR.

10.3.5.2 Environment

There are many areas within ESG. For example, an organization may choose to focus on employee satisfaction and/or labor concerns. Or a business may concentrate on supply chain issues to ensure that products and services are built by certified workers.

A company may choose an ESG area that is important to the organization's investors or customers. Because ESG is wide-ranging, there is likely an ESG area that important to the company's strategy, investors, employees, and customers.

Many organizations find that working on the environment and sustainability align with company strategy and the interests of owners, employees, and customers.

I recommend getting current information from management or company advisors, rather than reviewing only the sources below. The environmental component of ESG includes:

- Reporting: Senior management should understand SASB (Sustainability Accounting Standards Board) which is a reporting framework that works across industries.

---

29 SASB is Sustainability Accounting Standards Board – https://www.sasb.org/.

30 GRI is the Global Reporting Initiative – https://www.globalreporting.org/.

31 Chapter "Corporate Social Responsibility" in Adrian Cadbury's book, *Corporate Governance and Chairmanship: A Personal View*. Oxford, UK: Oxford University Press, 2002.

32 Chapter "Philanthropy, Social Responsibility, and Stakeholder Rights," J. Robert Brown, Jr., Lisa L. Casey, *Corporate Governance: Cases and Materials, Second Edition*, Durham, NC: Carolina Academic Press, 2016.

33 Chapters "Corporate Governance and Stakeholder Accountability" and "Responsible Investment" in Jill Solomon, *Corporate Governance and Accountability, Fifth Edition*. Hoboken, NJ: Wiley, 2020.

- Innovation, Risks, and Opportunities: What do your customers and owners expect when striving for environmental goals? What are the deficits that your organization must overcome? What are near-term innovations that the organization can pilot or implement?
- Regulation: US businesses likely will need to meet or exceed EU environmental regulations. What are those EU, global, and sometimes local regulations that companies need to meet or exceed?
- Climate Change: What is the climate science that impact the company's operations, supply chain, and reputation?
- Sustainability: How can the organization reduce energy, water consumption, and minimize waste? How can sustainability help with the organizations short- and long- term results?

Further reading on the Environment

See Dr. Yilmaz Argiiden's chapter, "Responsible Boards for a Sustainable Future" and Alice Korngold's chapter, "Corporate Governance to Advance Business and Society" in Richard Leblanc's book *The Handbook of Board Governance: A Comprehensive Guide for Public, Private, and Not-for-Profit Board Members*, Second Edition.[34]

See Ellie Mulholland, Sara Barker, Cynthis Williams and Robert G. Eccles' chapter, "Climate Change and Directors' Duties: Closing the Gap Between Legal Obligation and Enforcement Practice", and Patricia A. Koval "Board Oversight and Climate Change: What Directors Need to Know" in Richard Leblanc, *The Handbook of Board Governance: A Comprehensive Guide for Public, Private, and Not-for-Profit Board Members*, Second Edition.[35]

---

34 Chapters "Responsible Boards for a Sustainable Future," Alice Korngold "Corporate Governance to Advance Business and Society," Richard Leblanc's book *The Handbook of Board Governance: A Comprehensive Guide for Public, Private, and Not-for-Profit Board Members, Second Edition*. Hoboken, NJ: Wiley. 2020.
35 Chapters "Climate Change and Directors' Duties: Closing the Gap Between Legal Obligation and Enforcement Practice" and "Board Oversight and Climate Change: What Directors Need to Know," Richard Leblanc, *The Handbook of Board Governance: A Comprehensive Guide for Public, Private, and Not-for-Profit Board Members*, Second Edition. Hoboken, NJ: Wiley. 2020.

11 Conclusion

This book is written for everyone who wants to know what happens in the boardroom – this includes new board directors and professionals in many organizations (e.g., proxy advisory firms, investments banking, executive recruiting, institutional investors, compensation consultants, and more).

Good governance is a foundation of a growing organization. Board directors should help organizations grow and change.

> **Joyce Cacho**: Board work is integral to creating the future.
>
> Why do I want to do this work? It takes more than passion . . . it takes intentionality to be part of a living organism. It is to be part of corporates who see themselves as producers of tangible assets and services. That's the future that will turn companies into entities that serve a portfolio of stakeholders.
>
> If corporations can use the past three years of data during the pandemic years of 2020–2023 from crisis and business continuation challenges, then companies can understand how challenges impact different people. Companies can be part of an ecosystem, which acknowledges that they are here to not only produce things but also contribute to a society with fewer gaps.
>
> That is the script for companies to be trusted. Before 2020, corporations did not have a reason to understand where this gap in trust came from. But in 2023 they have the data to understand not only the source but also do something about it. This is what companies can do to be part of our society to help create the future.[1]

This book, *The Art of Director Excellence*, is intended as the first volume in a series; it is a roadmap to improve corporate governance. Reading all the stories from experienced board directors, I hope the reader understands the "how to" or roadmap to good governance. As board director Joyce Cacho says, good governance and board directors create a better future.

You may remember board director and CEO Michael Marquardt's opening quote in Chapter 1. Michael Marquardt is board chair and he imagines the board directors with their CEO achieving great things for the organization in the future.

This book describes the roadmap towards that future, which can be summarized as:

1. Understanding the role and responsibilities of board leadership and board directors (Chapters 1–4 and 7)
2. Overseeing risk, opportunities, and strategy through the Audit Committee and Entire Board (Chapters 5 and 9)
3. Motivating and selecting the CEO and senior management (Chapter 6)
4. Establishing the right overall board and committee structure, including Executive CEO, Lead Director, and Board Chair roles (Chapter 7)

---

1 Board director interview conducted on 12 January 2023.

https://doi.org/10.1515/9783110689129-011

5. Continuing a board director succession plan, transitioning directors off the board, selecting and orienting new board directors (Chapter 8)
6. Setting up a governance system that is improving continually (Chapter 10)

All the experienced corporate directors described the increasing amount of work for board directors. The board director role may have been an easy job 20 years ago, but it is not now. Because of the amount of internal and external pressures to organizations, there is a greater need for CEO leadership with board director support. See Deborah Hick Midanek's book, *The Governance Revolution: What Every Board Member Needs to Know, NOW!*[2]

> **Solange Charas**: The role of boards in the future is going to get more and more and more complex. Boards need to be more clear and to avoid living in the gray area, which is what a lot of boards do right now.
>
> What I think is going to happen in the future is that organizations are going to become much more sensitive and aware of human capital as a driver of sustainable value creation for stakeholders.
>
> So if I had to say, you know, what's the future for boards? I'd look at a matrix. The first thing I would look at is board composition and board qualifications or competencies. Who's on my board? What skills do they bring? . . .
>
> If you want to have a well-governed organization, you need to have the talent on the board to do that. So, the future is a shift in board composition that looks at more diverse sets of talents and skills. Not just a board composed of a bunch of CEOs sitting around being managers.[3]

Chapter 10, "Entire Board Agenda and Learning Topics," describes the many topics that will change and update constantly. These topics will continue to impact company strategy, risks, and opportunities. As board director Cacho says at the beginning of this chapter, a board director needs to have passion for board work and continually learn.

It was a pleasure interviewing my board director friends and colleagues during the COVID-19 pandemic from 2020 to 2023. As I described earlier, I asked my friends, "what surprised you when you became a board director?" and "what information would you want to share with students about corporate governance?" Their responses became the content of this book and it has been a pleasure compiling their wisdom and experience for the book's audience.

I look forward to interviewing more of my friends and colleagues to update this book and have much more content to put in another book, which I will call *The Art of Director Excellence*, Volume 2. I will also write articles for corporate governance publications.

If readers want to contribute to this book or the series, I can be reached at https://johnhotta.academia.edu/contact.

---

2 Chapter "Post 2000 Intensification of Focus on the Board," Deborah Hick Midanek, *The Governance Revolution: What Every Board Member Needs to Know, NOW!* Berlin, GE: De Gruyter Press, 2018.
3 Public company board director interview conducted on 12 January 2023.

Appendices

Appendix 1
Mapping between LeBlanc's *The Handbook of Board Governance: A Comprehensive Guide for Public, Private, and Not-for-Profit Board Members* and *The Art of Director Excellence, Volume 1*

The Handbook of Board Governance: A Comprehensive Guide for Public, Private, and Not-for-Profit Board Members[1]	The Art of Director Excellence, Volume 1
The Handbook of Board Governance: An Introduction and Overview 1	– CEO Succession Planning 6.2.1 – CEO Recruiting and Selection 6.3
CEO Succession Planning Trends and Forecast 2	
CEO Succession Planning 3	
CEO Succession: Lessons from the Trenches for Directors 4	
Model CEO Succession Planning Charter Appendix 1	
Model CEO Position Description Appendix 2	– CEO Performance 6.2.1.1
The Non-Executive Chairman: Toward a Shareholder Value Maximization Role 5	– Independent Board Chairs 7.1.2.7 – The Impact of Board Leadership 7.1.3
Great Boards Don't Exist Without Great Chairs 6	– Board Structure, CEOs, and Board Chairs 7.1
What's in a Name? The Lead Director Role at US Public Companies 7	– Lead Directors 7.1.2.6 – The Impact of Board Leadership 7.1.3
Model Board Chair Position Description Appendix 3	– Board Composition 8.1
Director Independence, Competency and Behavior 8	– Board Composition 8.1 – Board Director Evaluation 8.2
Board Behaviors: How Women Directors Influence Decision Outcomes 9	– Board Composition 8.1 – Dimensions of Diversity 8.1.4 and 8.1.4.1
The State of Gender Diversity in Boardrooms 10	

---

[1] Richard LeBlanc, *The Handbook of Board Governance: A Comprehensive Guide for Public, Private, and Not-for-Profit Board Members, second edition*. Hoboken, NJ: Wiley. 2020.

https://doi.org/10.1515/9783110689129-012

(continued)

The Handbook of Board Governance: A Comprehensive Guide for Public, Private, and Not-for-Profit Board Members	The Art of Director Excellence, Volume 1
Every Seat Matters 11	– Board Composition 8.1 – Board Director Skills, Knowledge, and Experience 8.1.3
The Art of Asking Questions as a Director 12	– What Board Directors Do 1.3 – Ask Questions 1.3.2
Board Succession, Evaluation, and Recruitment: A Global Perspective 13	– Board Composition 8.1 – Board Director Evaluation 8.2 – Board Director Recruiting 8.4 – Corporate Governance in Different Countries 1.6
Model Individual Director Position Description Appendix 4	– Board Director Evaluation 8.2
Model Conflict of Interest Policy for Directors Appendix 5	– Board Director Conflicts 7.2.1.1 – Board Culture 7.2 – Trust and Trustworthiness 7.2.1
Climate Change and Directors' Duties: Closing the Gap Between Legal Obligation and Enforcement Practice 14	– Purpose 9.1.3 – Corporate Social Responsibility (CSR), Environmental, Social, and Governance (ESG) 10.3.5
Board Oversight and Climate Change: What Directors Need to Know 15	
Responsible Boards for a Sustainable Future 16	
Corporate Governance to Advance Business and Society 17	– Shareholder Primacy and Stakeholder Capitalism 9.1.1 – Purpose 9.1.3
Technology and the Corporate Board 2020 and Beyond 18	– Board Composition 8.1 – Board Director Skills, Knowledge, and Experience 8.1.3 – Technology 8.1.3.1 – Technology and Cybersecurity 10.3.3 – Innovation and Disruption 10.3.4
Responsive Governance in a Digital World: The Need to Up-Skill 19	
The Impact of Blockchain Technology for Corporate Governance 20	
Blockchain: An Introduction for Boards of Directors 21	
Reflections of a Board Chair on the Christchurch Massacre: Governing Social Media 22	– Stakeholder Communication 9.4

(continued)

The Handbook of Board Governance: A Comprehensive Guide for Public, Private, and Not-for-Profit Board Members	The Art of Director Excellence, Volume 1
Financial Literacy and Audit Committees: A Primer for Directors and Audit Committee Members 23	– Financial Oversight 5.2 – Auditors and Other Professionals Supporting the Audit Committee 5.4
Corporate Governance in an Age of Populism 24	– Stakeholder Communications 9.4
A Call to Action for Geopolitical Governance 25	– Corporate Governance in Different Countries 1.6 – Cross-Border Corporate Governance 2.7 – International Regulatory Compliance 5.8.2 – Board Composition 8.1 – Board Director Skills, Knowledge, and Experience 8.1.3 – International 8.1.3.2
Governing Boards, Risk Management, and Deliberative Thinking 26	– Risks 9.2.1 – Risks and Opportunities 9.2.2
Lawyers' Advice to Directors on Overseeing Executive Pay 27	– Executive Compensation 6.1.2
Accountant's Advice to Company Directors: Directors' Obligation to Detect Top-10 Frauds 28 Ten Tell-Tale Signs of Possible Fraud: A Director's Primer 29	– Financial Oversight 5.2 – Fraud and Wrongdoing 5.3
100 Questions Directors Should Ask When Assessing the Effectiveness of Risk Systems 30 Risk Oversight for Directors: A Practical Guide 31 Risk Governance: Leading Practice and Demographic Impacts 32	– Transparency as an Organizational Value 5.6 – Internal Audit, Whistleblowing, and Ethics Programs 5.7 – Risk, Opportunity, Strategy, and Metrics 9.2
Agile Governance 33	– Board Culture 7.2 – Respect for Different Opinions and Experiences is a Boardroom Value 7.2.2 – It's Okay to Disagree – in a Respectful Manner 7.2.3 – Board Composition 8.1 – Dimensions of Diversity 8.1.4
The Three Dilemmas for Creating a Long-Term Board 34	– Board Composition 8.1 – Board Director Evaluation 8.2 – Board Director Recruiting 8.4

(continued)

The Handbook of Board Governance: A Comprehensive Guide for Public, Private, and Not-for-Profit Board Members	The Art of Director Excellence, Volume 1	
Strategic Blindspots in the Boardroom 35	–	Board Composition 8.1
	–	Board Evaluation 8.2
	–	Board Director Recruiting 8.4
	–	Strategy 9.2.5
	–	Conclusion 11
Winter Is Coming: The Approaching Human Capital Management Storm 36	–	Human Capital 10.3.2
The Effective Compensation Committee 37	–	Compensation Committee 6.1
Compensation Governance and Performance-Based Executive Compensation 38	–	Compensation Committee 6.1
	–	CEO Compensation 6.1.1
	–	Executive Compensation 6.1.2
	–	CEO Performance 6.2.1.1
Measuring and Improving Pay for Performance: Board Oversight of Executive Pay 39	–	Executive Compensation 6.1.2
Designing Performance for Long-Term Value: Aligning Business Strategy, Management Structure, and Incentive Design 40	–	CEO Compensation 6.1.1
	–	Executive Compensation 6.1.2
Mind the Gap: How Human Resources Can Become More Integral to the Corporate Boardroom Agenda 41	–	Human Capital 10.3.2
Board Risk and Responsibility Under Regulatory and Criminal Law 42	–	Risks 9.2.1
	–	Regulation, Compliance, and Reporting 5.8
Riding Between Cars: The Position of the Corporate Secretary 43	–	Board Books and Corporate Secretaries 10.1
Ensuring Good Governance and Business Success in International Subsidiaries	–	International Regulatory Compliance 5.8.2
The Rise of Investor Stewardship 45	–	Public Company Board Directors 2.0
Director/Shareholder Meetings 46	–	Stakeholder Communications 9.4
Dual-Class Share Firms in Developing Market Economies 47	–	Public Company Board Directors 2.0
For Directors: The Long-Term Relationship Between Directors, Companies, and Institutional Investors 48	–	Public Company Board Directors 2.0
Proxy Scorecards Will Empower Investors 49	–	Public Company Board Directors 2.0

(continued)

The Handbook of Board Governance: A Comprehensive Guide for Public, Private, and Not-for-Profit Board Members	The Art of Director Excellence, Volume 1
Charitable and Not-for-Profit Organization Governance 50	– Nonprofit Board Directors 4.0
	– Board Director Evaluation 8.2
The Best of Boards, the Worst of Boards: The Not-for-Profit Experience 51	– Succession Planning and Transitioning Directors off the Board 8.3
	– Board Director Recruiting 8.4
Fundraising Best Practices for Not-for-Profit Boards of Directors 52	
Governance of Small and Medium-Sized Entities 53	– Public Company Board Directors 2.0
	– Private Company Board Directors 3.0
Private Versus Public Company Governance: Top-13 Questions for Board Members to Consider 54	– Nonprofit Board Directors 4.0
Cannabis Governance: Advice for Current and Prospective Directors in This Emerging Industry 55	– n/a
Cross-Border Corporate Governance 56	– Corporate Governance in Different Countries 1.6
Corporate Governance in Asia-Pacific 57	– Cross-Border Corporate Governance 2.7
Boards of Directors of Chinese Companies 58	– International Regulatory Compliance 5.8.2
	– Board Composition 8.1
The Russian Corporate Governance Story 59	– Board Director Skills, Knowledge, and Experience 8.1.3
CARICOM (Caribbean Community Governance 60	
King IV: Taking Corporate Governance to the Next Level 61	– International Experience 8.1.3.2

Appendix 2
Mapping between *Bainbridge's Advanced Corporation Law: A Practical Approach to Corporate Governance* and *The Art of Director Excellence, Volume 1*

Advanced Corporation Law: A Practical Approach to Corporate Governance[1]	The Art of Director Excellence, Volume 1
Regulating Corporate Governance in a Federal System 1	– Regulation, Compliance, and Reporting 5.8 – US Regulatory Compliance 5.8.1
The Roles and Duties of the Board of Directors 2	– What Board Directors Do 1.3 – Duty of Care and Duty of Loyalty 1.4 – Business Judgment Rule 1.5 – Internal Audit, Whistleblowing, and Ethics Programs 5.7
Director Independence 3	– Trust and Trustworthiness 7.2.1 – Board Director Conflicts 7.2.1.1 – Duty of Care and Duty of Loyalty 1.4 – Nominating and Governance Committee 8 – Board Composition 8.1 – Dimensions of Diversity 8.1.4 – Selecting Board Candidates 8.5
Operationalizing the Monitoring Model: State Corporate Law 4	– Enterprise Risk Management (ERM) 9.2.1.1
Operationalizing the Monitoring Model: Federal Law 5	– Audit Committee 5 – Fraud and Wrongdoing 5.3 – Auditors and Other Professionals Supporting the Audit Committee 5.4 – Internal Audit, Whistleblowing, and Ethics Programs 5.7 – Regulation, Compliance, and Reporting 5.8
Executive Compensation 6	– Compensation Committee 6.1 – CEO Compensation 6.1.1 – Executive Compensation 6.1.2 – Board Director Compensation 8.4.2

---

[1] Stephen M. Bainbridge, *Advanced Corporate Law: A Practical Approach to Corporate Governance*, St. Paul, MN, West Academic, 2021.

https://doi.org/10.1515/9783110689129-013

(continued)

Advanced Corporation Law: A Practical Approach to Corporate Governance	*The Art of Director Excellence, Volume 1*
Executive Duties 7	– CEO Performance 6.2.1.1
	– CEO Succession Planning 6.2.1
Insider Trading 8	– Fraud and Wrongdoing 5.3
	– Integrity as an Organizational Value 5.5
Voting Proxies 9	– Stakeholder Communication 9.4
Shareholder Activism 10	– Board Directors in Public Companies Representing
Shareholder Activism via Proxy Contest 11	Activist Investors 2.2
Shareholder Activism via Proposal 12	– Board Directors in Public Companies Thinking Like an Activist 2.3
ESG Activism 13	– Shareholder Primacy and Shareholder Capitalism 9.1.1
	– Purpose 9.1.3
	– Corporate Social Responsibility (CSR), and Environmental, Social, and Governance (ESG) 10.3.5

Appendix 3
Mapping between Brown and Casey's *Corporate Governance Cases and Materials* and *The Art of Director Excellence, Volume 1*

Corporate Governance Cases and Materials[1]	The Art of Director Excellence
An Introduction to Corporate Governance 1	– What Board Directors Do 1.3 – Public Company Board Directors 2.0 – Private Company Board Directors 3.0 – Nonprofit Board Directors 4.0
Corporate Governance, Path Dependency, and the Sources of Regulations 2	– Public Company Board Directors 2.0 – Regulation, Compliance, and Reporting 5.8
The Public Company Board 3	– Public Company Board Directors 2.0 – Board Structure, CEOs, and Board Chairs 7.1 – Board Structure 7.1.1 – Nominating and Governance Committee 8.0 – Board Composition 8.1 – Dimensions of Diversity 8.1.4 – Succession Planning and Transitioning Directors off the Board 8.3 – Board Director Recruiting 8.4 – Board Director Compensation 8.4.2 – Selecting Board Candidates 8.5
Duties of Corporate Fiduciaries 4	– Duty of Care and Duty of Loyalty 1.4
The Duty of Loyalty 5	– Business Judgment Rule 1.5 – Board Director Conflicts 7.2.1.1
Executive Compensation 6	– Executive Compensation 6.1.2
The Role of Shareholders in the Governance Process 7	– Public Company Board Directors 2.0 – Board Directors and Institutional Investors 2.4 – Stakeholder Communications 9.4

---

1 Robert J. Brown and Lisa L. Casey *Corporate Governance: Cases and Materials*, Second Edition. Durham, NC: Carolina Academic Press. 2016.

https://doi.org/10.1515/9783110689129-014

(continued)

Corporate Governance Cases and Materials	The Art of Director Excellence
The Market for Corporate Control: Hostile Tender Offers and Proxy Contests 8	– Public Company Board Directors 2.0 – Board Directors in Public Companies Representing Activist Investors 2.2 – Board Directors in Public Companies Thinking Like an Activist 2.3 – Some Board Directors are Appointed by Investors and Owners 8.1.2
The Role of Disclosure in the Governance Process 9	– Integrity as an Organizational Value 5.5 – Transparency as an Organizational Value 5.6 – Regulation, Compliance, and Reporting 5.8 – Board Structure 7.1.1 – Board Composition 8.1 – Dimensions of Diversity 8.1.4 – Corporate Social Responsibility and ESG 10.3.5
Shareholders' Derivative Litigation 10	– Public Company Board Directors 2.0 – Public Company Board Directors Thinking Like an Activist 2.3 – Audit Committee 5.0
Philanthropy, Social Responsibility, and Stakeholder Rights 11	– Shareholder Primacy and Stakeholder Capitalism 9.1.1 – Purpose 9.1.3 – Stakeholder Communications 9.4 – Corporate Social Responsibility and ESG 10.3.5 – Nonprofit Board Directors 4.0
Comparative Corporate Governance 12	– Corporate Governance in Different Countries 1.6 – Cross-Border Corporate Governance 2.7 – International Regulatory Compliance 5.8.2 – Board Composition 8.1 – Board Director Skills, Knowledge, and Experience 8.1.3 – International 8.1.3.2 – Shareholder primacy and Stakeholder Capitalism 9.1.1 – Values 9.1.2 – Culture is More Important Than Strategy 9.1.4
How Does Corporate Governance Matter? 13	– Book's Purpose 1.2

Appendix 4
Mapping between Mallin's *Corporate Governance* and *The Art of Director Excellence, Volume 1*

Corporate Governance by Mallin[1]	*The Art of Director Excellence*
Introduction 1	– Book's Purpose 1.2
Theoretical Aspects of Corporate Governance 2	– n/a
Development of Corporate Governance Codes 3	– n/a
Shareholders and Stakeholders 4	– Public Company Board Directors 2.0 – Private Company Board Directors 3.0 – Nonprofit Board Directors 4.0 – Shareholder Primacy and Stakeholder Capitalism 9.1.1 – Purpose 9.1.3
Family-Owned Firms 5	– Family-Owned Business Directors 3.5 – Private Company Board Directors 3.0
The Role of Institutional Investors 6	– Public Company Board Directors 2.0 – Board Directors and Institutional Investors 2.4 – Board Directors, Micro-Caps, And Small-Cap Companies 2.6
Socially Responsible Investment 7	– Shareholder Primacy and Stakeholder Capitalism? 9.1.1 – Values 9.1.2 – Purpose 9.1.3 – Corporate Social Responsibility (CSR), Environmental, Social, and Governance (ESG) 10.3.5

---

1 Christine Mallin, *Corporate Governance,* Sixth Edition. Oxford, UK: Oxford University Press. 2019.

https://doi.org/10.1515/9783110689129-015

(continued)

Corporate Governance by Mallin	*The Art of Director Excellence*
Directors and Board Structure 8	– What Board Directors Do 1.3 – Board Committees 5.1 – Audit Committee 5.0 – Compensation Committee 6.0 – CEOs and Board Chairs 7.1 – Board Structure 7.1.1 – Decision to Combine or Separate the CEO and Chair Roles 7.1.2 – Nominating and Governance committee 8.0 – Board Composition 8.1 – Dimensions of Diversity 8.1.4 – Board Director Evaluation 8.2 – Succession Planning 8.3 – Board Director Recruiting 8.4 – Corporate Secretaries 10.1
Directors' Performance and Remuneration 9	– Board Composition 8.1 – Board Director Evaluation 8.2 – Succession Planning and Transitioning Directors off the Board 8.3 – Board Director Recruiting 8.4 – Board Director Compensation 8.4.2
Corporate Governance in Continental Europe 10	– Corporate Governance in Different Countries 1.6 – Cross-Border Corporate Governance 2.7 – International Regulatory Compliance 5.8.2 – Board Composition 8.1 – Board Director Skills, Knowledge, and Experience 8.1.3 – International Experience 8.1.3.2
Corporate Governance in Central and Eastern Europe 11	
Corporate Governance in the Asia-Pacific 12	
Corporate Governance in South Africa, Egypt, India, and Brazil 13	
Conclusions 14	– Conclusion 11.0

Appendix 5
Mapping between Monks and Minow's *Corporate Governance* and *The Art of Director Excellence, Volume 1*

Corporate Governance by Monks and Minow[1]	*The Art of Director Excellence*
What is a Corporation? 1	– Board Structure 7.1.1 – Shareholder Primacy and Stakeholder Capitalism 9.1.1 – Purpose 9.1.3 – Strategy 9.2.5 – Metrics 9.2.6 – Corporate Social Responsibility (CSR), Environmental, Social, and Governance (ESG) 10.3.5
Shareholders: Ownership 2	– Directors Represent Owners and Stakeholders 1.3.7 – Public Company Board Directors 2.0 – Private Company Board Directors 3.0
Directors: Monitoring 3	– What Board Directors Do 1.3 – Oversee the Organization 1.3.6 – Directors Represent Owners and Stakeholders 1.3.7 – Duty of Care and Duty of Loyalty 1.4 – Public Company Board Directors 2.0 – Private Company Board Directors 3.0 – Nonprofit Board Directors 4.0 – Audit Committee 5.0 – CEO Succession Planning 6.2.1 – Decision to Combine or Separate the CEO and Chair Roles 7.1.2 – Board Composition 8.1 – Dimensions of Diversity 8.1.4 – Unexpected Events and Crisis 9.3

1 Robert Monks and Nell Minow, *Corporate Governance, Fifth Edition*. West Sussex, UK: Wiley. 2011.

https://doi.org/10.1515/9783110689129-016

(continued)

Corporate Governance by Monks and Minow	*The Art of Director Excellence*
Management: Performance 4	– Audit Committee 5.0 – CEO Compensation 6.1.1 – Executive Compensation 6.1.2 – CEO Succession 6.2.1 – Decision to Combine or Separate the CEO and Chair Roles 7.1.2 – Executive Chairs 7.1.2.5 – Risks 9.2.1
International Corporate Governance 5	– Corporate Governance in Different Countries 1.6 – Cross-Border Corporate Governance 2.7 – International Regulatory Compliance 5.8.2 – Board Composition 8.1 – Board Director Skills, Knowledge, and Experience 8.1.3 – International 8.1.3.2
Afterword: Final Thought and Future Directors 6	– Board Composition 8.1 – Board Director Skills, Knowledge, and Experience 8.1.3 – Dimensions of Diversity 8.1.4 – Conclusion 11.0

Glossary

This glossary provides a broader definition of some of the terms used throughout the book to enhance readers' understanding of corporate governance and what happens in a boardroom. This glossary is also a good summary of this book's key concepts.

The 25+ glossary terms below will help readers understand corporate governance and what happens in a boardroom.

Chapters	Glossary Terms
1. Introduction and What Board Directors Do	– Business Judgment Rule – Duty of Care – Duty of Loyalty
2. Public Company Board Directors	– Activist Investors – B Corporations – Institutional Investors – Public Companies
3. Private Company Board Directors	– ESOP – Family-Owned Business – IPO – Micro-Cap and Small-Cap – Private Companies – PE Firms – SPAC – Start-Up – VC or Venture Capital Firms (see PE Firms)
4. Nonprofit Board Directors	– Nonprofit Organization – NGO (Non-Governmental Organization; see Nonprofit Organization)
6. Compensation Committee and Ad Hoc Committees	– D&O insurance
7. Board Leadership and Culture	– Independent Chair – Independent Director – Lead Director – Non-Executive Chair (see Independent Chair)
9. Entire Board Responsibilities	– Shareholder Primacy – Stakeholder Capitalism

https://doi.org/10.1515/9783110689129-017

(continued)

Chapters	Glossary Terms
10. Entire Board Agenda and Learning Topics	– Board Book
	– Board Calendar
	– Board Secretary (see Corporate Secretary)
	– Company Secretary (see Corporate Secretary)
	– Corporate Secretary
	– ESG
	– Executive Session

Activist Investors

Activist investors are individuals or entities that acquire a significant stake in a publicly traded company to influence the company's management, strategy, operations, or financial structure.

Their goal is often to create change within the target company to improve its financial performance, enhance shareholder value, or address specific corporate governance, environmental, or social issues.

Activist investors typically undertake various actions and strategies to achieve their objectives:

- Engaging with management: Activist investors typically begin private discussions with the company's management to express their concerns and propose changes. They may suggest strategic shifts, operational improvements, cost reductions, or changes in capital allocation.
- Public campaigns: If private discussions do not yield the desired results, activist investors may launch public campaigns to garner support from other shareholders and put pressure on the company's management. These campaigns can involve issuing open letters, making public statements, or using media and social platforms to highlight their concerns and proposals.
- Proxy fights: Activist investors may initiate proxy fights by soliciting votes from other shareholders to gain control of the company's board of directors. The goal is to replace existing board members with their nominees, who would be more supportive of their proposed changes.
- Shareholder proposals: Activist investors can submit shareholder proposals for consideration and vote at the company's annual general meeting. These proposals often address specific corporate governance, environmental, or social issues and can serve as a means to pressure the company to take action on the proposed matters.

By employing these tactics, activist investors can drive changes within a company that may ultimately lead to improved financial performance, enhanced shareholder value, and better corporate governance.

Activist investors can have both positive and negative impacts on a company.

On the one hand, they can help unlock value, improve corporate governance, and encourage greater transparency and accountability. On the other hand, their involvement can create distractions, increase short-term focus, and lead to conflicts with management and other shareholders.

B Corporations

A "B Corporation" (or Benefit Corporation) is a type of for-profit company that emphasizes social and environmental responsibility in addition to pursuing financial profit. The purpose of these companies is to create a positive impact on society, the environment, and their stakeholders (employees, customers, and communities), while also generating profit for shareholders. Some well-known B Corps include Patagonia, Ben & Jerry's, and Etsy.

B Corps are certified by the nonprofit organization B Lab, which assesses a company's social and environmental performance, accountability, and transparency. To become a B Corp, companies must meet rigorous standards and go through a comprehensive certification process.

B Corporations differ from traditional corporations in that they are legally obligated to consider the impact of their decisions on all stakeholders, not just shareholders.

Board Book

A board book is a collection of documents and materials provided to board director members in advance of a board meeting.

The purpose of the board book is to provide board members with the necessary information to make informed decisions and participate in productive discussions during the board meeting.

The board book typically includes a variety of information related to the organization's operations, finances, strategic direction and specific items on the meeting agenda.

The contents of a board book can vary depending on the organization and the specific meeting, but may include items such as:
- Agenda for the meeting
- Minutes from the previous meeting
- Financial reports and statements
- Performance reports on key metrics
- Information on upcoming projects or initiatives
- Reports from committees or task forces
- Legal or regulatory updates
- Other relevant materials, such as articles, research reports, or presentations.

The board book is usually prepared by the organization's staff or executive team in consultation with the board or committee chairs.

Board Calendar

A board calendar is a schedule of upcoming meetings and events for the board of directors of an organization.

The calendar provides information on dates, times, and locations of board meetings, including other important dates and deadlines, such as committee meetings, regulatory filings, or shareholder meetings.

The board calendar is created by the organization's staff or executive team in consultation with the board chair or other board members and is distributed to board members in various formats.

It is designed to help board members plan their schedules, attend meetings and events as needed, while ensuring that the organization stays on track with important tasks and deadlines.

Business Judgment Rule

The "business judgment rule" is a legal principle that protects the decision-making authority of directors and officers in companies and organizations.

It grants them a presumption of good faith and reasonable judgment when making decisions on behalf of the organization, as long as they act in accordance with their fiduciary duties such as the duty of care and duty of loyalty.

Under the business judgment rule, courts generally defer to the judgment of directors and officers and do not second-guess their decisions, even if the outcome of those decisions is unfavorable.

The rule is based on the understanding that decision-makers should have the freedom to take risks and make strategic choices without the fear of constant legal challenges or liability, which could hinder their ability to effectively manage the organization.

To be protected by the business judgment rule, directors and officers must meet certain criteria:

- They must have acted in good faith, genuinely believing that their decision was in the best interests of the organization.
- They must have conducted an appropriate level of due diligence, gathering relevant information and considering the potential risks and benefits of their decision.
- They must have acted without conflicts of interest, putting the organization's interests above their personal interests or those of third parties.
- Their decision-making process must be rational and reasonable, even if the outcome of the decision ultimately proves to be unfavorable.

If these criteria are met, courts are unlikely to hold directors and officers personally liable for losses resulting from their decisions.

It is important to note that the business judgment rule does not protect directors and officers who engage in misconduct, self-dealing or gross negligence. If a plaintiff can demonstrate that a director or officer breached their fiduciary duties; the business judgment rule will not shield them from liability.

Corporate Secretary

The corporate secretary is an officer of the company responsible for ensuring that the company complies with legal and regulatory requirements and maintaining accurate records of corporate actions and decisions.

The role and responsibilities of a corporate secretary can vary depending on the size, industry, and jurisdiction of the company, but some common duties include:

- Board meetings and communication: The corporate secretary is responsible for organizing and facilitating board meetings, preparing agendas, distributing materials, and recording minutes. They also ensure that board members are informed about relevant issues and developments within the company.
- Compliance and governance: The corporate secretary ensures that the company complies with applicable laws, regulations, and stock exchange requirements. They also oversee the development and implementation of corporate governance policies and practices, such as codes of conduct, conflict of interest policies, and whistleblower programs.
- Record-keeping and reporting: The corporate secretary maintains the company's official records, including articles of incorporation, bylaws, board meeting minutes, and shareholder records. They are also responsible for filing various reports and documents with regulatory authorities, such as annual reports, proxy statements, and stock exchange filings.
- Shareholder relations: The corporate secretary serves as the primary point of contact between the company and its shareholders. They manage shareholder communications, oversee the organization

and administration of annual general meetings, and ensure that shareholder rights are respected and protected.

– Advising the board: The corporate secretary often provides guidance and advice to the board on matters related to corporate governance, legal compliance, and fiduciary duties. They may also be involved in board member recruitment, orientation, and evaluation.

The Board Secretary, on the other hand, is a role specifically related to the board of directors, responsible for managing the administrative and logistical aspects of board meetings and activities.

The board secretary works closely with the corporate secretary to ensure that board meetings are conducted efficiently and effectively, and that the board's decisions and actions are properly recorded and communicated.

The board secretary's duties may include:

– Scheduling and coordinating board meetings, preparing agendas and meeting materials.
– Taking minutes of board meetings and ensuring that they accurately reflect the board's decisions and actions.
– Managing the flow of information between the board and management, and between board members.
– Ensuring compliance with legal and regulatory requirements related to board meetings and activities.

Overall, while the roles of corporate secretary and board secretary share some similarities, they have distinct responsibilities and focus areas within a company's governance structure.

D&O Insurance

Directors and Officers (D&O) insurance is a type of liability insurance that provides financial protection to directors and officers of a company in the event of a legal action or claim against them.

D&O insurance protects directors and officers from personal financial losses due to legal claims brought against them in connection with their work for the company.

D&O insurance is usually purchased by the company on behalf of its directors and officers, and the premiums are typically paid by the company.

Claims may arise from a variety of sources, such as shareholders, creditors, employees, customers, or regulators, and may allege a breach of fiduciary duty, mismanagement, fraud, or other wrongful acts.

The coverage and costs of D&O insurance can vary depending on the size of the company, the industry, and the specific risks and exposures faced by the directors and officers.

Overall, D&O insurance is an important risk management tool for companies and their leadership, providing financial protection and peace of mind in the event of legal action.

Duty of Care

Duty of care is a legal and ethical obligation of a company or organization to take reasonable steps to ensure the safety and well-being of its employees, customers, and other stakeholders.

Duty of care requires a company to identify and assess potential risks, and to take appropriate measures to minimize or prevent harm.

Duty of care to an organization or company can encompass various aspects, such as:

– Health and safety: Ensuring that the workplace is safe for employees and that the organization complies with relevant health and safety regulations to prevent accidents, injuries, or illness.

- Product and service quality: Ensuring that products and services offered by the company are of a certain standard and do not cause harm or injury to customers. This includes proper labelling, safety measures, and adherence to relevant industry standards.
- Corporate governance: Directors and officers of the company have a duty to act in the best interests of the company and its shareholders. This includes making informed decisions, avoiding conflicts of interest, and ensuring that the company's resources are used responsibly.
- Environmental responsibility: Companies have a duty to minimize their impact on the environment by reducing pollution, managing waste, and complying with environmental regulations.
- Financial management: Organizations have a duty to manage their finances responsibly, ensuring that they maintain financial stability, avoid fraud, and comply with relevant financial regulations.
- Legal compliance: Companies have a duty to comply with all applicable laws and regulations, such as labor laws, taxation, and industry-specific regulations.
- Data protection and privacy: Organizations have a duty to protect the personal information of their customers, employees, and other stakeholders by implementing appropriate data protection measures and adhering to privacy regulations.

By upholding their duty of care, organizations can minimize the risk of legal liability, protect their reputation, and maintain the trust of their stakeholders.

Duty of Loyalty

"Duty of loyalty" is a legal principle that applies to individuals in positions of trust and authority within an organization or company, such as directors, officers, and sometimes employees.

The duty of loyalty requires these individuals to act in the best interests of the organization, putting the organization's interests above their own or those of any other party.

The duty of loyalty is an essential component of corporate governance and helps maintain the integrity of the company.

The duty of loyalty to an organization or company generally includes the following components:

- Conflicts of interest: Individuals subject to the duty of loyalty must avoid conflicts of interest that could compromise their ability to act in the organization's best interests. This means avoiding situations where personal interests, relationships, or financial gain could potentially influence their decision-making on behalf of the organization.
- Confidentiality: Individuals must protect and maintain the confidentiality of the organization's sensitive information, including trade secrets, intellectual property, and other proprietary information. This obligation continues even after the individual's relationship with the organization ends.
- Good faith and fair dealing: Individuals must act in good faith, treating the organization fairly and honestly, and make decisions with the organization's best interests in mind.
- Corporate opportunities: Individuals must not take advantage of business opportunities that belong to the organization for their personal benefit. This includes not competing with the organization or diverting its resources, customers, or business opportunities for personal gain.
- Proper use of company assets: Individuals must use the organization's assets responsibly and for legitimate business purposes, rather than for personal benefit or other unauthorized purposes.

By adhering to the duty of loyalty, individuals in positions of trust and authority within an organization help ensure the organization's long-term success and stability, protect its reputation, and maintain the trust of its stakeholders.

Breaches of the duty of loyalty can result in legal consequences, reputational damage, and potential financial losses for the company.

ESG

ESG stands for Environmental, Social, and Governance, and refers to a set of criteria used to evaluate the sustainability and social impact of a company or organization.

The environmental factors of ESG include a company's impact on the environment, such as its carbon footprint, resource consumption, and waste management practices.

The social aspect considers how a company's operations impact society, including issues such as human rights, labor practices, and community engagement.

The governance aspect considers how a company is governed and managed, including issues such as executive compensation, board diversity, and shareholder rights.

Investors and companies use ESG criteria to assess the long-term financial and non-financial risks or opportunities associated with a company's operations and investments.

Companies that prioritize ESG factors are seen as more sustainable and better able to manage risks and opportunities related to environmental, social, and governance issues.

ESOP (Employee Stock Ownership Plan)

An ESOP company is an enterprise that has established an Employee Stock Ownership Plan (ESOP) for its employees. An ESOP is a type of employee benefit plan that provides employees with an ownership stake in the company. In an ESOP company, employees become partial owners of the company through the purchase of company stock, which is held in a trust. Over time, as the company grows and becomes more valuable, the value of the employees' stock holdings also increases.

ESOP companies can range in size from small, privately-owned businesses to large, publicly-traded corporations. The goal of an ESOP is to align the interests of employees and the company by providing employees with an incentive to work towards the success of the company.

Executive Session

An executive session is a private meeting of governing body members, such as a board of directors, without the presence of others, such as staff or the public.

Executive sessions are held to discuss sensitive or confidential matters that require a higher level of privacy, such as legal issues, personnel matters, or financial information.

Only board members and any required staff are allowed to attend the executive session. Any decisions or actions taken during the session are generally reported in the minutes of the next regular board meeting.

The content of executive sessions is usually kept confidential and may be subject to legal restrictions on disclosure or public access.

Family-Owned Business

A family-owned business is a company that is owned and operated by members of a single family, often spanning multiple generations.

These businesses are typically managed by family members, who may hold executive or board positions and significantly influence the company's operations and decision-making.

The family's values, culture, and traditions may play a significant role in the company's operations and decision-making.

Family-owned businesses face unique challenges, such as balancing family dynamics with business decisions, succession planning, and inter-generational transfer of ownership and leadership.

Family members may also have different interests, priorities, and skill sets, leading to conflicts and challenges in managing the business.

Despite these challenges, family-owned businesses often have advantages, such as a strong sense of commitment and loyalty, a long-term perspective, and a focus on relationships and trust.

They may also benefit from the knowledge, experience, and expertise of family members who have grown up in the business and understand its values and culture.

Independent Chair

An Independent Chair, also called an Independent Chairman or Non-Executive Chair, is a leadership position within a company's board of directors. An Independent Chair is not an employee or executive of the company and does not have any material or significant relationship with the company or its management.

The Independent Chair is responsible for presiding over the board and ensuring that it functions effectively while maintaining a high degree of independence from the company's management and operations.

A Non-Executive Chair is a member of the board of directors of a company who is not involved in the day-to-day operations but instead provides oversight and guidance to the executive management team.

This independence ensures that the board remains objective and unbiased in its decision-making and oversight responsibilities.

Key roles and responsibilities of an Independent Chair often include:

Setting the agenda for board meetings and ensuring that meetings are conducted effectively.

Facilitating open and constructive communication among board members, encouraging the expression of diverse viewpoints, and fostering a culture of collaboration and accountability.

Overseeing the performance and effectiveness of the board, as well as the CEO and other top executives.

Ensuring that the board is focused on its governance responsibilities, including strategic planning, risk management, financial oversight, and regulatory compliance.

Serving as a liaison between the board and management and representing the interests of shareholders and other stakeholders.

The role of the Non-Executive Chair is to provide an independent perspective on the company's strategic direction, performance, and risk management, and to ensure that the executive management team is acting in the best interests of the company and its stakeholders.

Independent Director

An independent director is a board member not affiliated with the company or its management team in a way that could compromise their objectivity or independence.

An independent director is not an employee or executive of the company, and does not have any personal or business ties that could create a conflict of interest or compromise their objectivity.

The purpose of having independent directors is to ensure that the board has a balanced perspective and that decisions are made in the company's and shareholders' best interests.

Independent directors bring a diverse range of skills, experience, and expertise to the board, contributing to its overall effectiveness.

They play a crucial role in corporate governance by overseeing management, monitoring financial performance, and providing objective oversight on matters such as executive compensation, mergers and acquisitions, and risk management.

Institutional Investors

Institutional investors are entities or organizations that pool and manage large amounts of money to invest in various financial instruments, such as stocks, bonds, and other securities. These investors typically have significant financial resources and professional expertise, which allows them to make large-scale investments and exert considerable influence in financial markets.

There are many types of institutional investors, including:

Pension funds: These are investment funds that manage retirement savings for employees. Pension funds collect contributions from employers and employees and invest the pooled funds to generate returns that are used to pay retirement benefits.

Mutual funds: These are investment vehicles that pool money from multiple individual investors and use that capital to buy a diversified portfolio of stocks, bonds, or other securities. Mutual funds are managed by professional investment managers who make decisions on behalf of the fund's shareholders.

Institutional investors often have access to better investment opportunities, more resources, and professional expertise than individual investors.

Institutional investors can also influence corporate governance and management decisions by exercising their voting rights as shareholders in publicly traded companies.

IPO (Initial Public Offering)

An initial public offering (IPO) is the process by which a private company offers shares of its stock to the public for the first time, enabling it to raise capital and become a publicly traded company.

During an IPO, the company works with investment banks to prepare and file a prospectus that provides information about the company's financial performance, operations, and management, including risks associated with investing in the company's stock.

Once the prospectus is filed with the Securities and Exchange Commission (SEC), the company goes on a "roadshow" to pitch the stock to institutional and individual investors.

After a period of time, typically several weeks, the company sets an IPO price for its shares based on the demand from investors, and the shares are then sold to the public through the stock exchange.

The process of going public through an IPO can be complex and expensive, involving significant regulatory requirements and fees, including the need to disclose detailed financial and operational information to the public.

However, an IPO can also provide significant benefits, such as raising large amounts of capital, increase public awareness and credibility, and enable the company's founders and early investors to sell their shares to realize a return on their investment.

Overall, an IPO is an important event in the life of a company, marking its transition from a private enterprise to a publicly traded entity with access to a wider pool of capital and investors.

Lead Director

A lead director is a member of a company's board of directors who is appointed to serve as an intermediary between the independent directors and the company's management, particularly the CEO and the Chairman of the board.

The lead director is usually an independent director, which means they have no material or significant relationship with the company, its management, or its shareholders that could compromise their objectivity.

The lead director plays a crucial role in corporate governance, particularly in situations when the roles of CEO and Chairman are combined as an Executive Chair.

Key responsibilities of a lead director often include:

- Providing guidance and leadership to the board on corporate governance, strategy, and risk management.
- Ensuring that the board's agenda is focused on critical issues and that sufficient time is allocated to discuss these matters.
- Facilitating communication and collaboration among independent directors and between the board and management, particularly in situations where there might be potential conflicts of interest or disagreements.
- Leading executive sessions, which are meetings of independent directors without management present, to discuss sensitive issues or evaluate the performance of the CEO and other top executives.
- Serving as a liaison between the board and shareholders, addressing their concerns and representing their interests.

The lead director helps to promote a culture of transparency, integrity, and accountability within the organization, contributing to its overall effectiveness and success.

Micro-Cap and Small-Cap Companies

Micro-cap and small-cap companies are publicly traded companies differentiated by their market capitalization, which is the total value of a company's outstanding shares.

Micro-cap companies have a market capitalization ranging between $50 million and $300 million. They are smaller in size, often operate in niche markets or emerging industries, and may have limited financial resources compared to larger companies. They also usually have lower trading volumes and less coverage by financial analysts, which can result in less available information for investors. Micro-cap companies are often considered riskier investments than small-cap companies due to their smaller size, limited resources, higher volatility, and lower liquidity.

Small-cap companies generally have a market capitalization between $300 million and $2 billion. While considered small compared to mid-cap and large-cap companies, they are larger and more established than micro-cap companies. They typically have a broader market presence, more resources, and greater stability than micro-cap companies. Small-cap companies may also have more extensive analyst coverage and higher trading volumes, which can provide more available information and liquidity for investors.

Nonprofit Organization

A nonprofit organization or NGO (non-governmental organization) operates for a specific charitable, social, educational, or religious purpose rather than to generate profit.

Nonprofits are typically mission-driven and aim to benefit the public or a specific group of individuals, rather than individual shareholders or owners.

Nonprofits are governed by a board of directors or trustees and may be structured as a foundation, association, or corporation.

They rely on donations, grants, and other forms of funding to support their operations and programs rather than generating revenue from the sale of goods or services.

Nonprofits often have tax-exempt status, which means they are not required to pay federal or state income taxes as long as they meet certain criteria set by the Internal Revenue Service (IRS).

They can work in various fields, such as health care, education, environmental conservation, social services, and more.

Overall, nonprofits play an important role in promoting social welfare, advancing public interests, and providing services and programs that benefit society.

PE Firms (Private Equity Firms)

Private equity (PE) firms are investment management companies that raise capital from various sources, such as institutional investors, high-net-worth individuals, and pension funds, to acquire ownership or stakes in private or public companies to take them private.

The primary goal of private equity firms is to generate significant returns on their investments by improving the financial and operational performance of the companies they invest in and eventually selling them or taking them public through an initial public offering (IPO).

Venture capital is a subset of private equity, a type of financing that investors provide to early-stage companies with high growth potential. Venture capital investments typically focus on innovative start-ups and emerging industries, such as technology or biotechnology.

Private equity firms play a significant role in the investment landscape and are known for their hands-on approach to managing their portfolio companies. They often work closely with the management teams of the companies they invest in, providing strategic guidance, operational expertise, and financial resources to create value and drive growth.

Private Companies

A private company is a business that is owned by private individuals or a small group of investors and is not publicly traded on a stock exchange.

Private companies can be small or large and operate in any industry or sector.

Private companies may raise funds from private investors, such as venture capitalists or angel investors, or from debt financing. They may also choose to go public through an IPO if they want to raise additional capital or provide liquidity for their owners.

Private companies may also have more flexibility in terms of their management structure and decision-making processes, as they are not subject to the same scrutiny as public companies by shareholders and regulatory bodies.

Public Companies

A public company is a business that has issued shares of stock to the public and is listed and traded on a public stock exchange, such as the New York Stock Exchange (NYSE) or NASDAQ.

Shares in public companies are bought and sold by investors through public markets, such as stock exchanges or electronic trading platforms, allowing for broad public ownership and liquidity.

Public companies can raise capital by issuing new shares of stock, selling bonds, or obtaining loans from financial institutions.

They also have a larger number of shareholders, who can buy and sell shares freely on the stock exchange, and have a greater say in the company's decision-making through their voting rights.

Public companies are typically large, well-established, and operate in a variety of industries or sectors.

Public companies are required to follow strict regulatory requirements and reporting obligations,

Shareholder Primacy

Shareholder primacy is a corporate governance principle that prioritizes the interests of shareholders above all other stakeholders, including employees, customers, suppliers, and the community. Under this principle, the primary responsibility of the board of directors and management is to maximize shareholder value, as measured by financial metrics such as stock price and return on investment. The concept of shareholder primacy has also been criticized for its narrow focus on short-term financial performance and for ignoring the interests of other stakeholders. Some argue that it can lead to a neglect of environmental, social, and governance (ESG) issues, and can result in decisions that are harmful to employees, customers, and the community.

SPAC

A Special Purpose Acquisition Company (SPAC) is a shell company formed specifically to raise capital through an IPO to acquire or merge with an existing company.

SPACs are typically founded by investors with expertise in a specific industry or sector, who seek to identify and acquire a promising target company.

The SPAC then uses the funds raised to identify and acquire an operating company that fits its investment criteria, typically within a timeframe of two years.

Once the SPAC identifies a suitable target company, it will negotiate and execute a merger or acquisition, which results in the target company becoming a public company.

SPACs have recently gained popularity as an alternative to traditional IPOs for companies seeking to go public.

SPACs offer several advantages, such as a quicker and more streamlined process for going public and reduced regulatory requirements.

Stakeholder Capitalism

Stakeholder capitalism is an approach to corporate governance that recognizes that corporations have a broader set of responsibilities beyond maximizing shareholder value. The concept of stakeholder capitalism holds that corporations have a responsibility to all of their stakeholders, including shareholders, employees, customers, suppliers, the community, and the environment.

Stakeholder capitalism has gained increasing attention in recent years, as a response to the shortcomings of shareholder primacy and the growing recognition of the need for a more sustainable and equitable form of capitalism. By considering the interests of all stakeholders, stakeholder capitalism seeks to create value in a more sustainable and equitable manner, and to promote the long-term success of the enterprise.

Startup

A startup is a newly established business venture founded by an entrepreneur with an innovative idea, product, or service.

Startups often face challenges such as limited resources, raising capital, and competition and may seek external financing from sources like angel investors or venture capital firms.

About the Author

John Hotta was born and raised in Berkeley, California. He grew up among the children of professors and deans. He graduated with honors with degrees from Harvard University, the Wharton School at the University of Pennsylvania, and UCLA. He has published research in artificial intelligence that can be found in Academia.edu.

He has been a board director of multi-billion-dollar organizations since the early 2010s. After a career at Microsoft, Accenture, and AT&T, and now a board director, he is fortunate to have friends and colleagues who are board directors at startups and nonprofits as well as the largest ten global public companies.

He is privileged to be able to live a purpose-driven life. He builds a culture of governance to improve better businesses and organizations and is happy to conduct training sessions for young professionals (in investment banking, proxy advisory firms, executive compensation, executive recruiting, corporate legal affairs offices, etc.) and undergraduate and graduate students in corporate governance classes.

He can be reached at https://johnhotta.academia.edu/contact.

Acknowledgments: Many people are involved in creating a good book. First, I want to thank Jaya Dalal, Stefan Giesen, Alexandra Lajoux, Ishwarya Mathavan, and their teams at De Gruyter. And infinite thanks to my colleagues, friends, loved ones, and dogs who guided me during writing – and make life worthwhile.

https://doi.org/10.1515/9783110689129-018

About the Series Editor

Alexandra Reed Lajoux is Series Editor for Walter De Gruyter, Inc. The series has an emphasis on governance, corporate leadership, and sustainability. Dr. Lajoux is chief knowledge officer emeritus (CKO) at the National Association of Corporate Directors (NACD) and founding principal of Capital Expert Services, LLC (CapEx), a global consultancy providing expert witnesses for legal cases. She coauthored *Making Money: The History and Future of Society's Most Important Technology* with Peet van Biljon (Walter de Gruyter, 2020). She has served as editor of *Directors & Boards*, *Mergers & Acquisitions*, *Export Today*, and *Director's Monthly*, and has coauthored a series of books on M&A for McGraw-Hill, including *The Art of M&A* and eight spin-off titles on strategy, valuation, financing, structuring, due diligence, integration, bank M&A, and distressed M&A. For Bloomberg/Wiley, she coauthored *Corporate Valuation for Portfolio Investment* with Robert A. G. Monks. Dr. Lajoux serves on the advisory board of Campaigns and Elections, and is a Fellow of the Caux Round Table for Moral Capitalism. She holds a B.A. from Bennington College, a Ph.D. from Princeton University, and an M.B.A. from Loyola University in Maryland. She is an associate member of the American Bar Association.

https://doi.org/10.1515/9783110689129-019

Index

https://doi.org/10.1515/9783110689129-020